The Sounds of the Southern Tier

Patti Schwartz

The Southern Tier of New York plays host to a diverse local music scene. On any given day of the week, you would be hard pressed not to find one of the local indie bands playing, a performance of the local opera company, the sounds of one of the local celtic pipe and drum bands, choirs singing or local residents participatng in karaoke or a piano bar.

As a photographer, I have had the pleasure of capturing many of these moments over the years. This is my way of paying tribute to the sounds that echo throughout the rolling hills of the Southern Tier of New York and the talented people responsible for those sounds.

Patti Schwartz

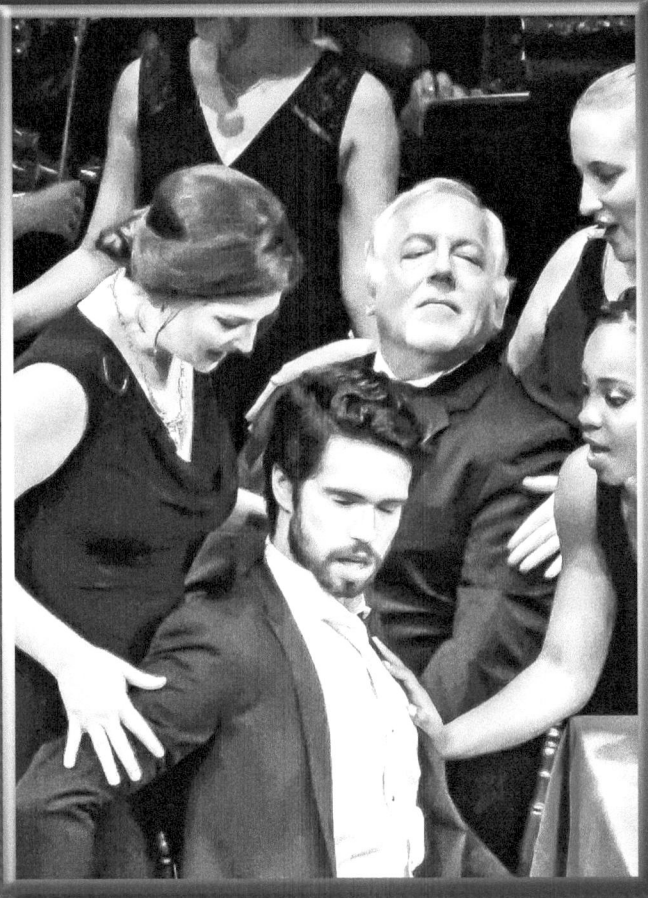
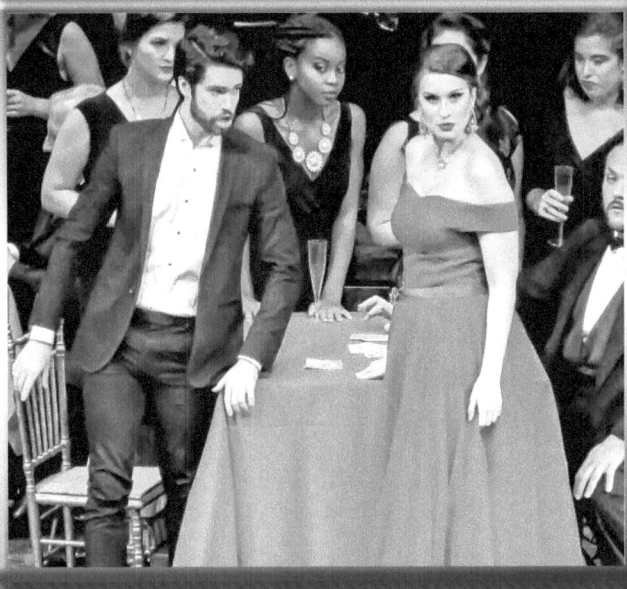
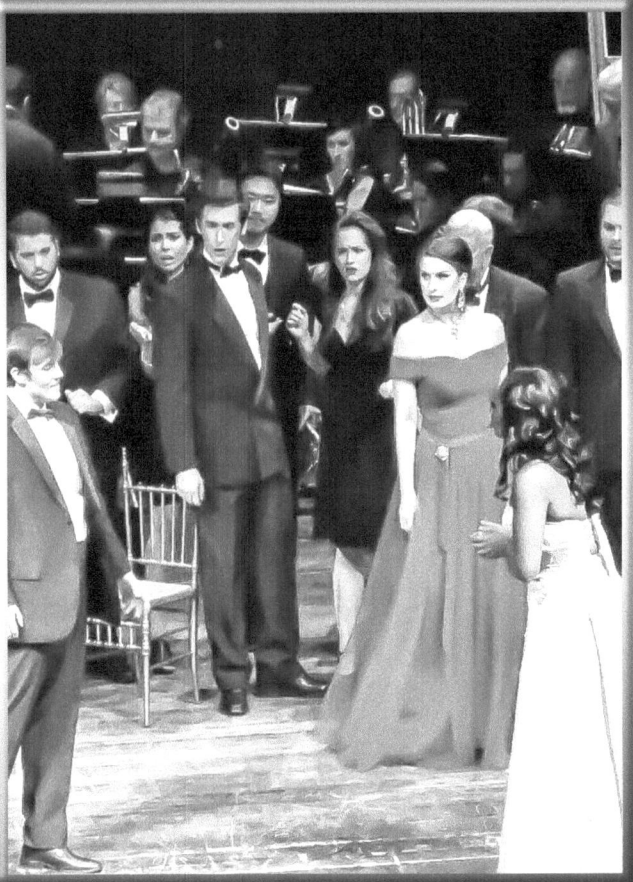
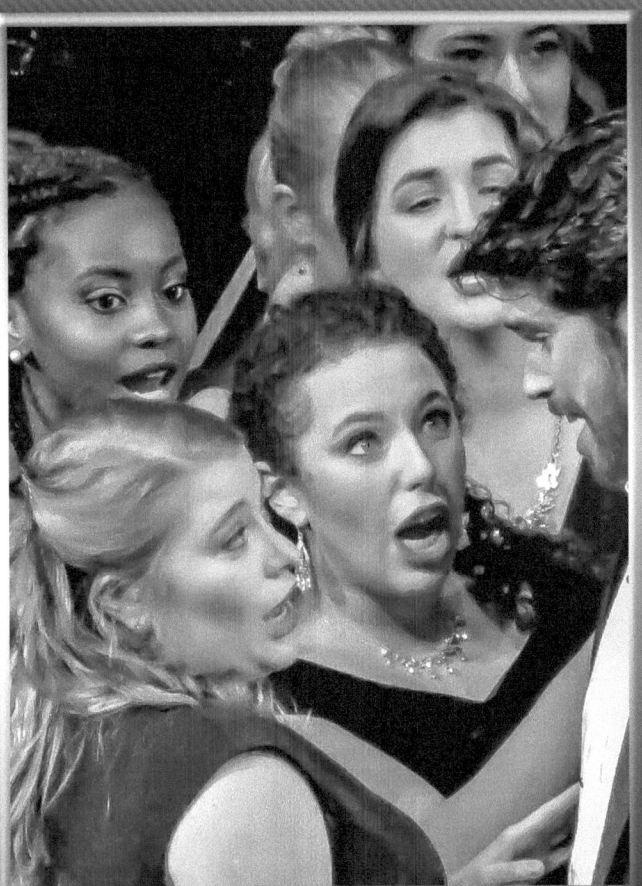

Tri-Cities Opera presents world class opera that appeals to an ever growing audience.

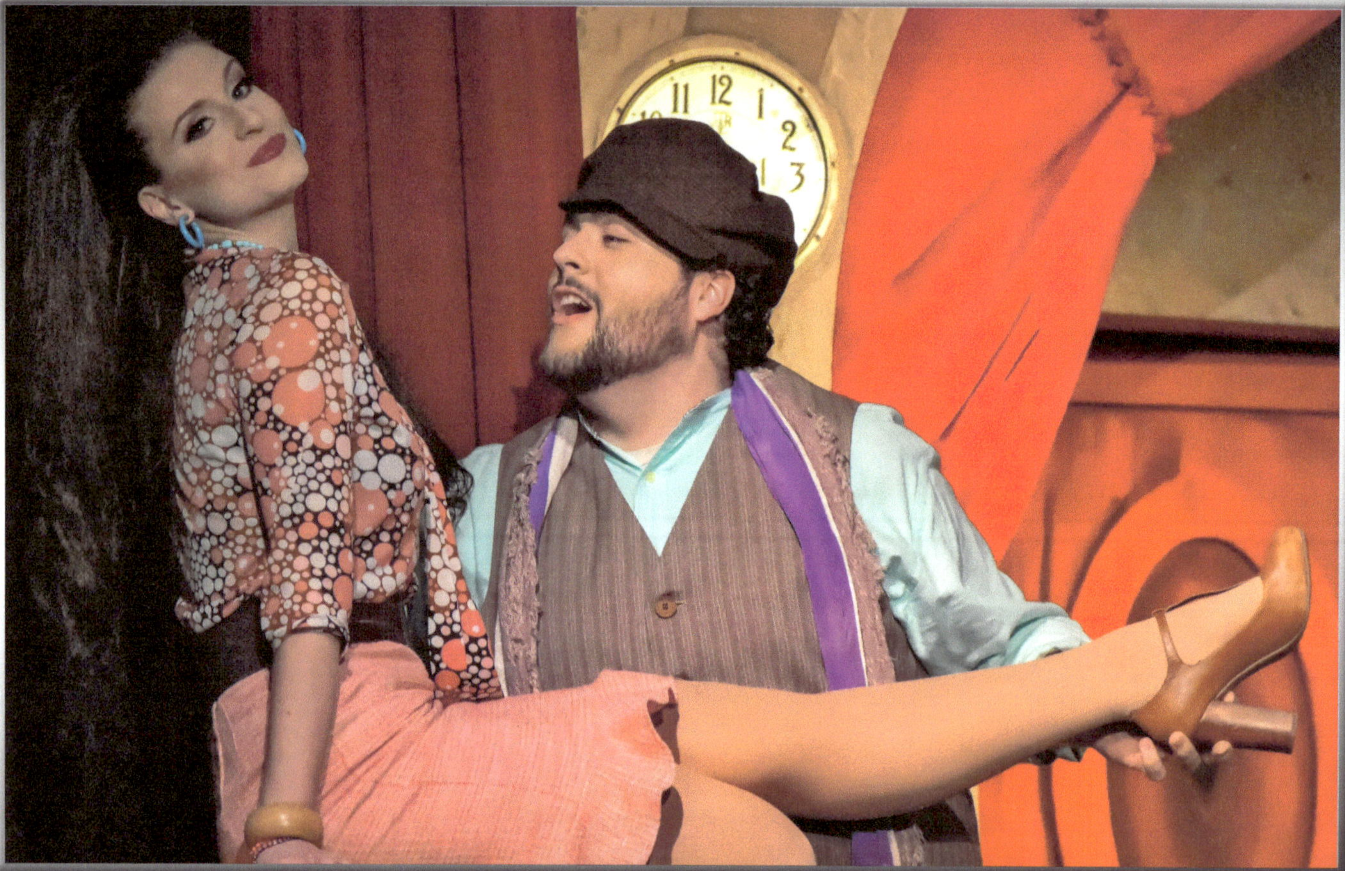

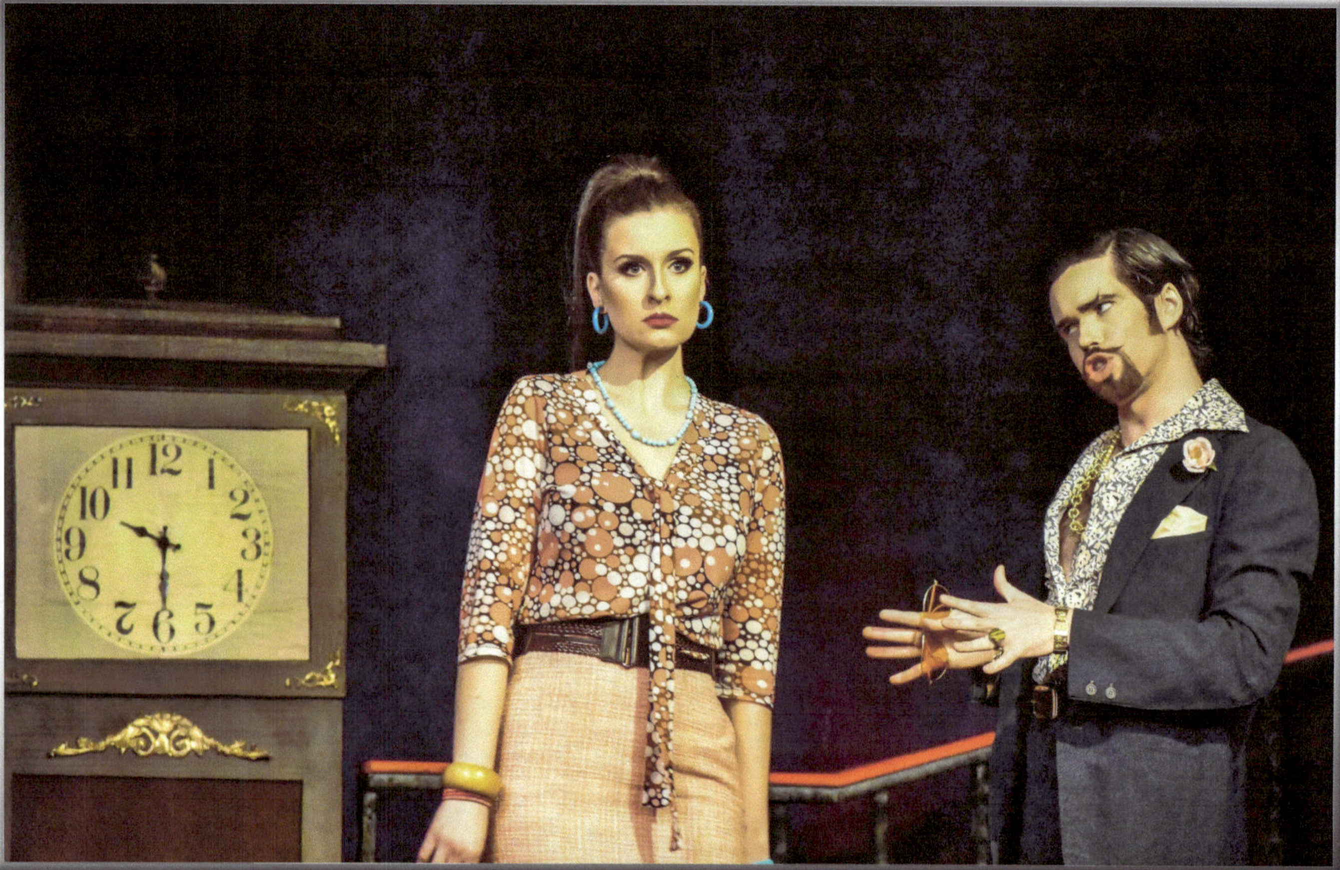

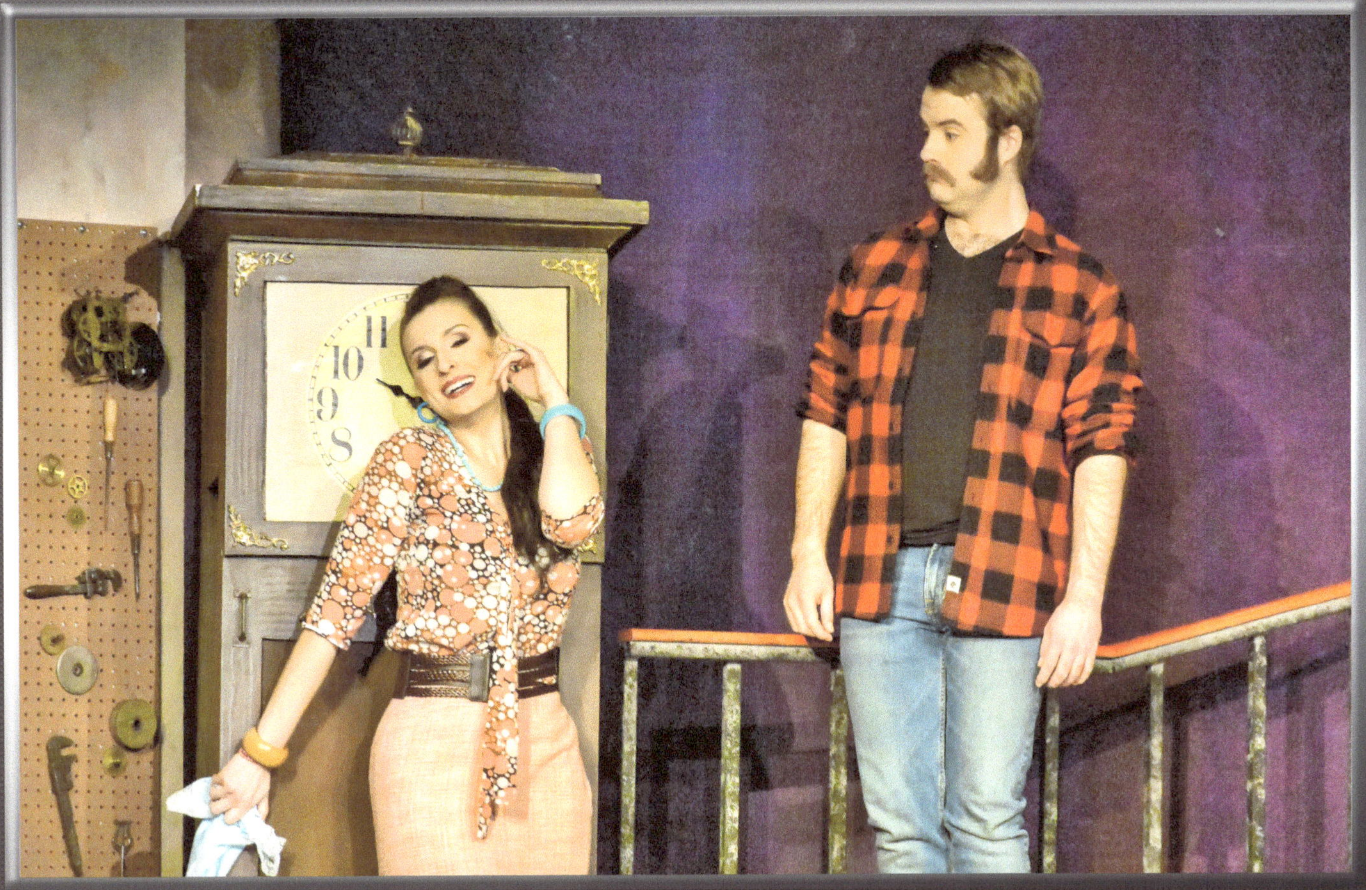

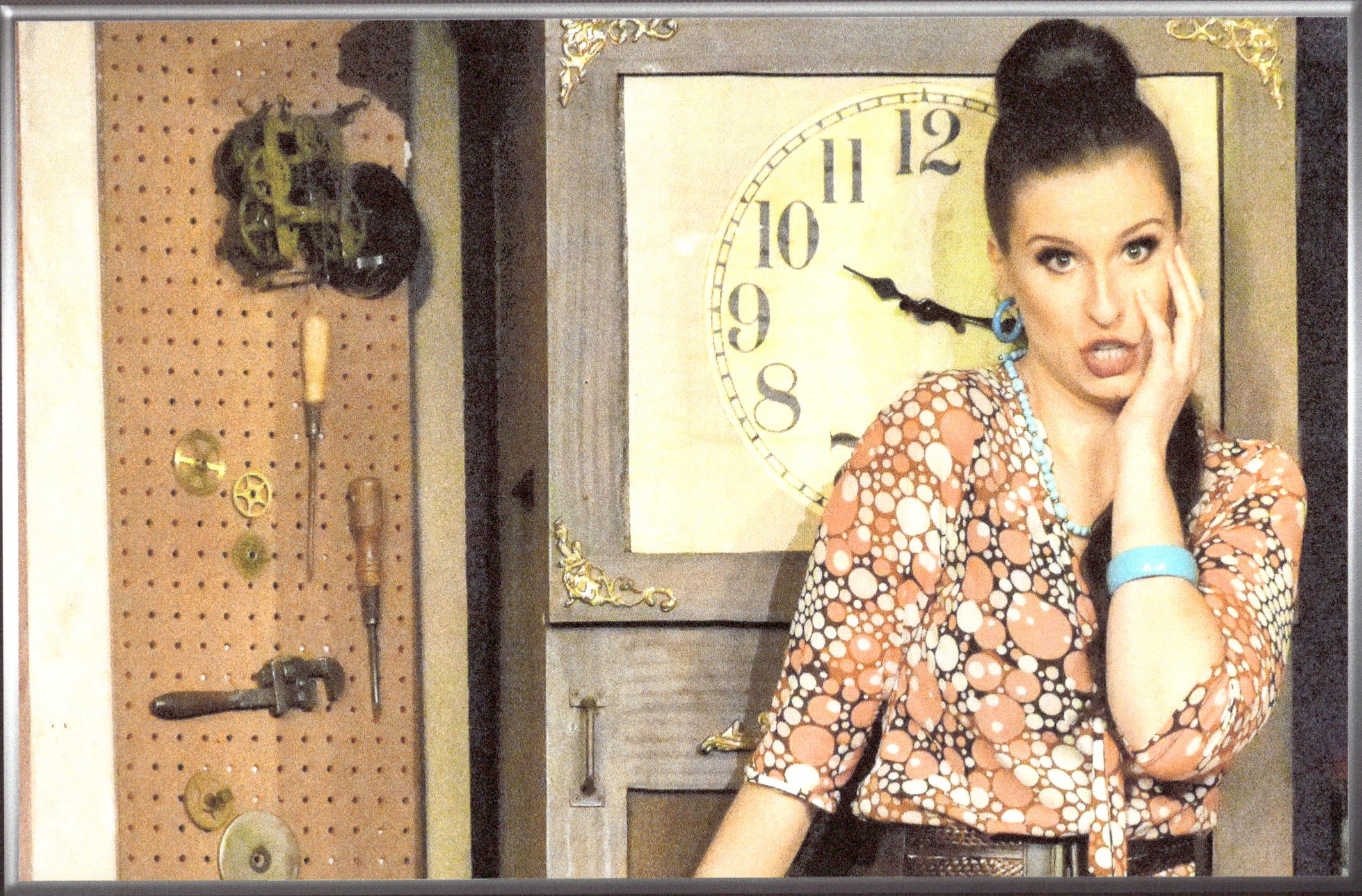

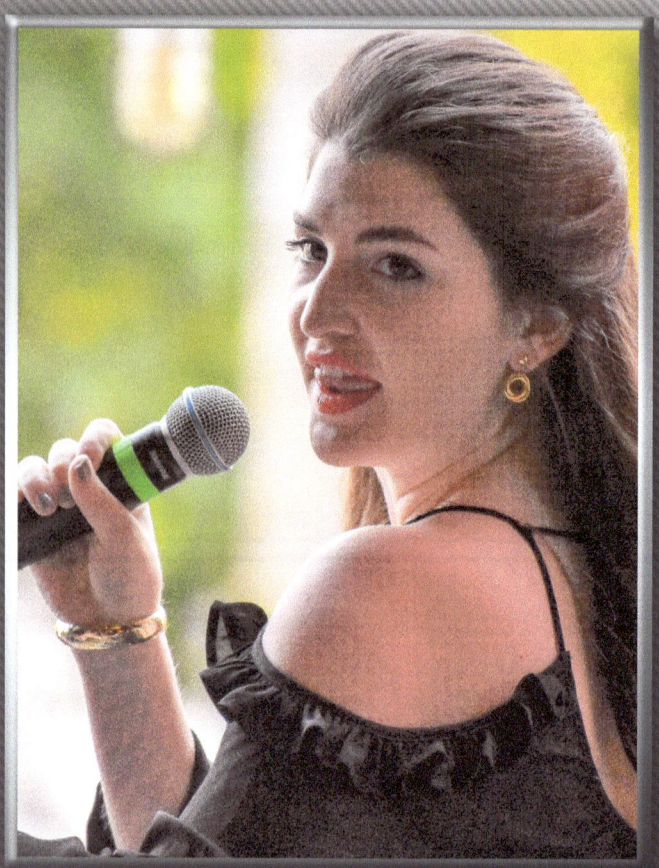
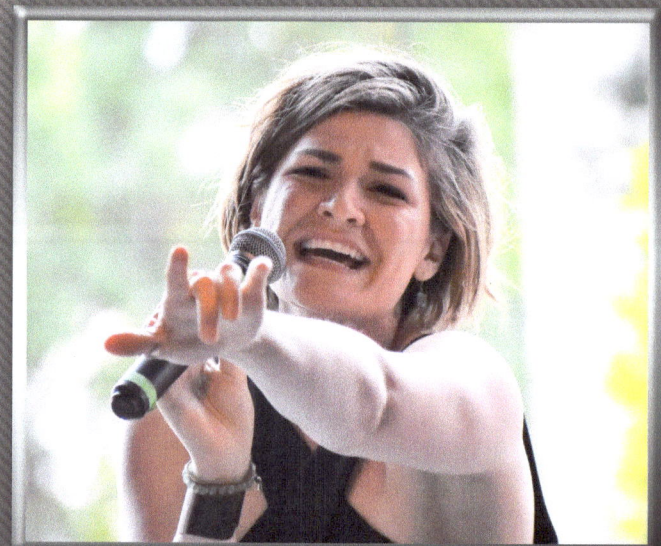

The Tri-Cities Opera also holds a yearly fundraiser, "Opera & Beer", where their resident artists perform contemporary tunes for their audience.

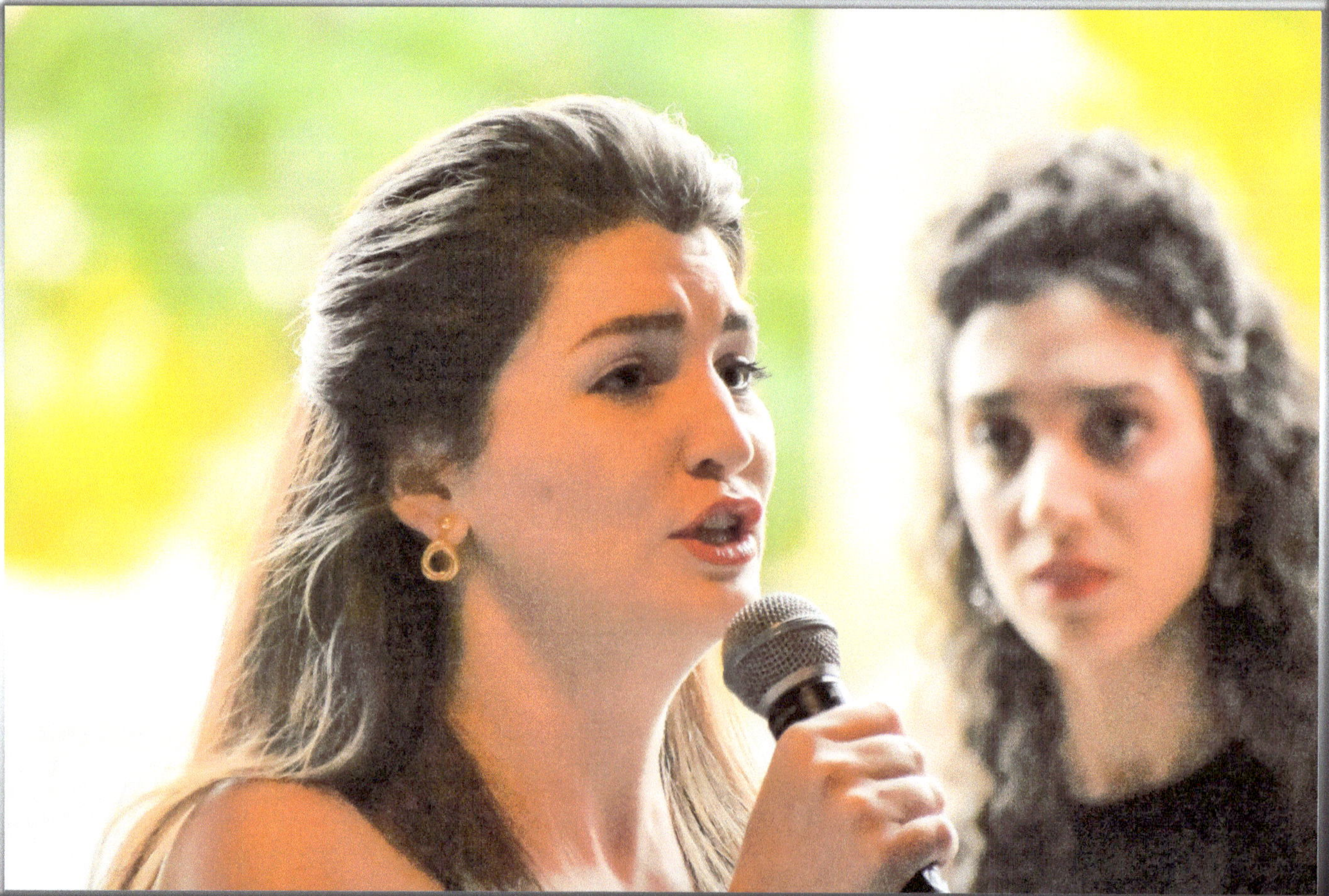

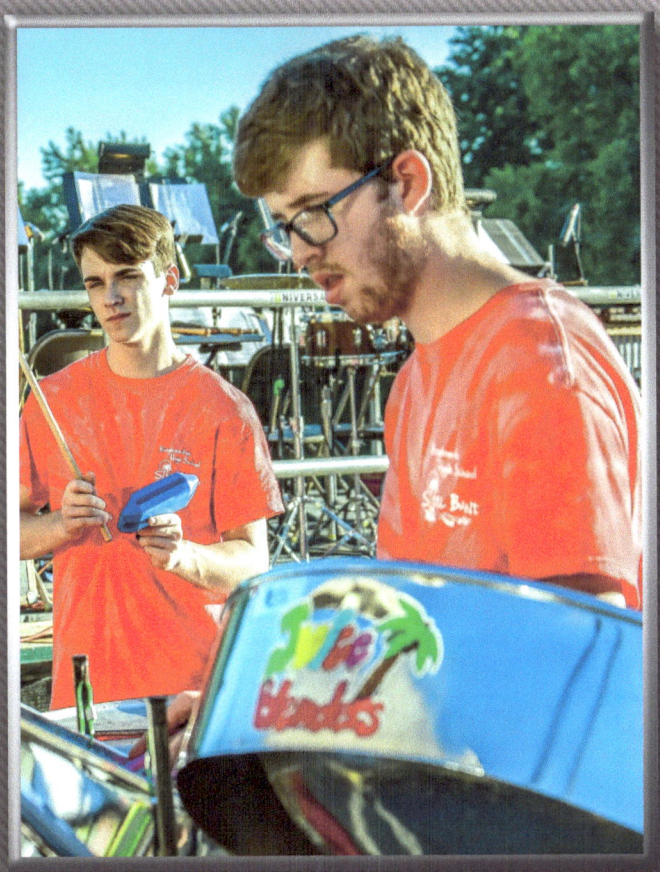
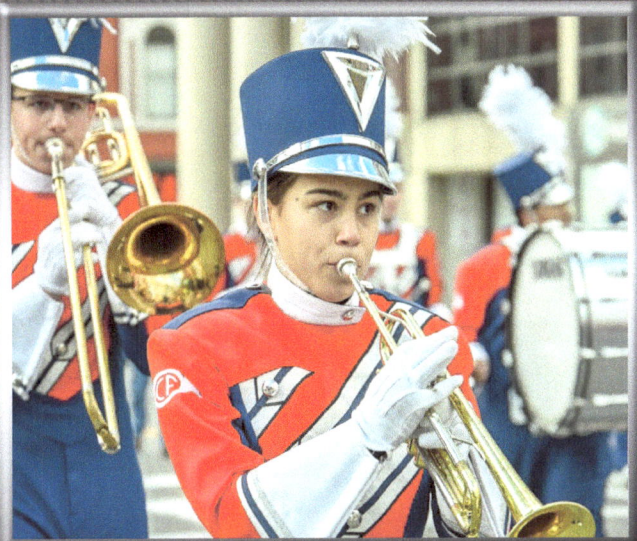

Whether it's marching, stage, concert or symphonic or steel drum band, the Southern Tier's school districts pride themselves in their music programs; and, well they should.

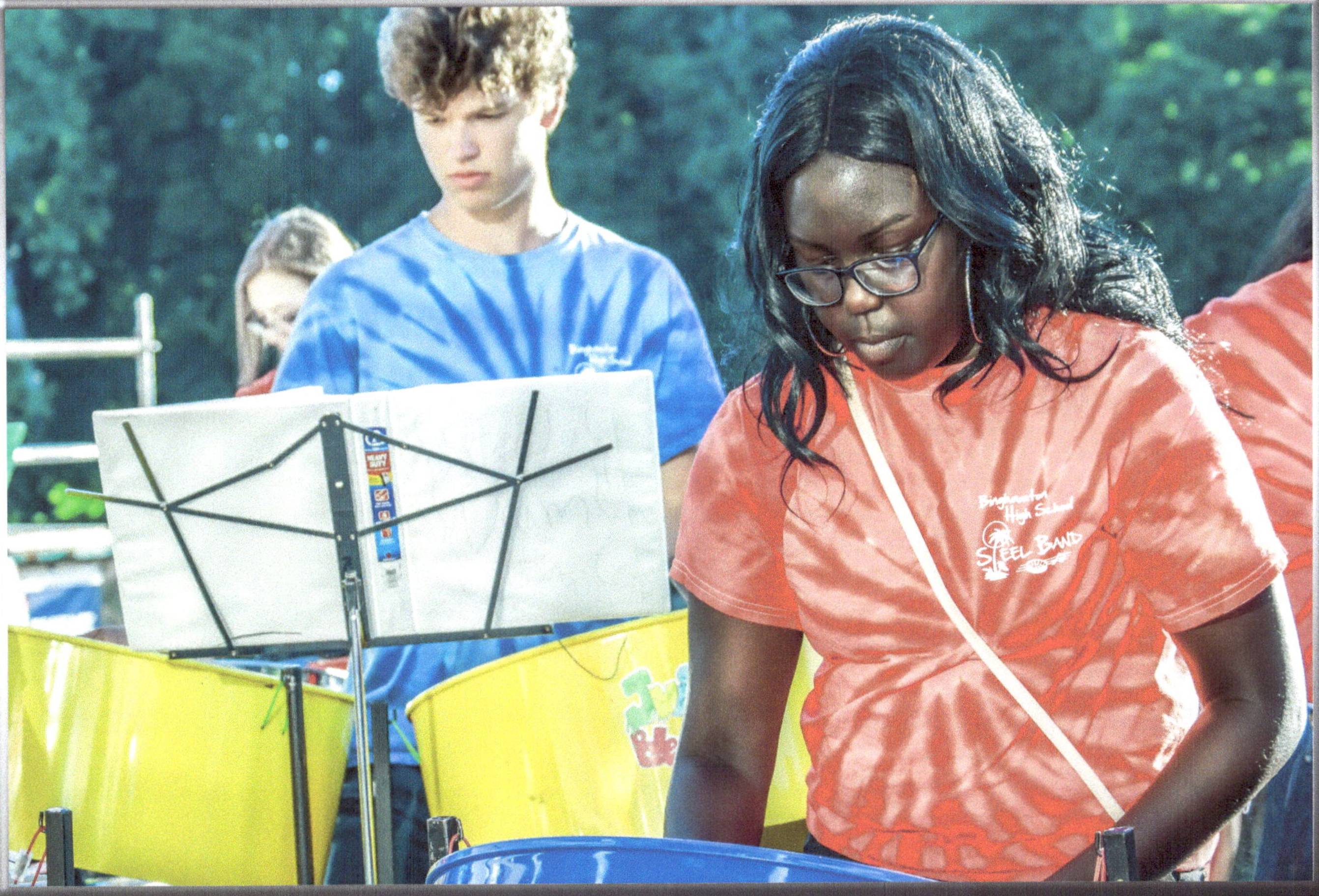

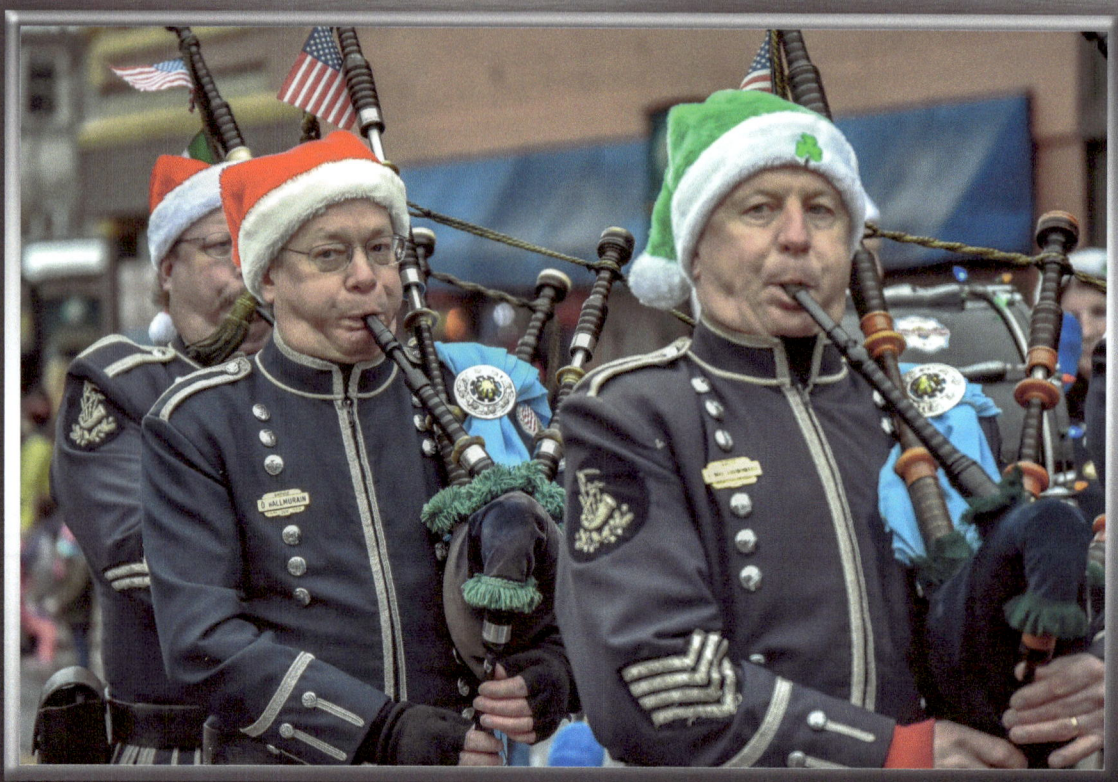

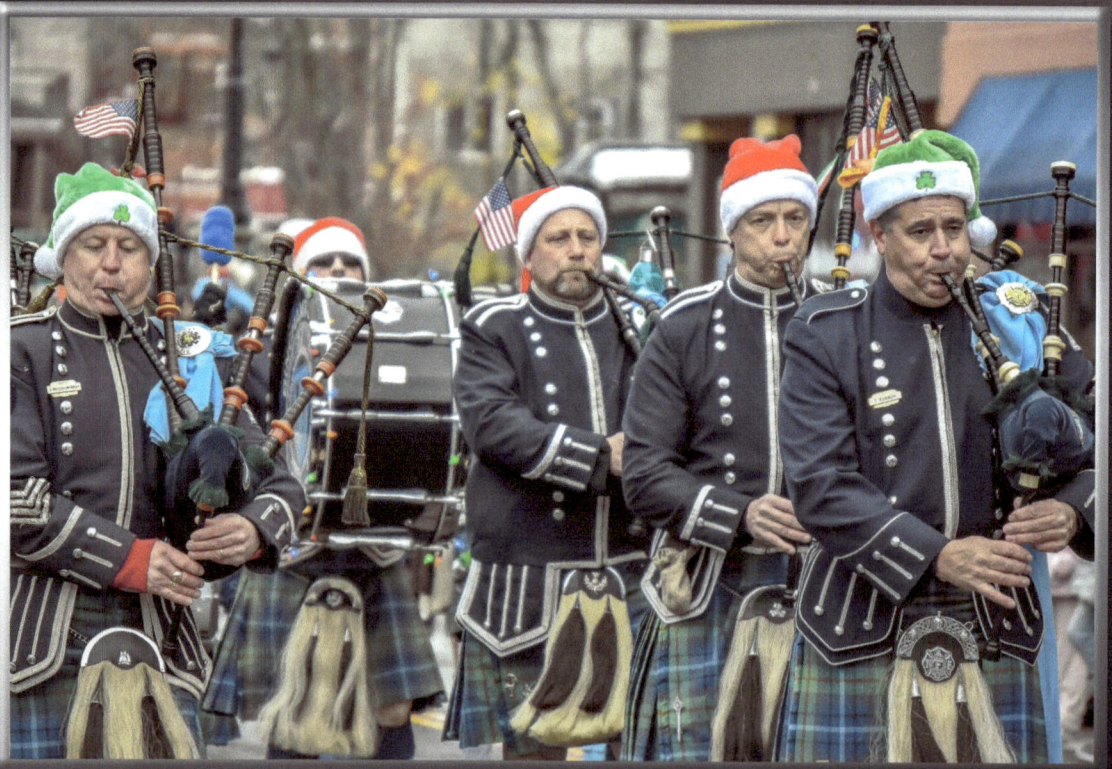

The Southern Tier is home to several celtic pipe and drum bands. They perform at music festivals, in parades, and at special events throughout the year. They have even traveled the globe representing the Southern Tier with pride.

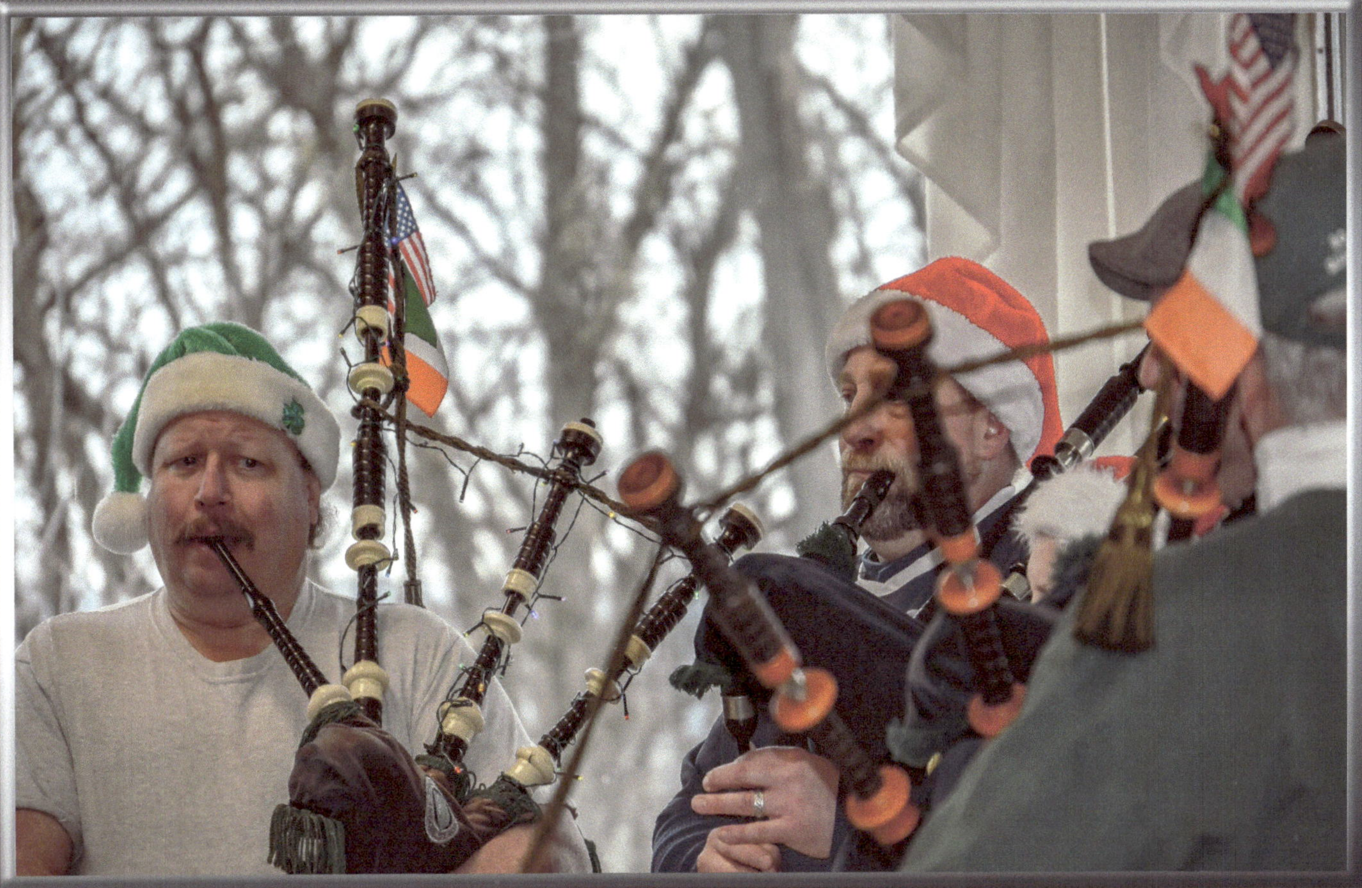

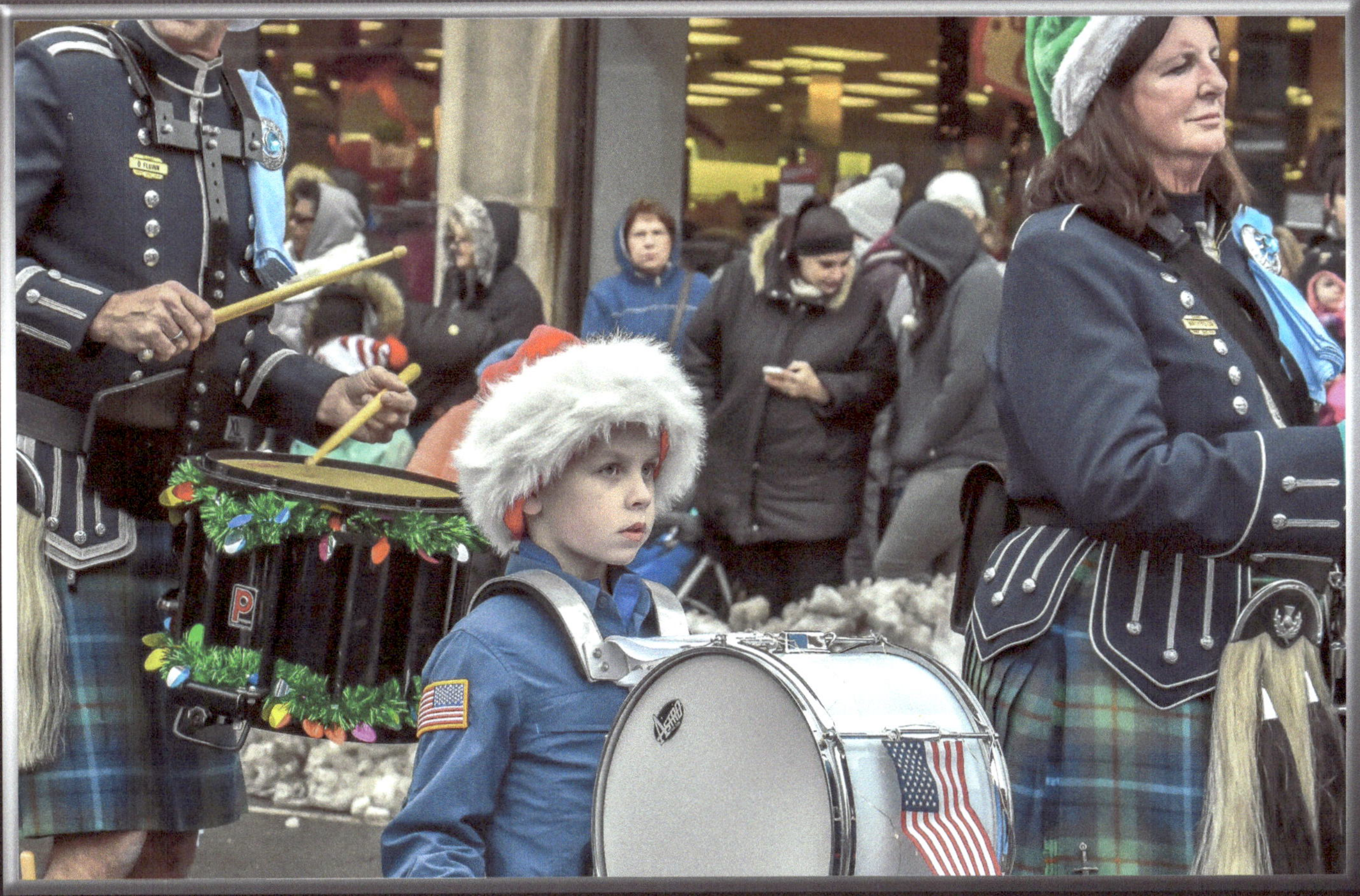

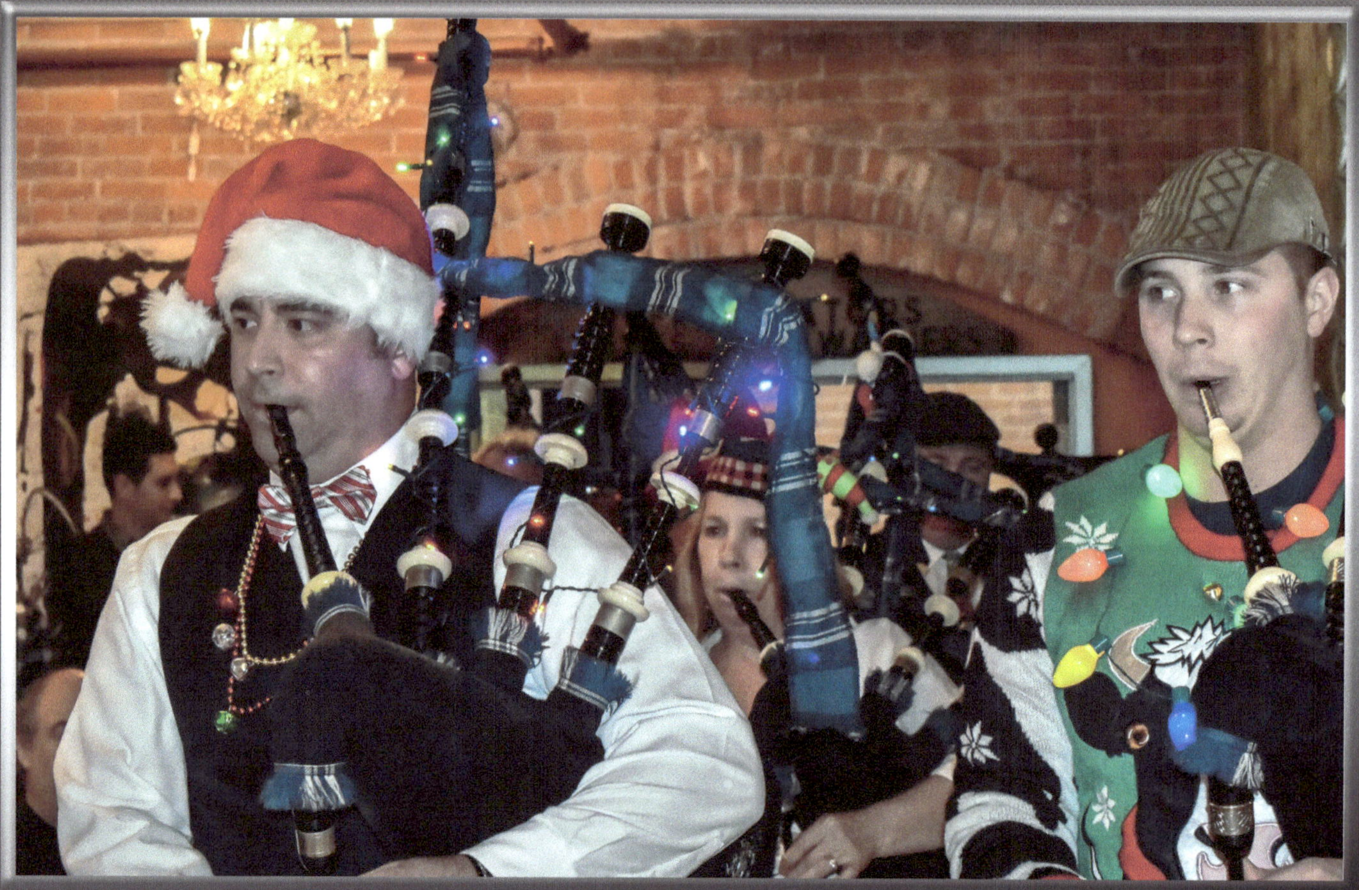

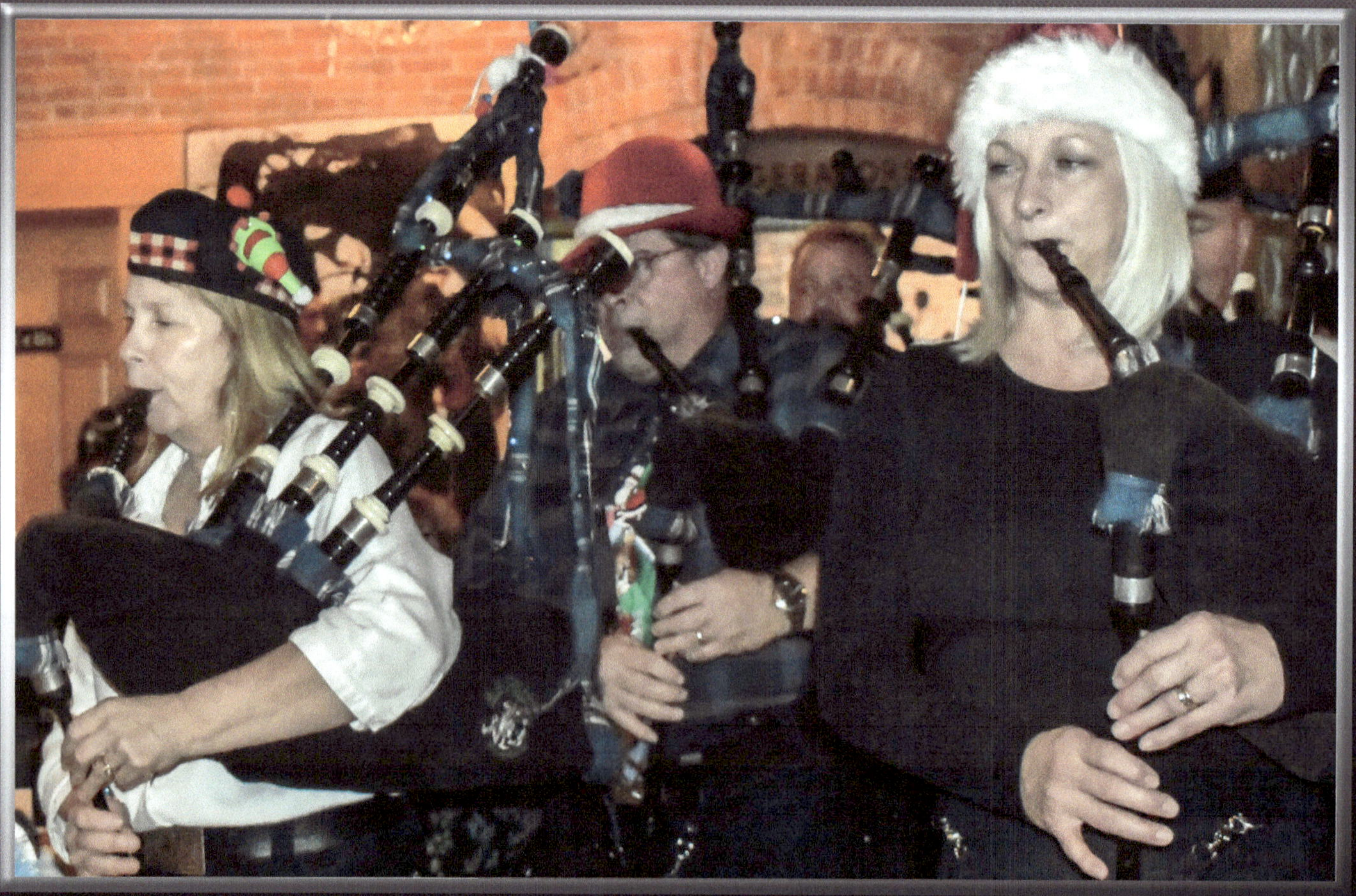

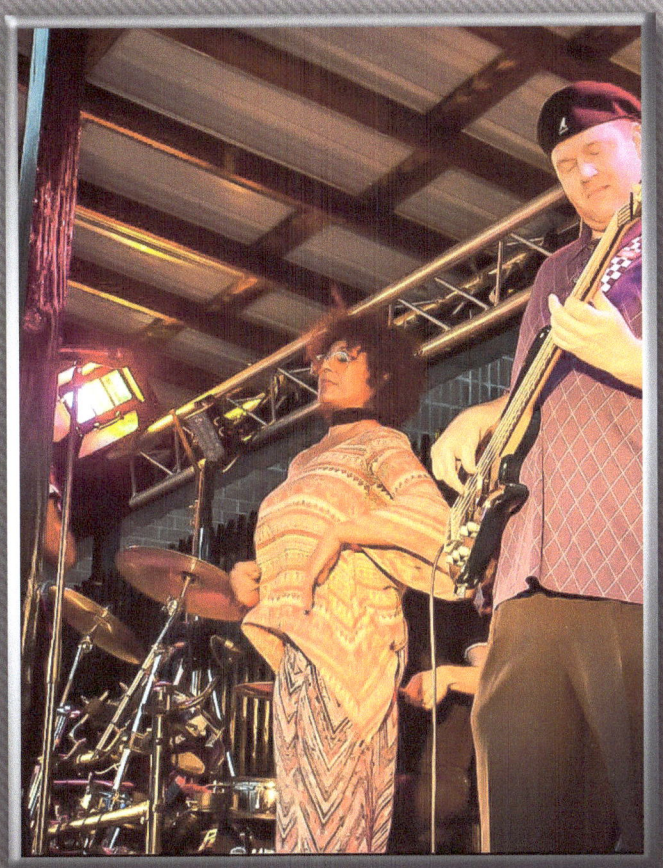

Nothing says summer in the Southern Tier better than gathering with friends on a Friday night listening to live local music. One such way to achieve this is by attending Cans N' Clams, a popular event among the locals.

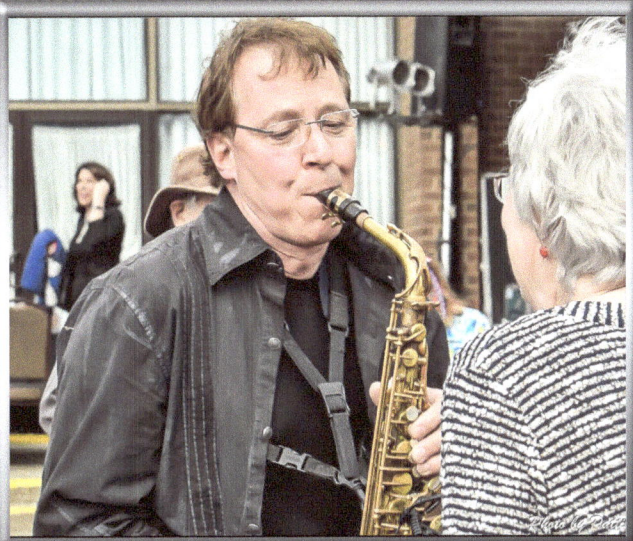

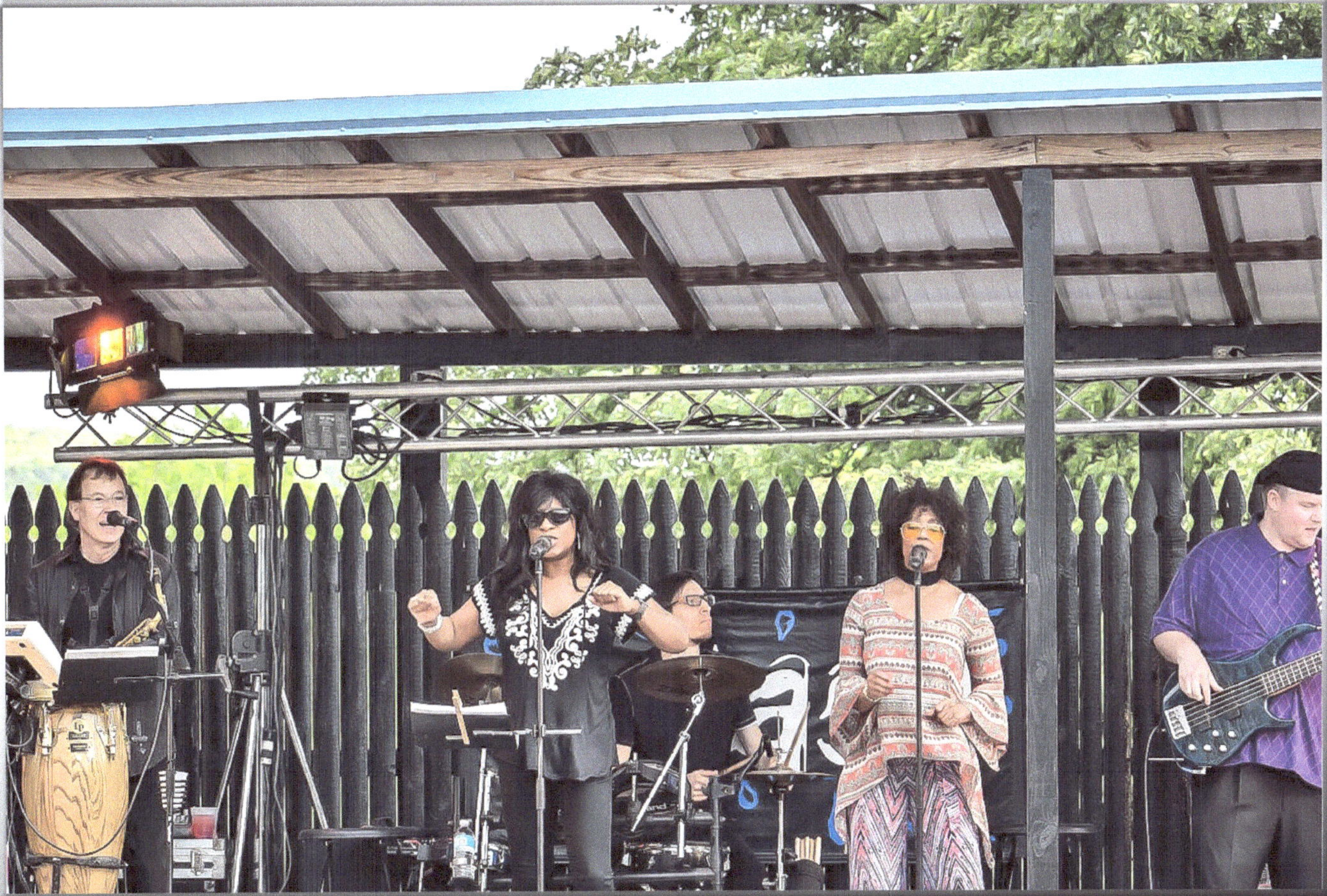

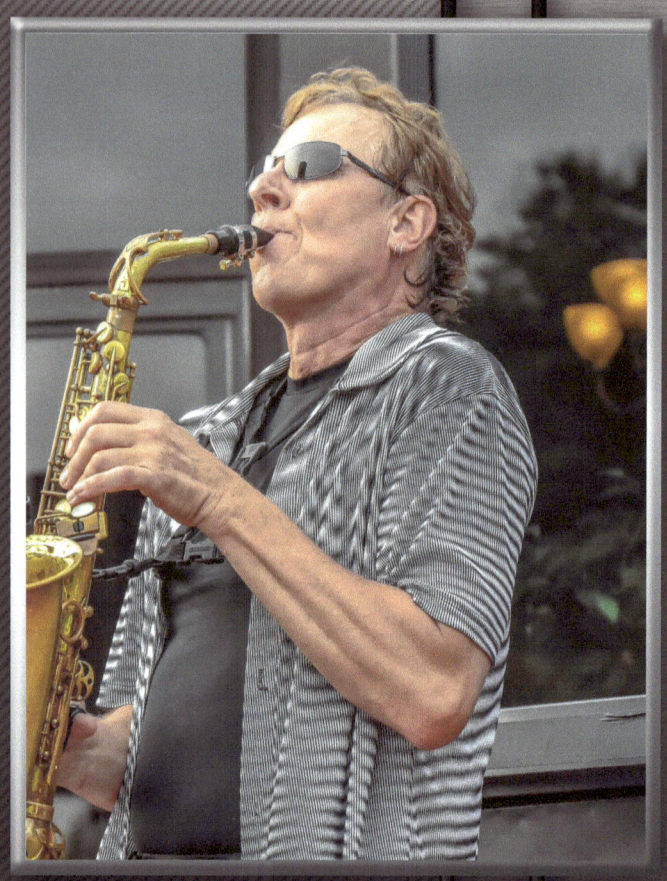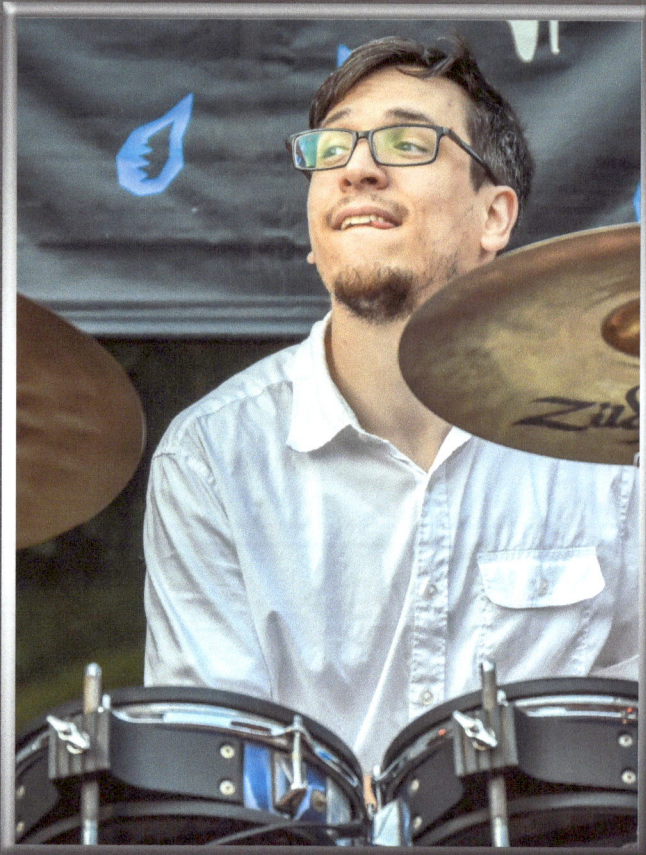

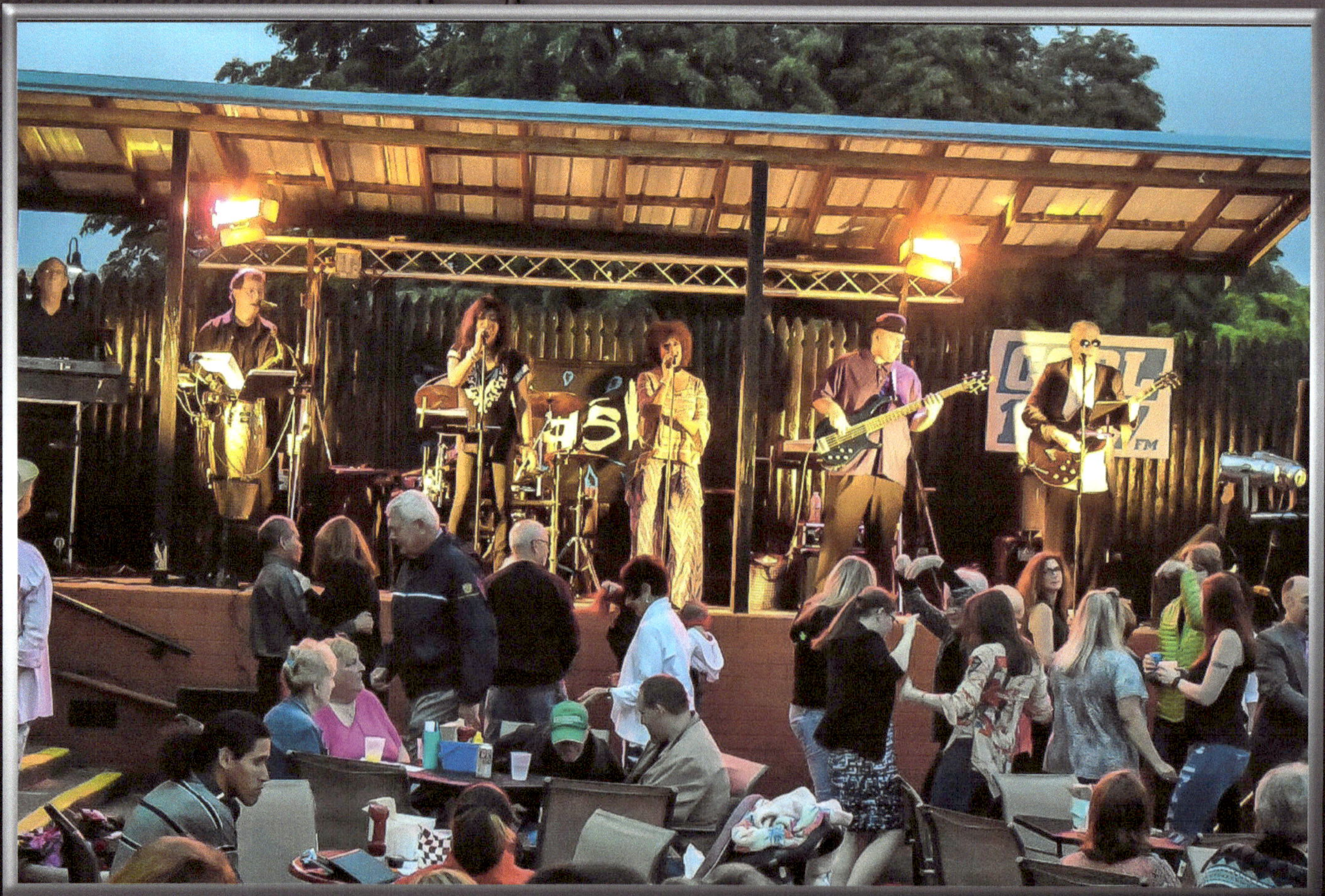

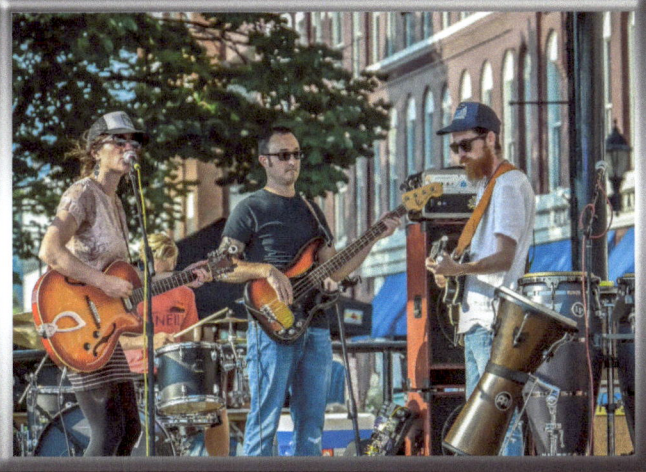
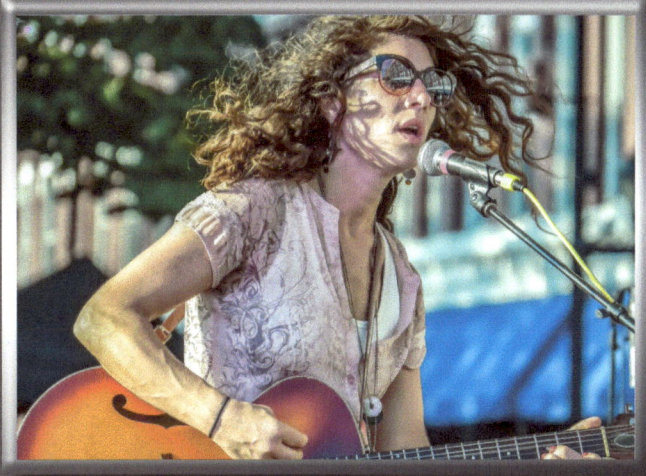
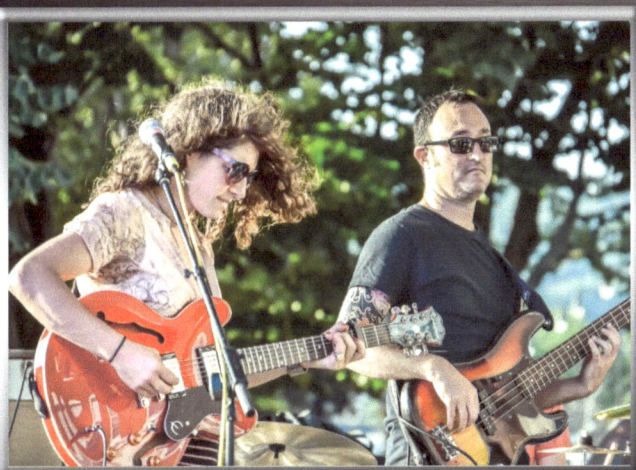
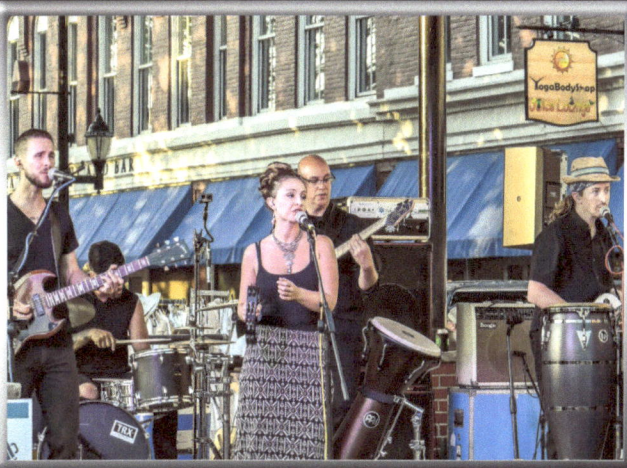
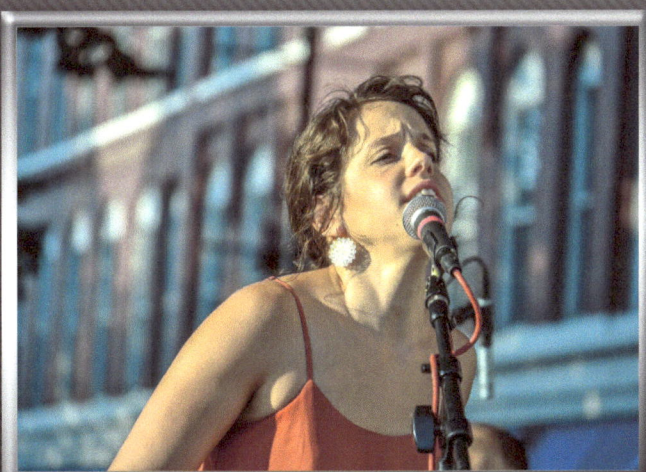
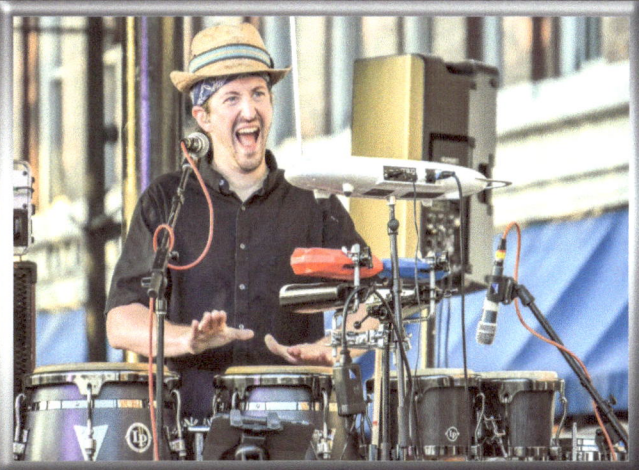

Another outdoor live music option during the summer is always Binghamton Live on the Waterfront. A perfect way to unwind after work.

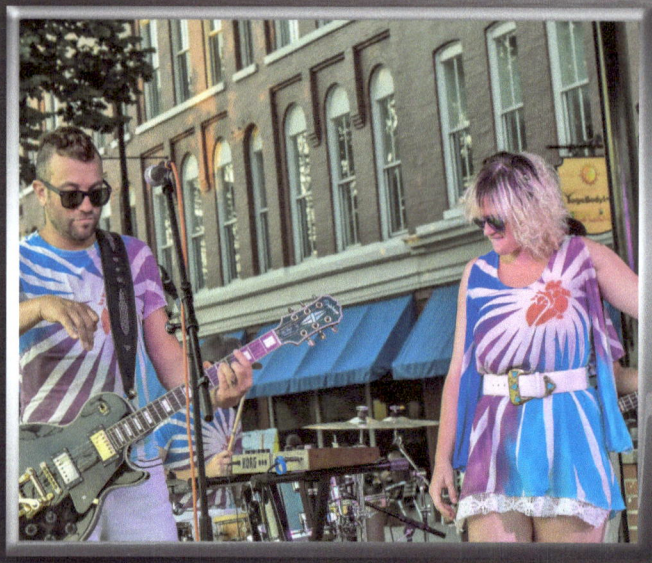
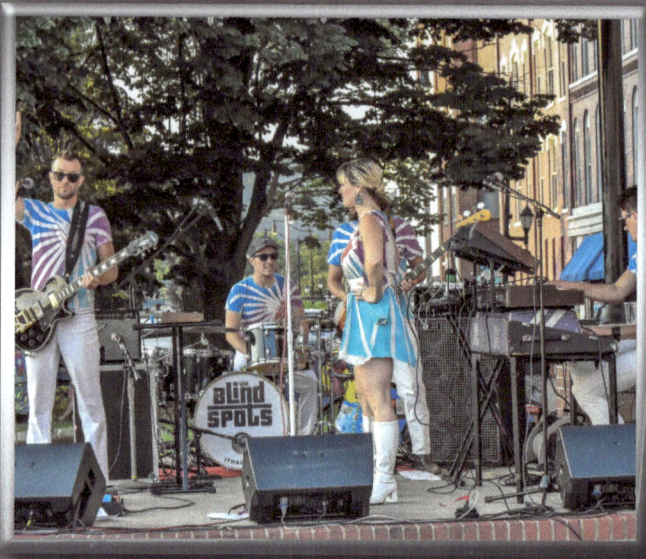
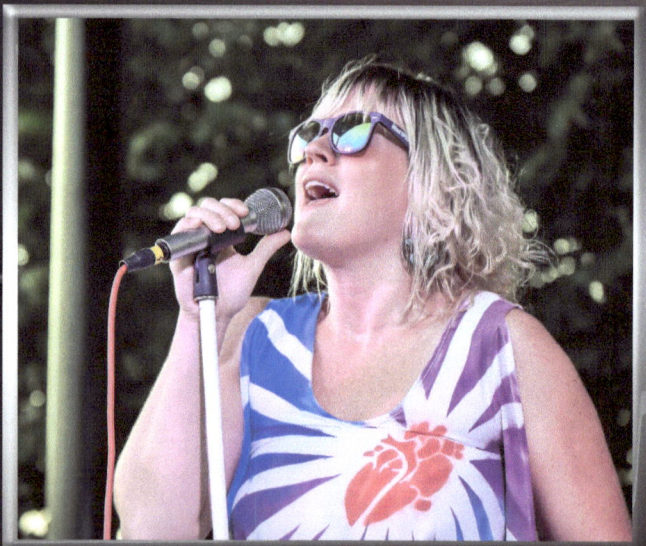
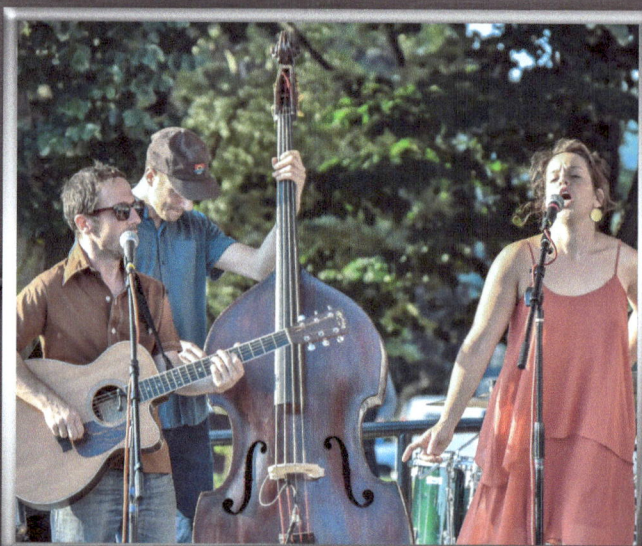
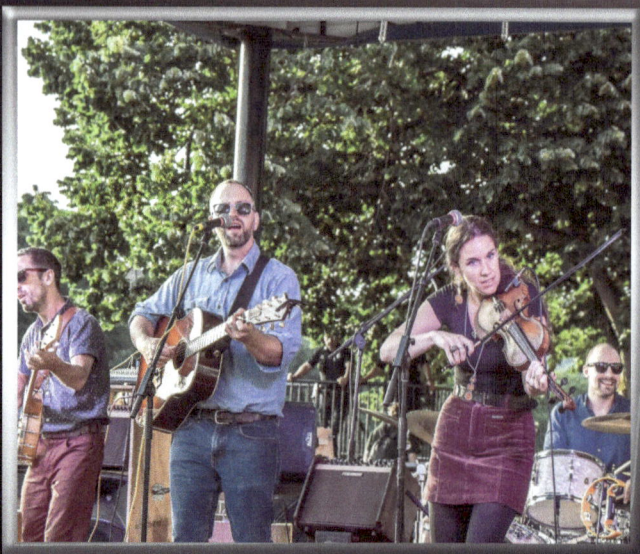
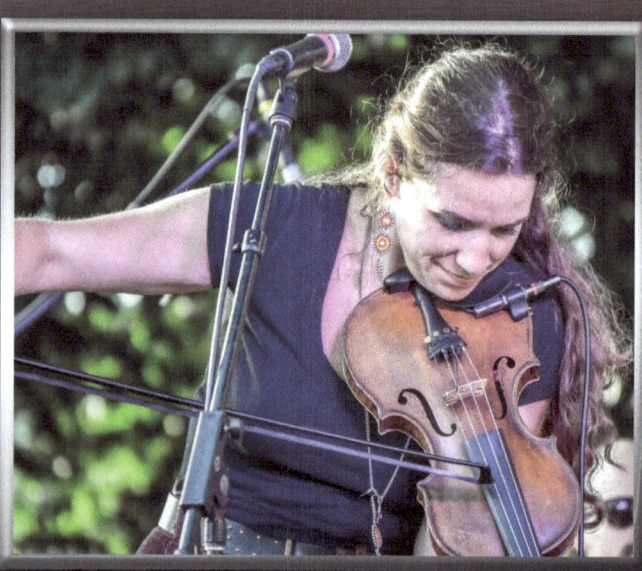

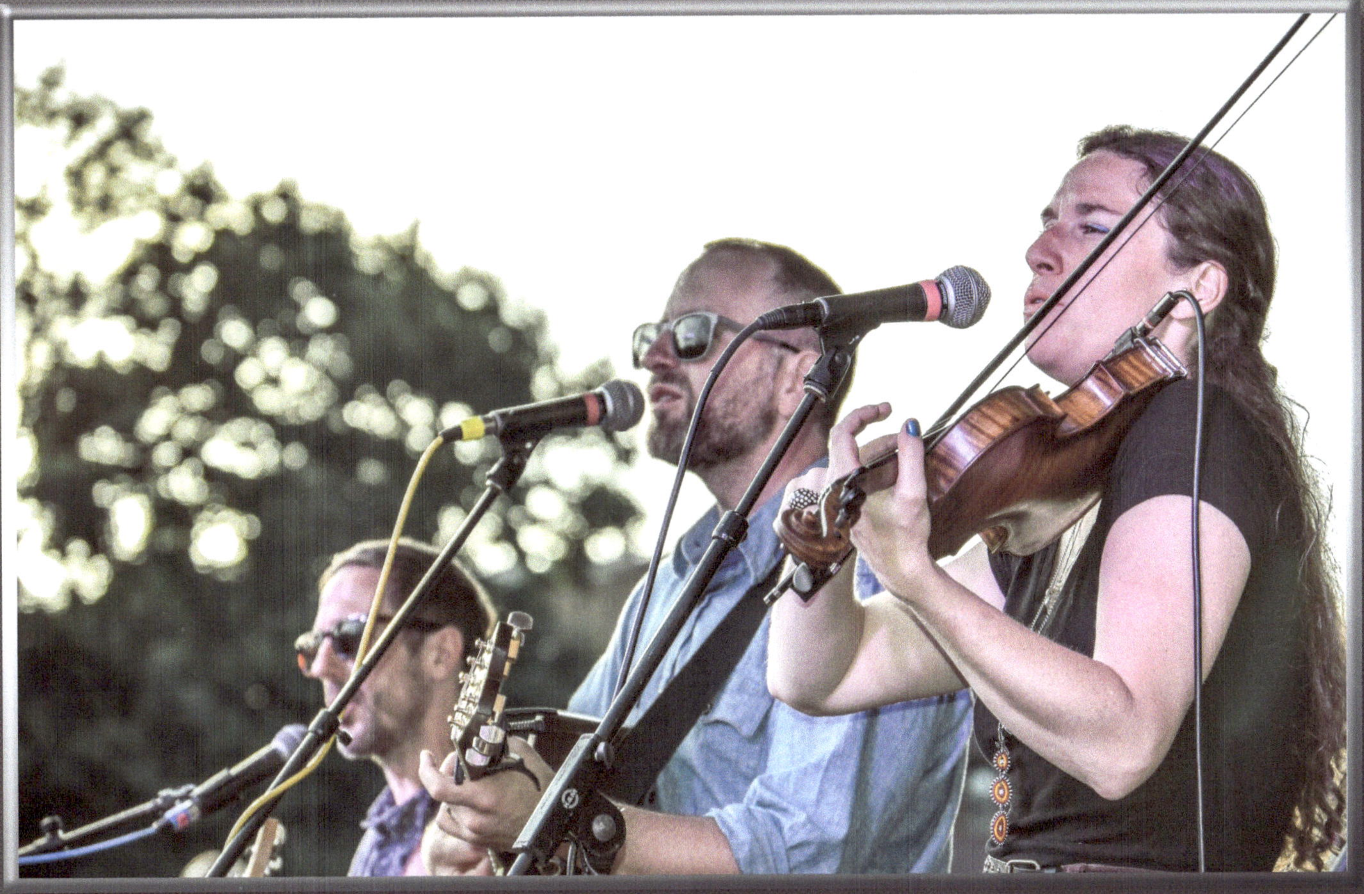

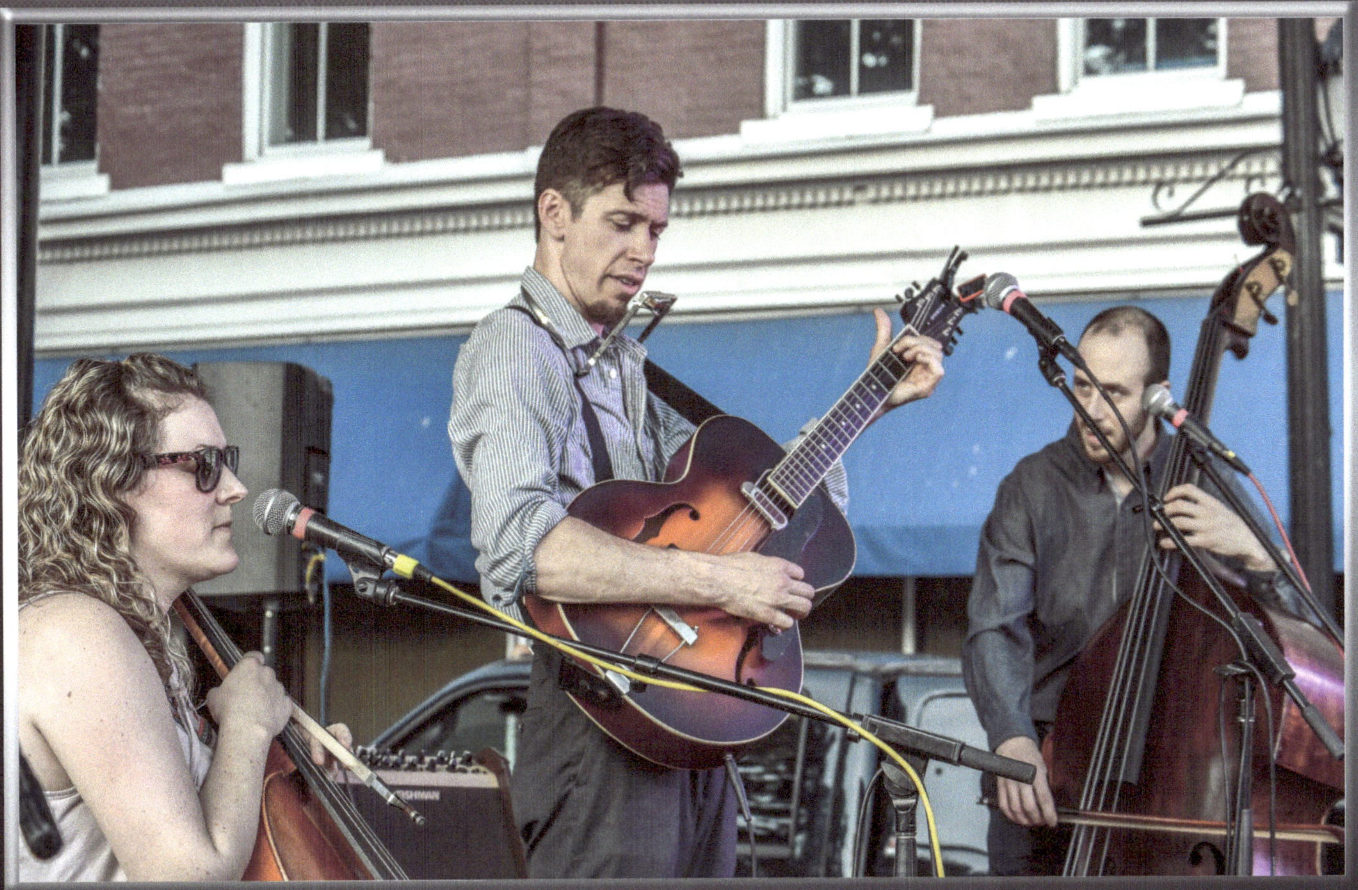

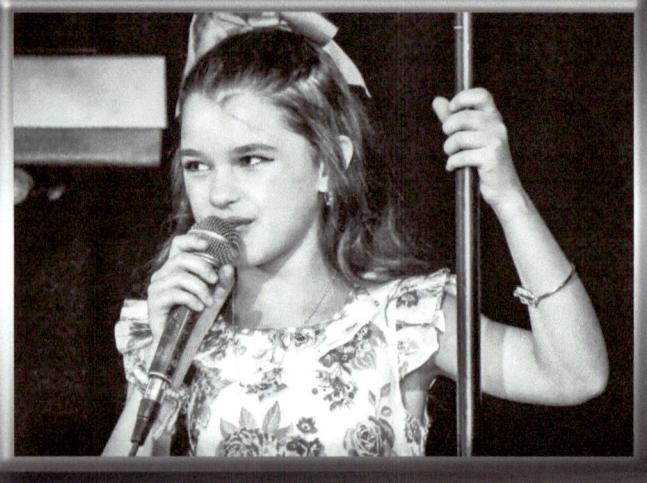
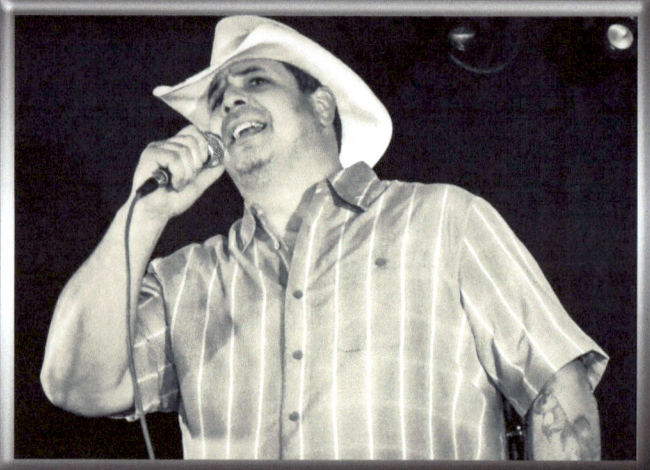
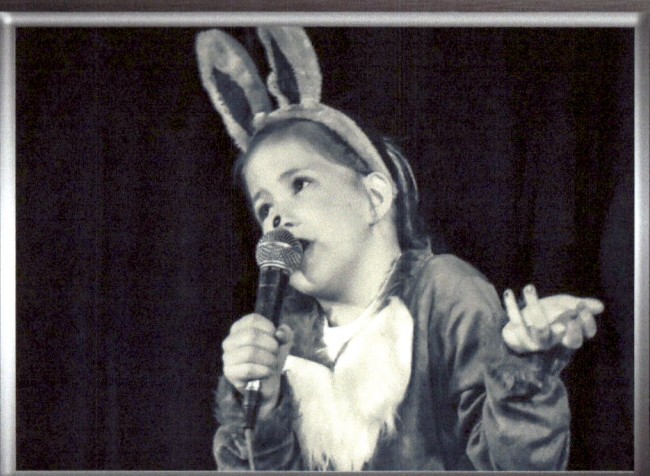
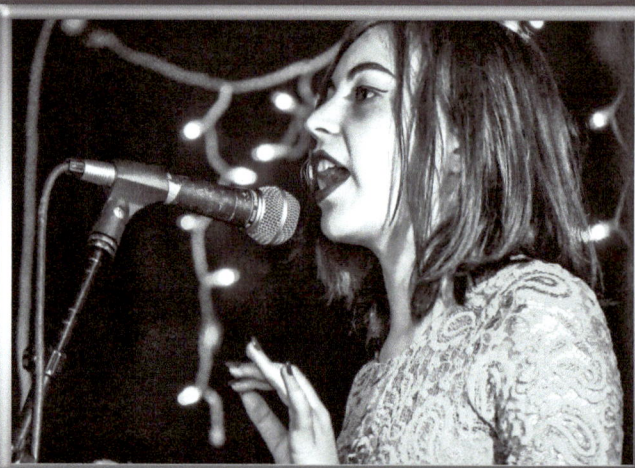
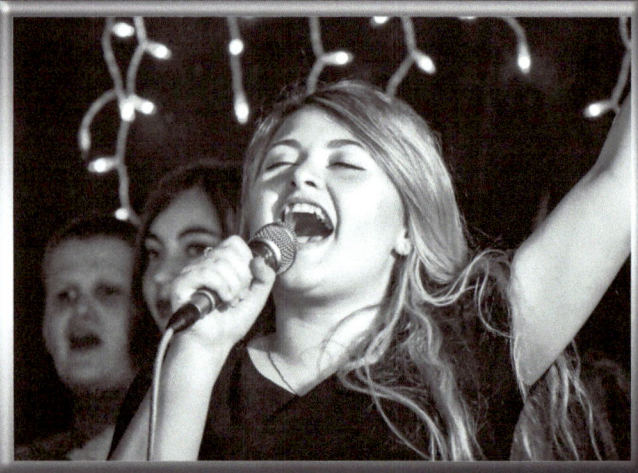
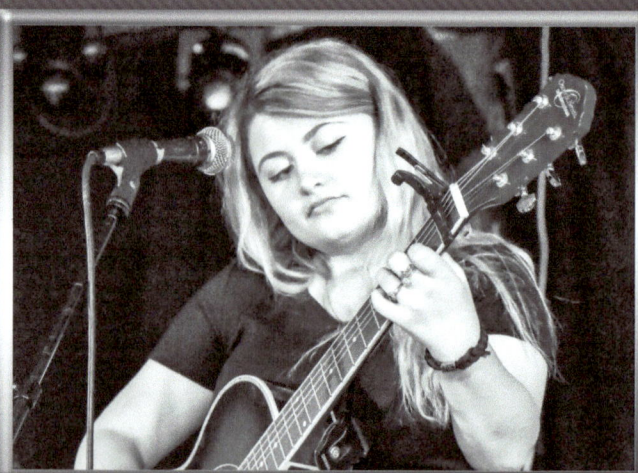

The local music scene would not exist without the several music education programs throughout the area. These programs can be found both within the public school systems and through private enterprise.

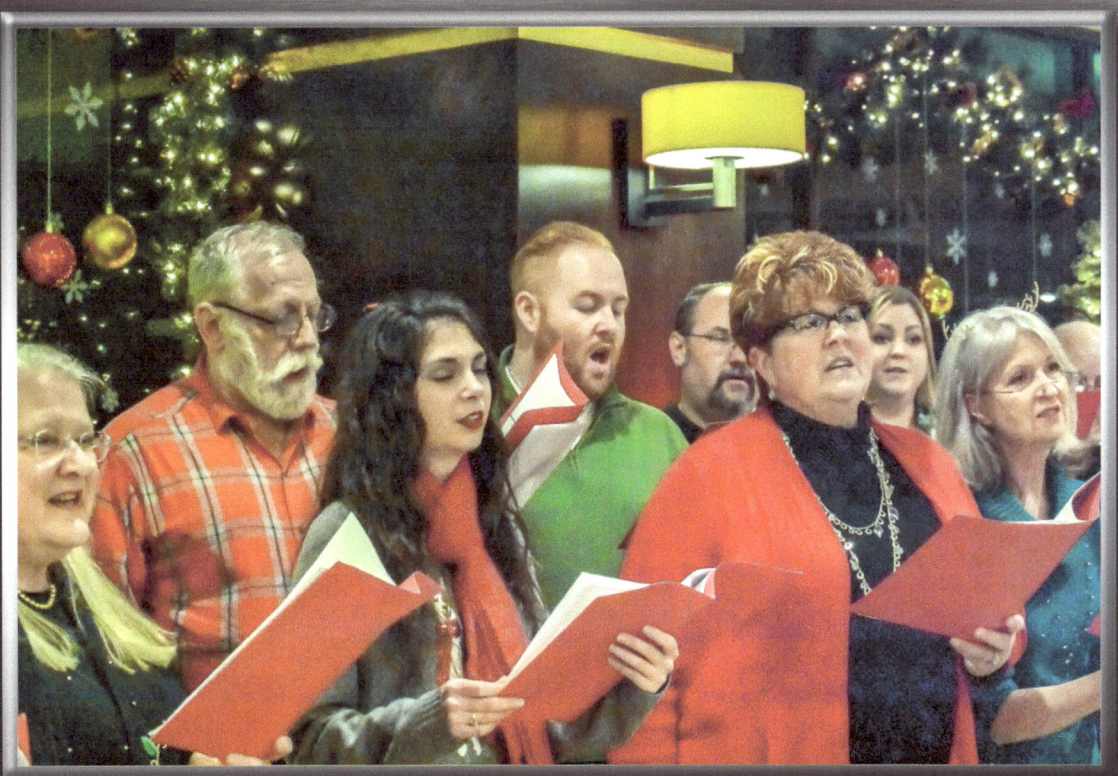

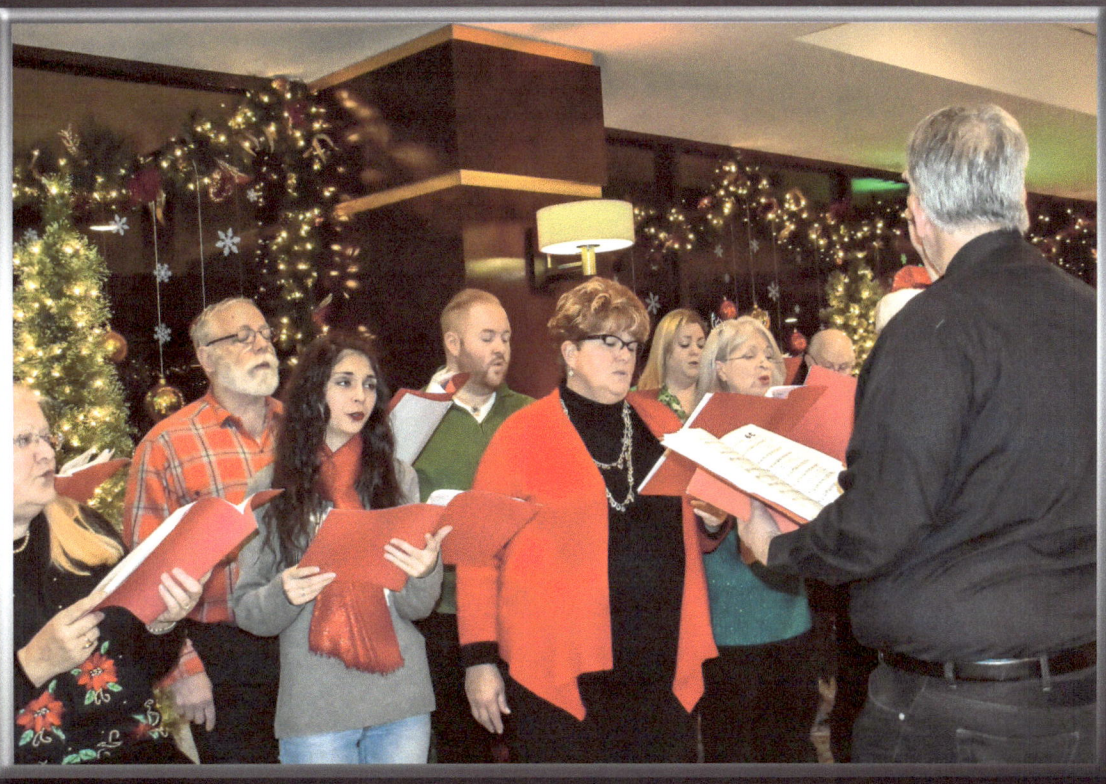

You never know where you will find one of the local choral groups performing throughout the year.

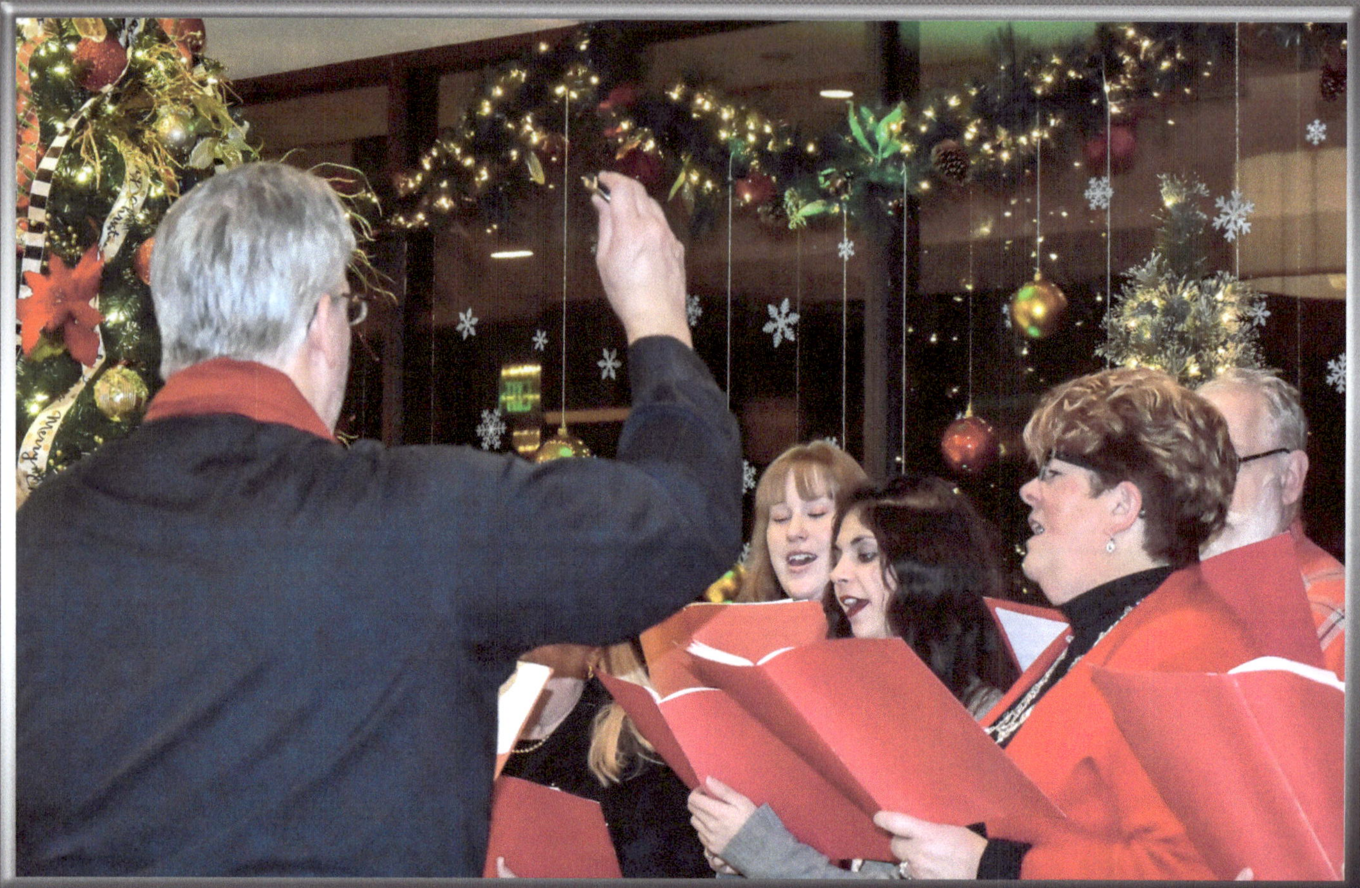

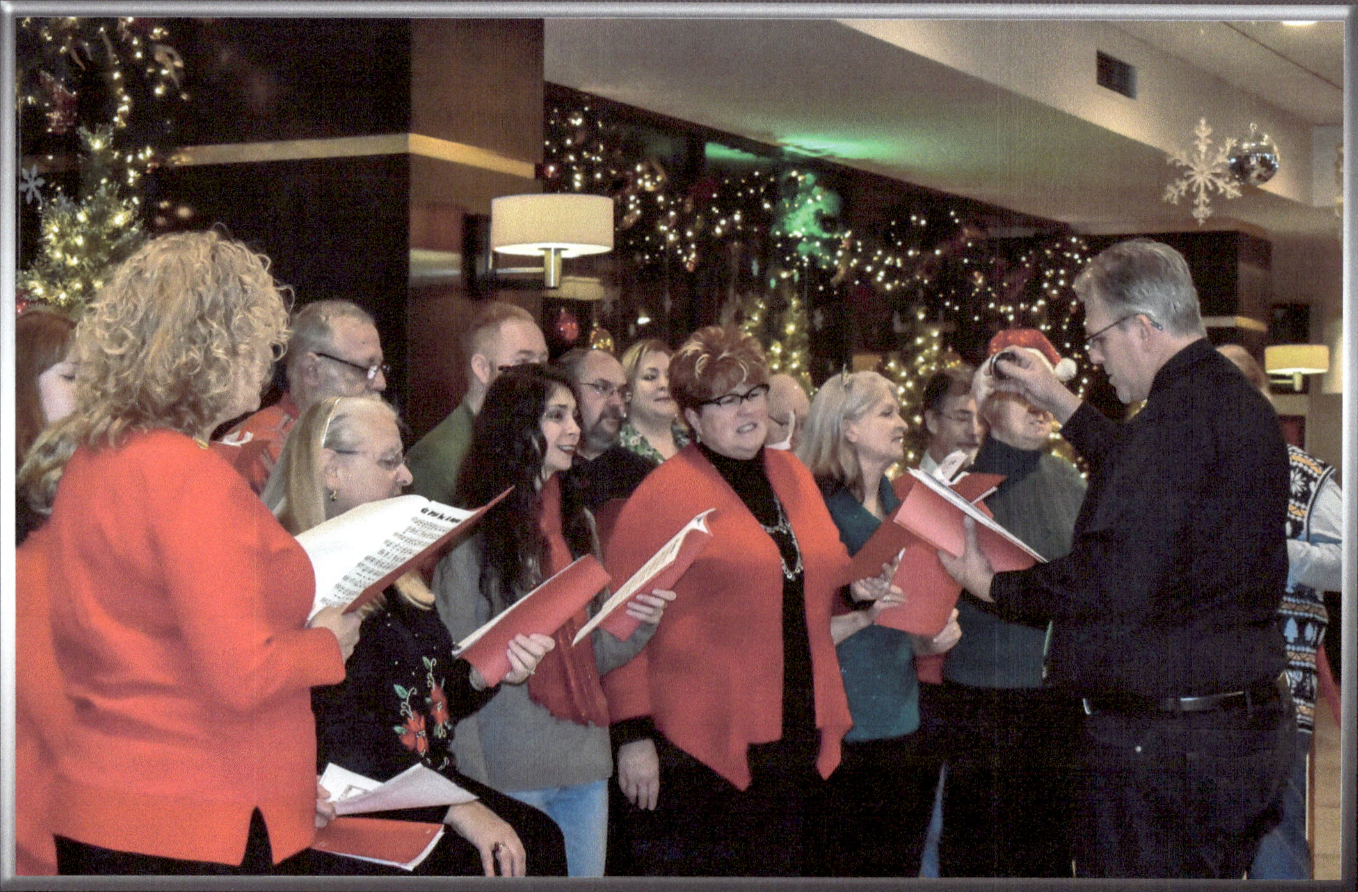

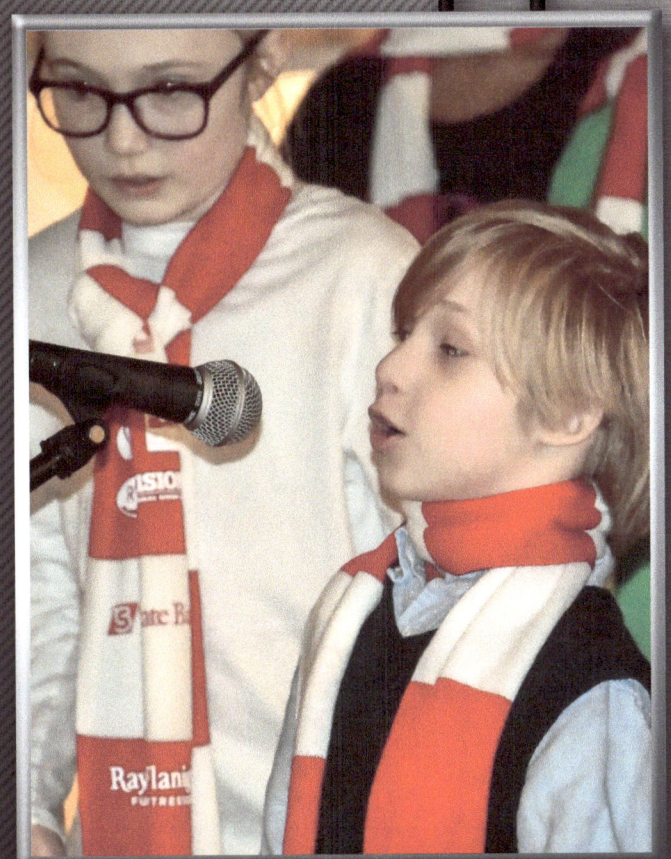
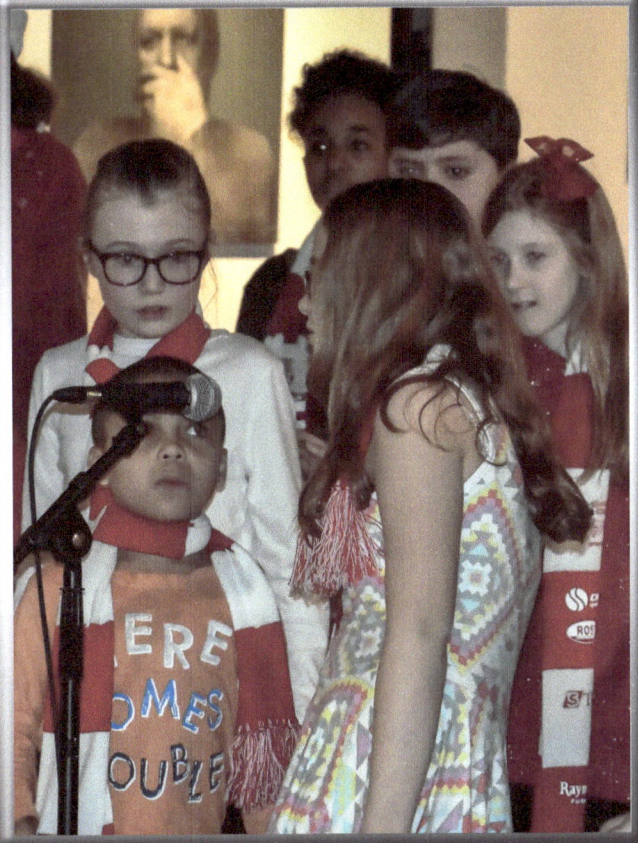

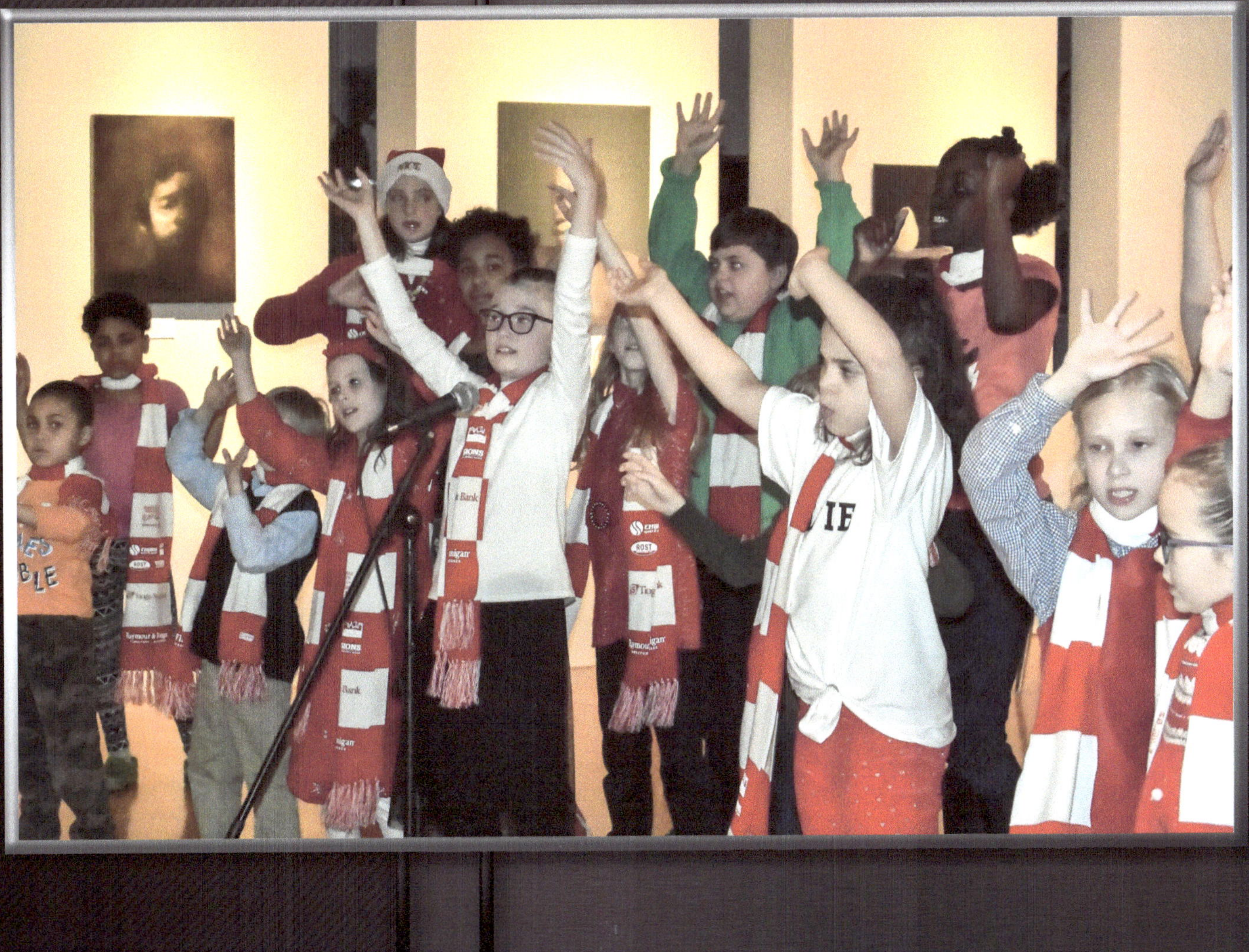

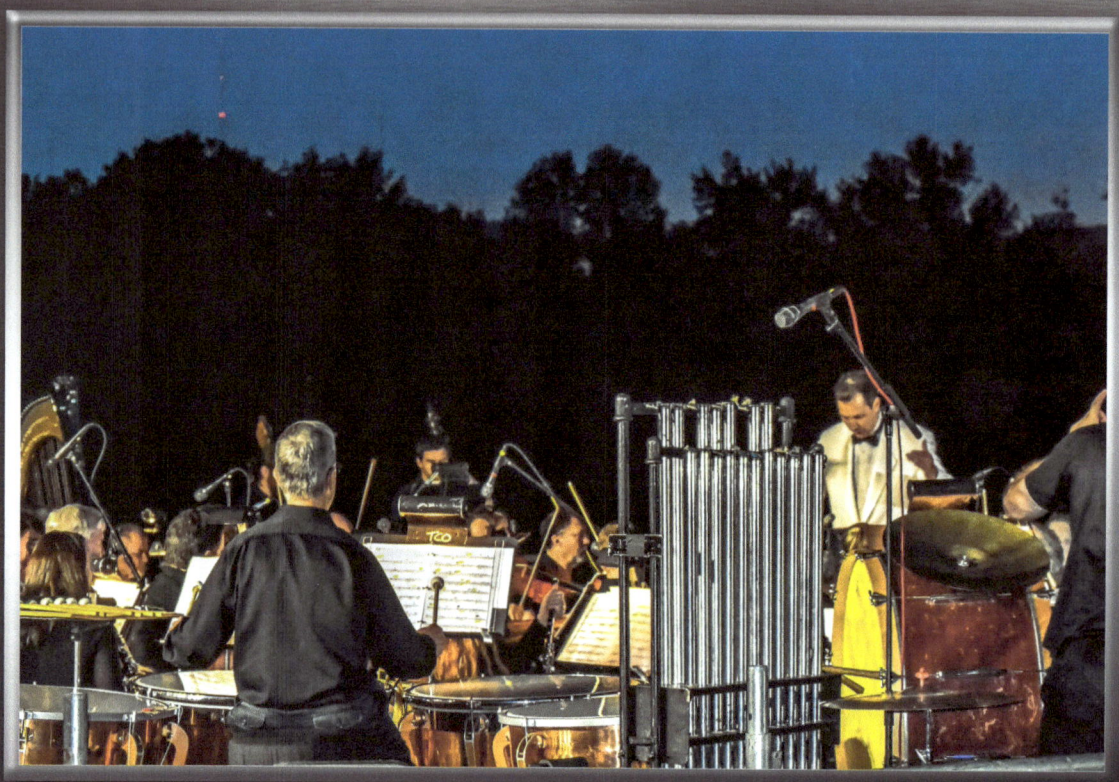

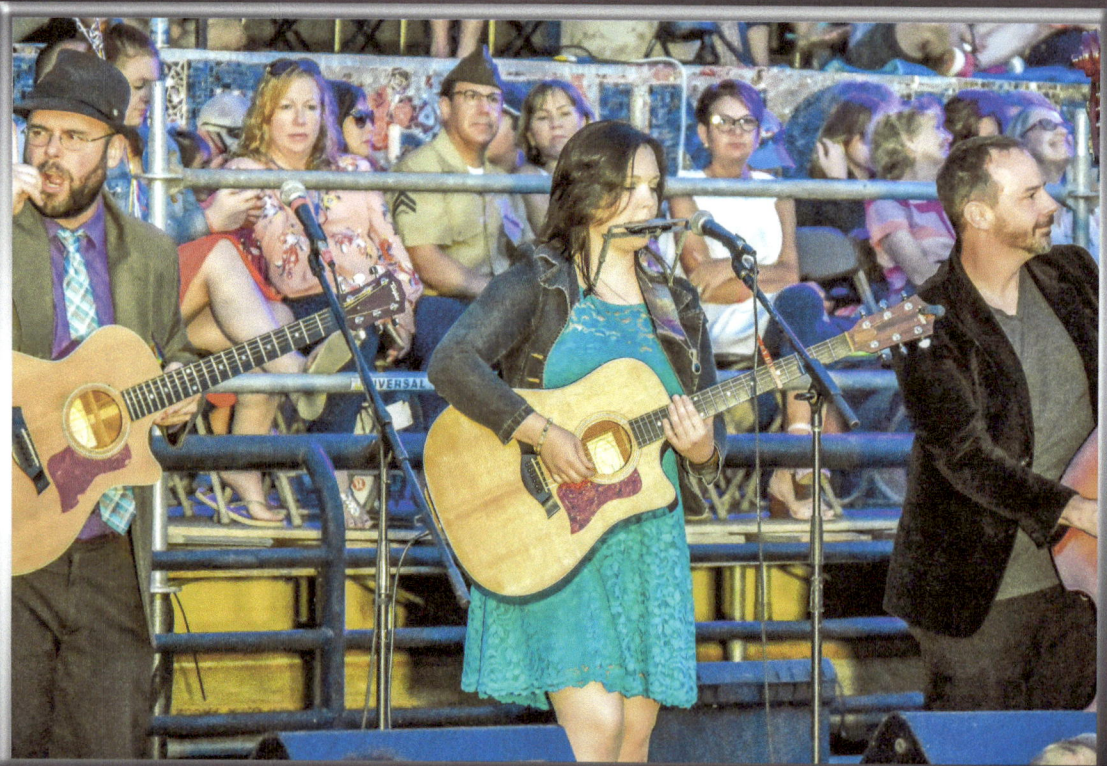

What do you get when you combine the local philharmonic orchestra with an acoustic trio, a steel drum band and a pipe & drum band? An amazing night of music on the river.

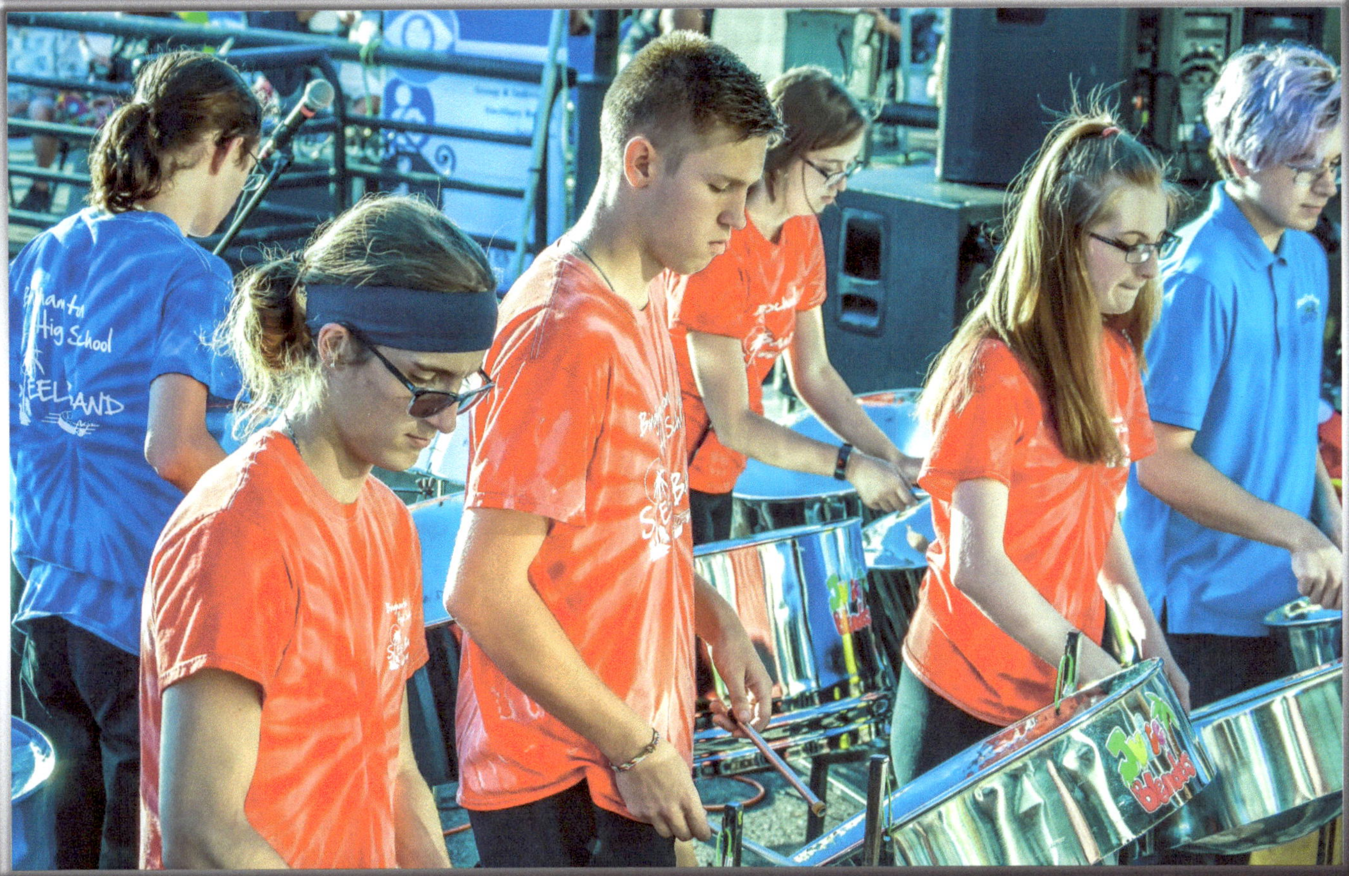

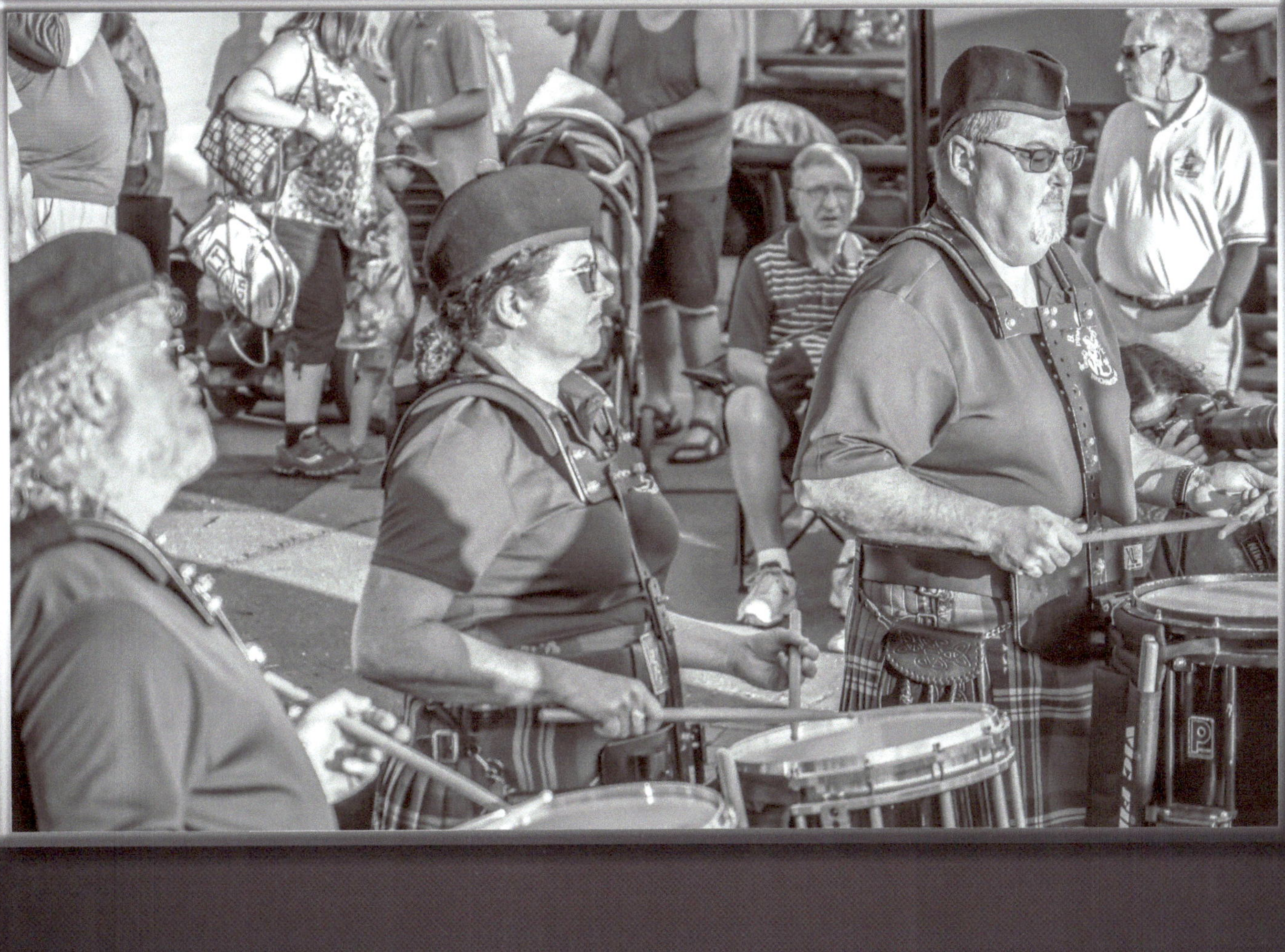

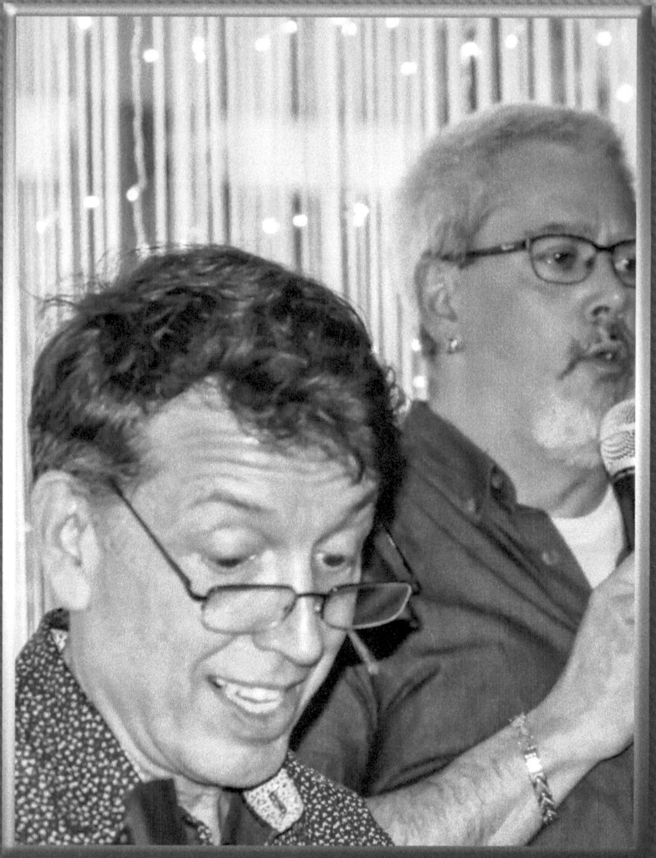

Growing in popularity this past year has been the NYC-style Piano Bar.

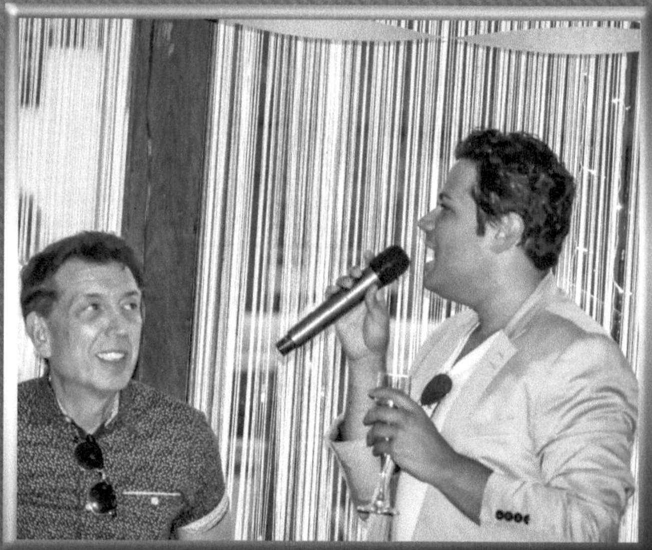

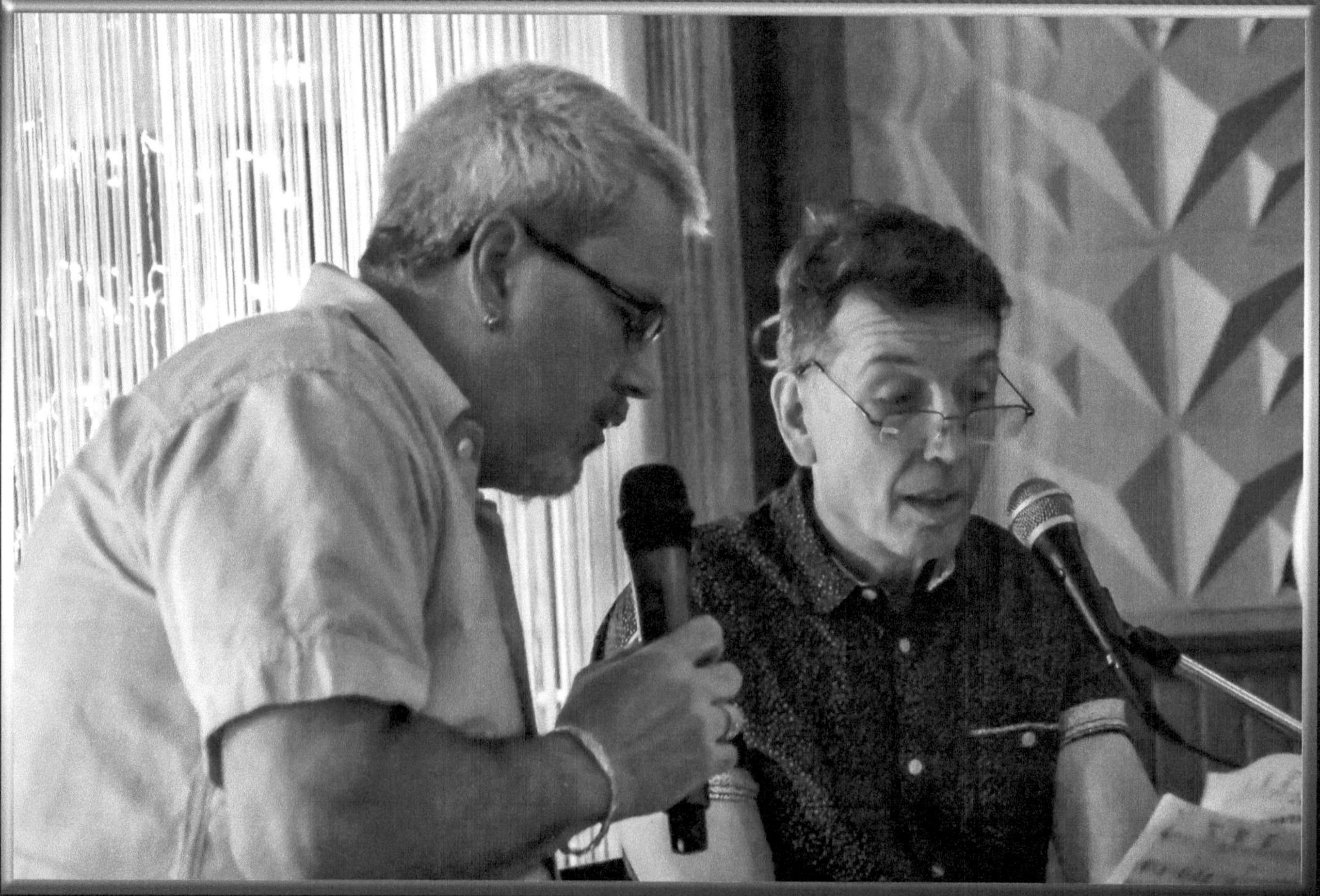

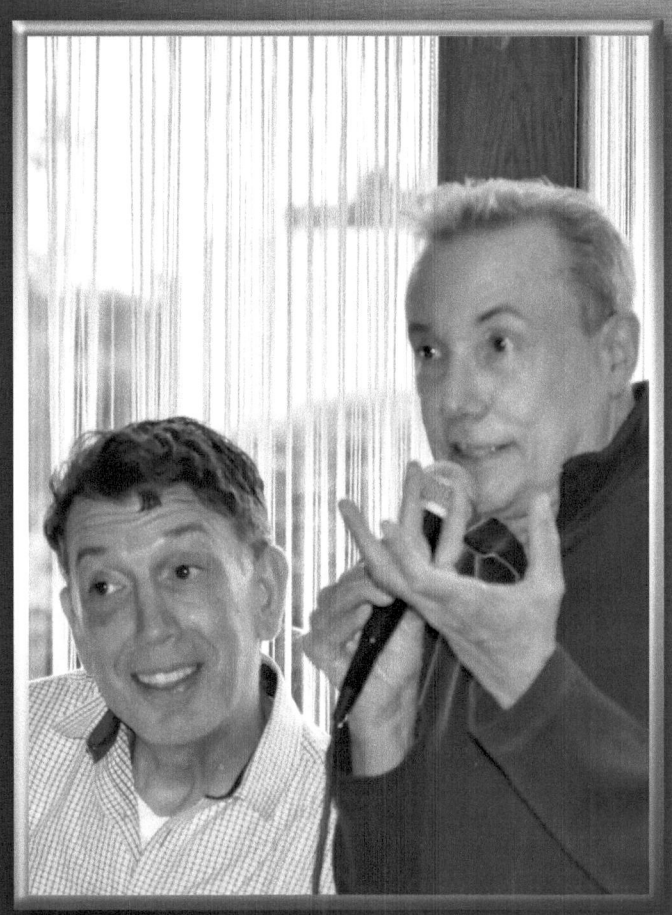

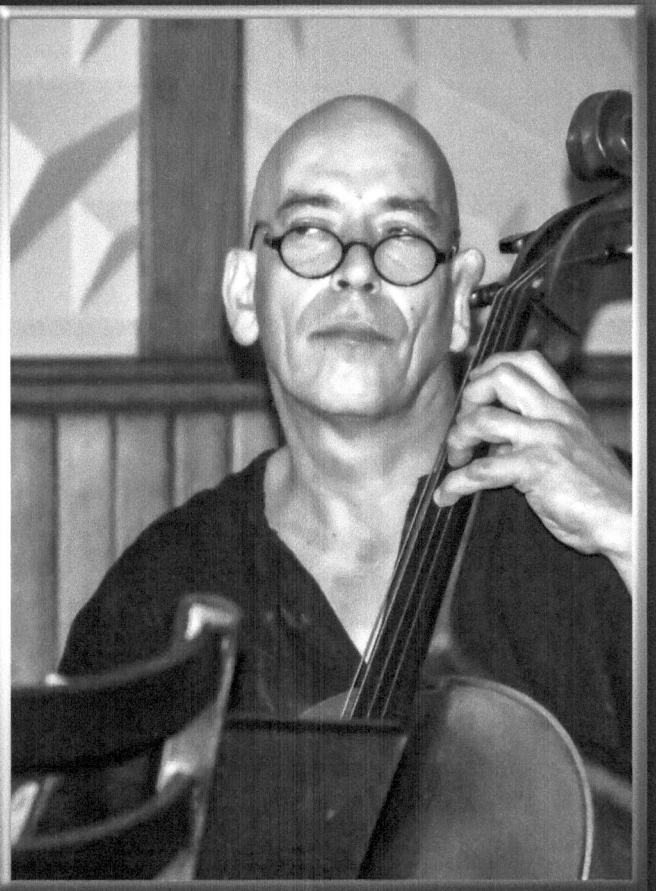
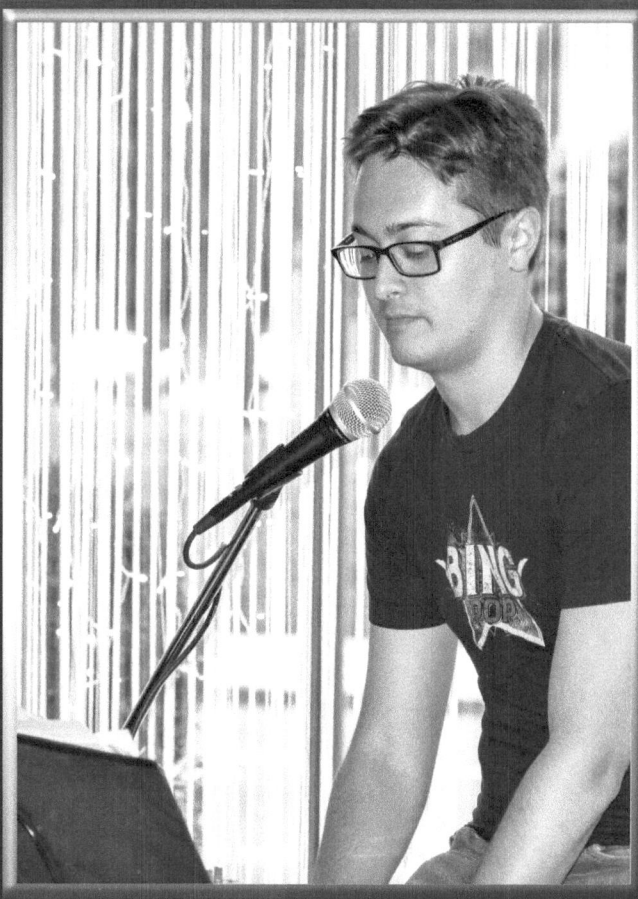

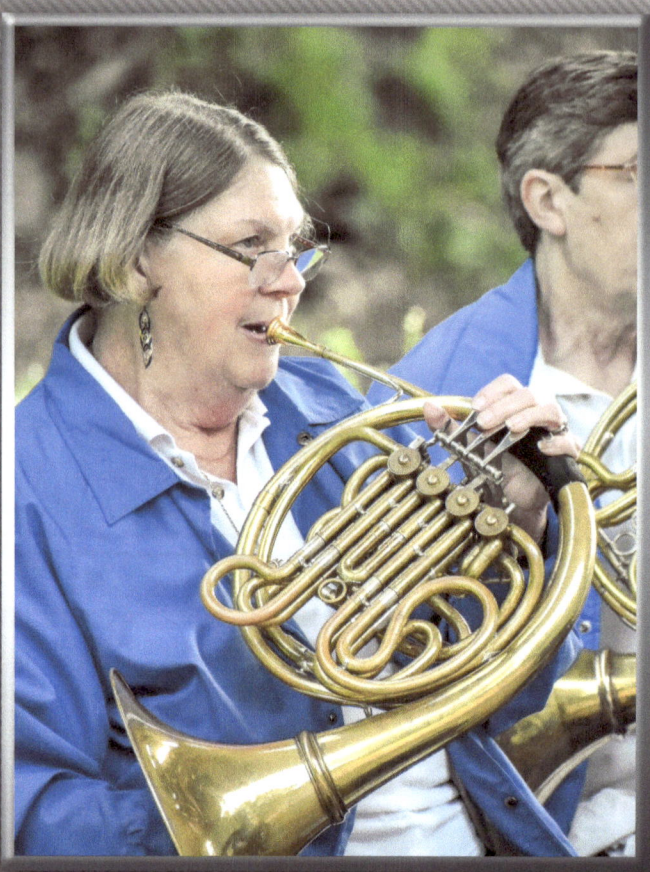
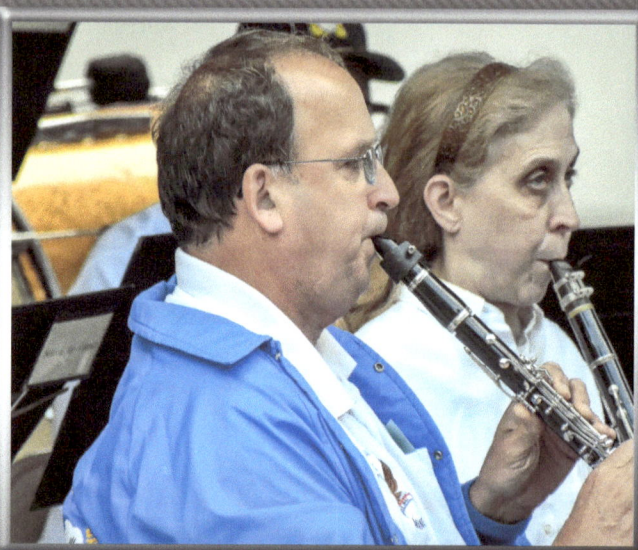

Community bands provide an outlet for adult musicians to continue their love of playing. Many are retirees, teachers, corporate executives and business owners.

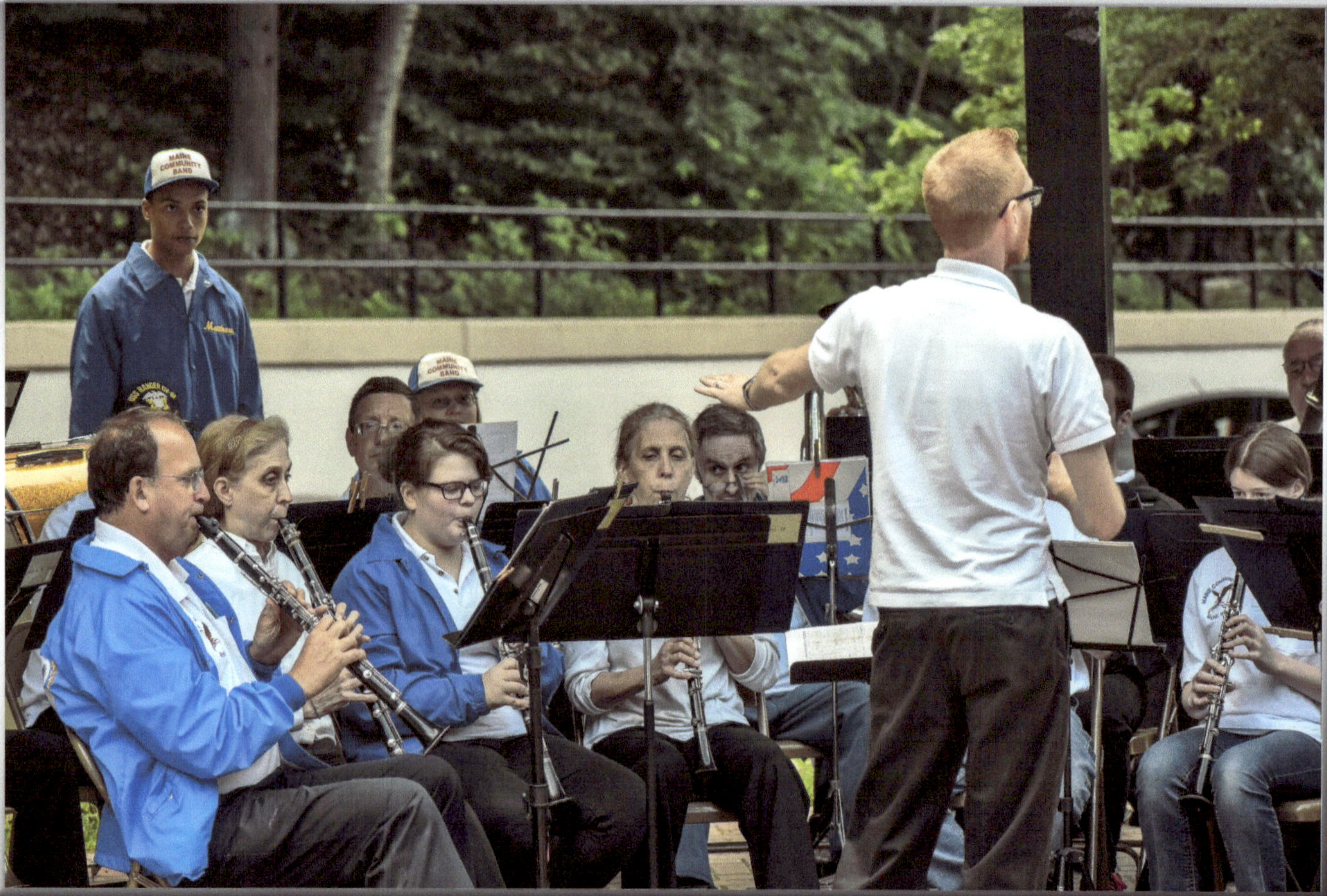

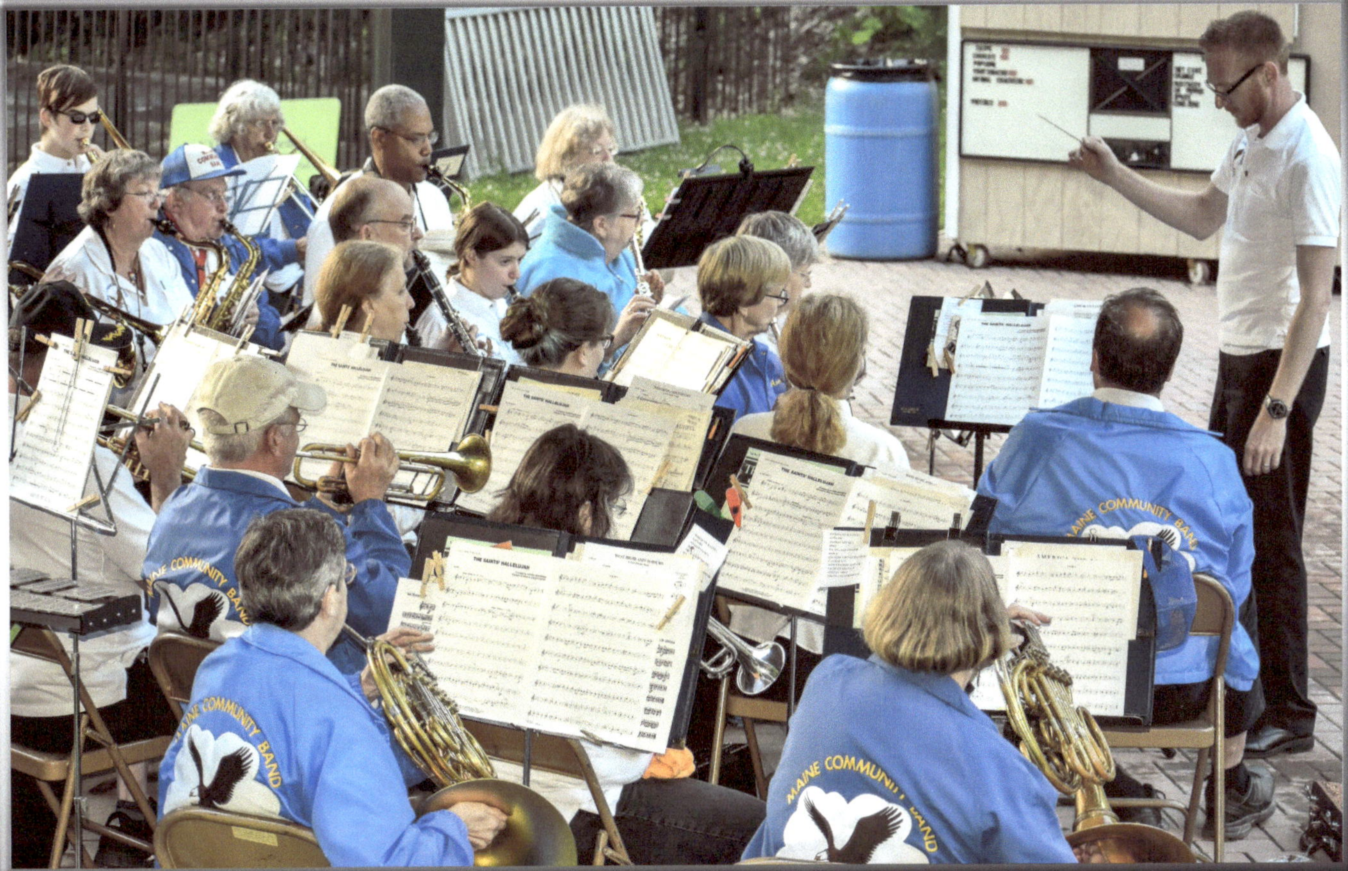

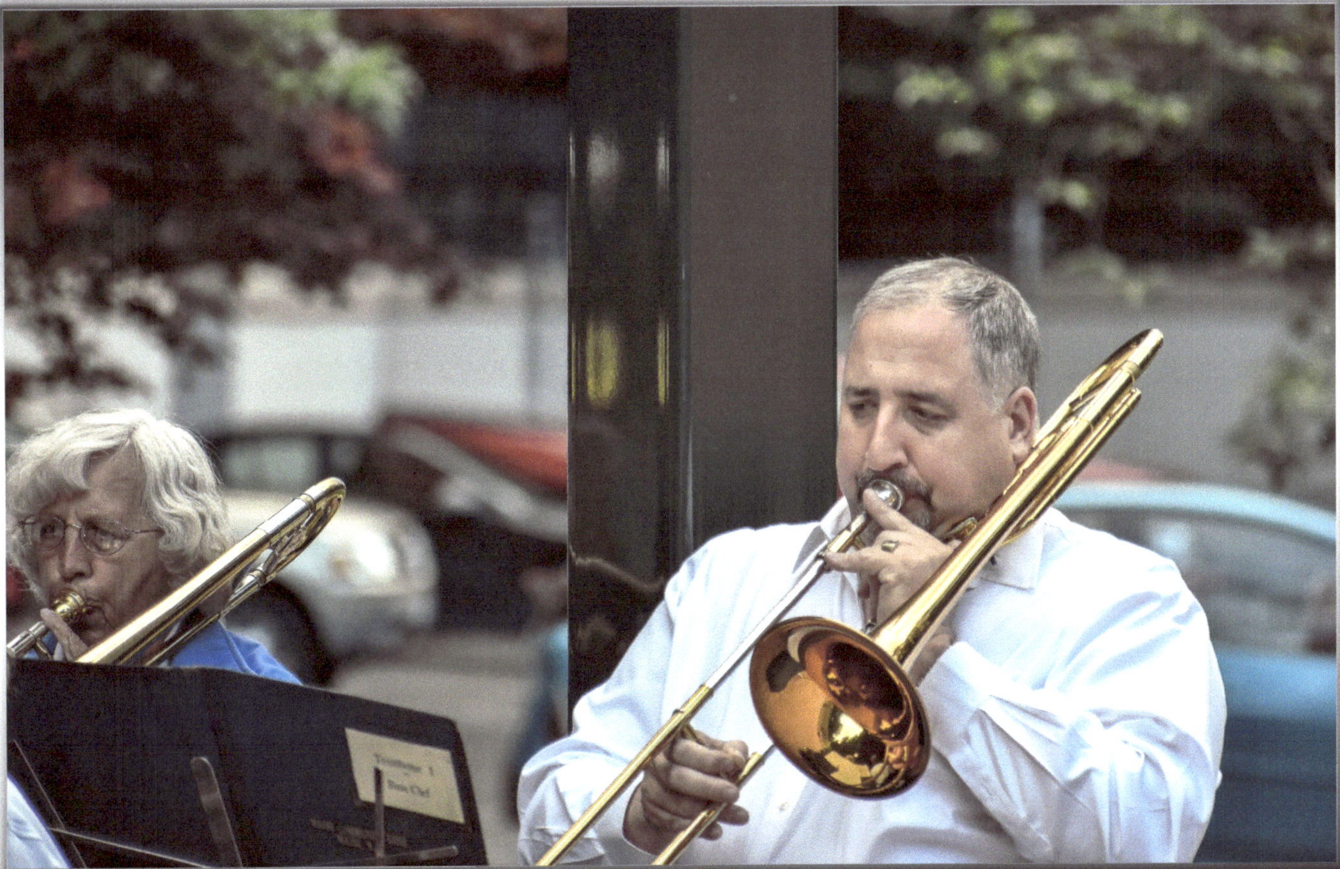

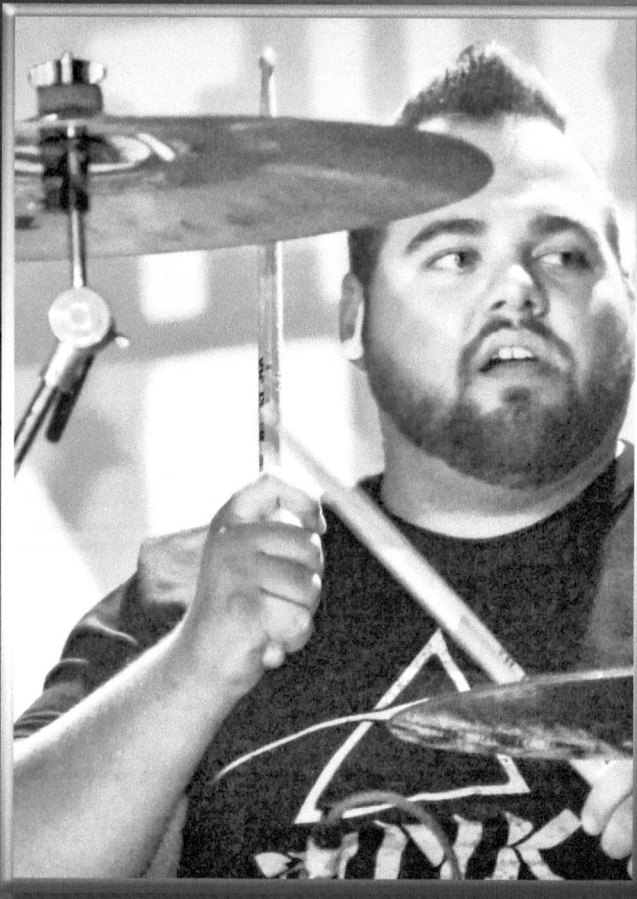
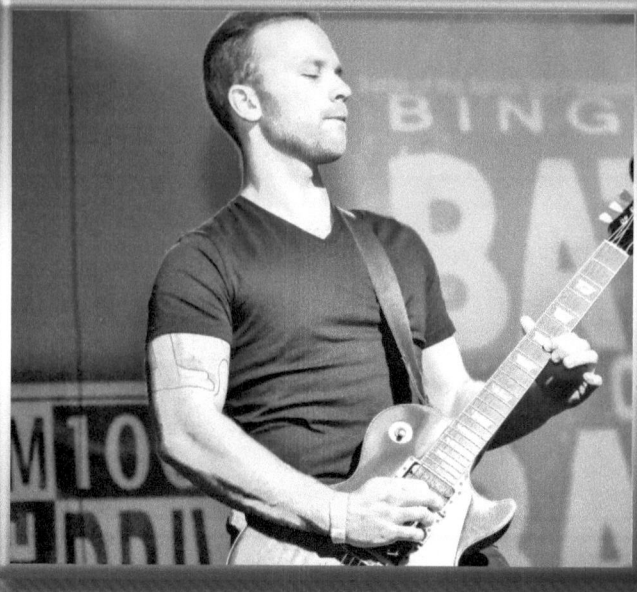
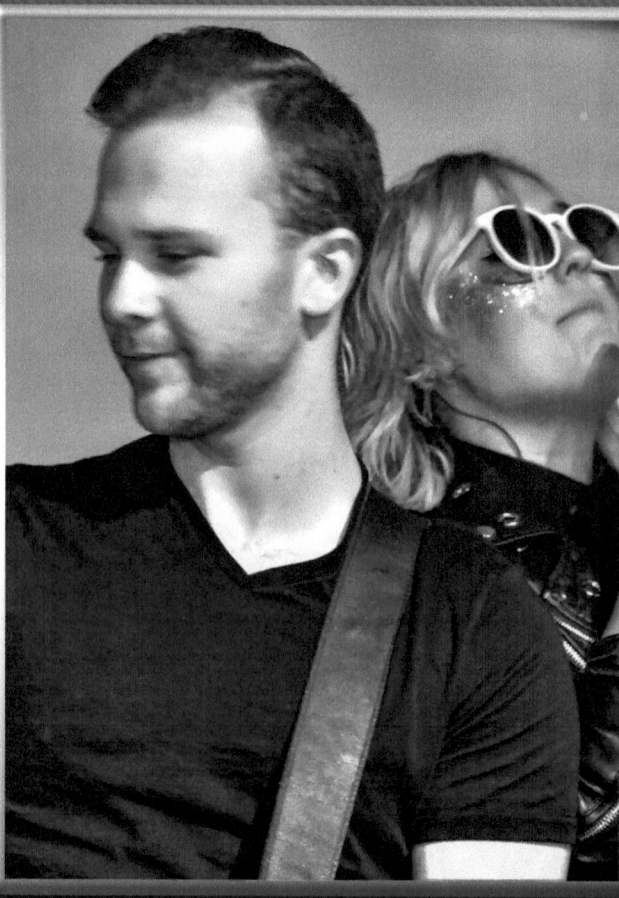
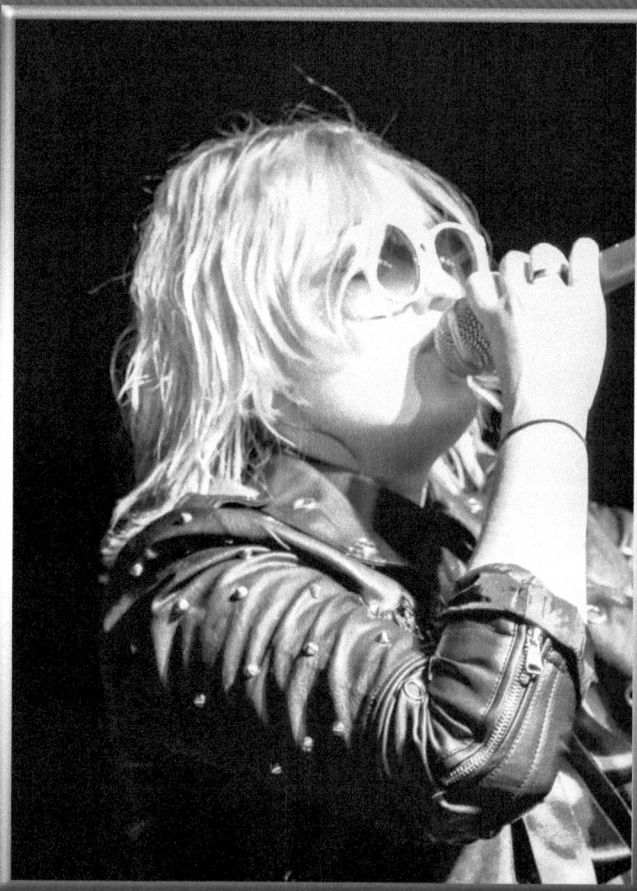

Local bands will occasionally compete against each other for the title of the best band in the Southern Tier. It's the perfect way to experience the diversity of the music scene.

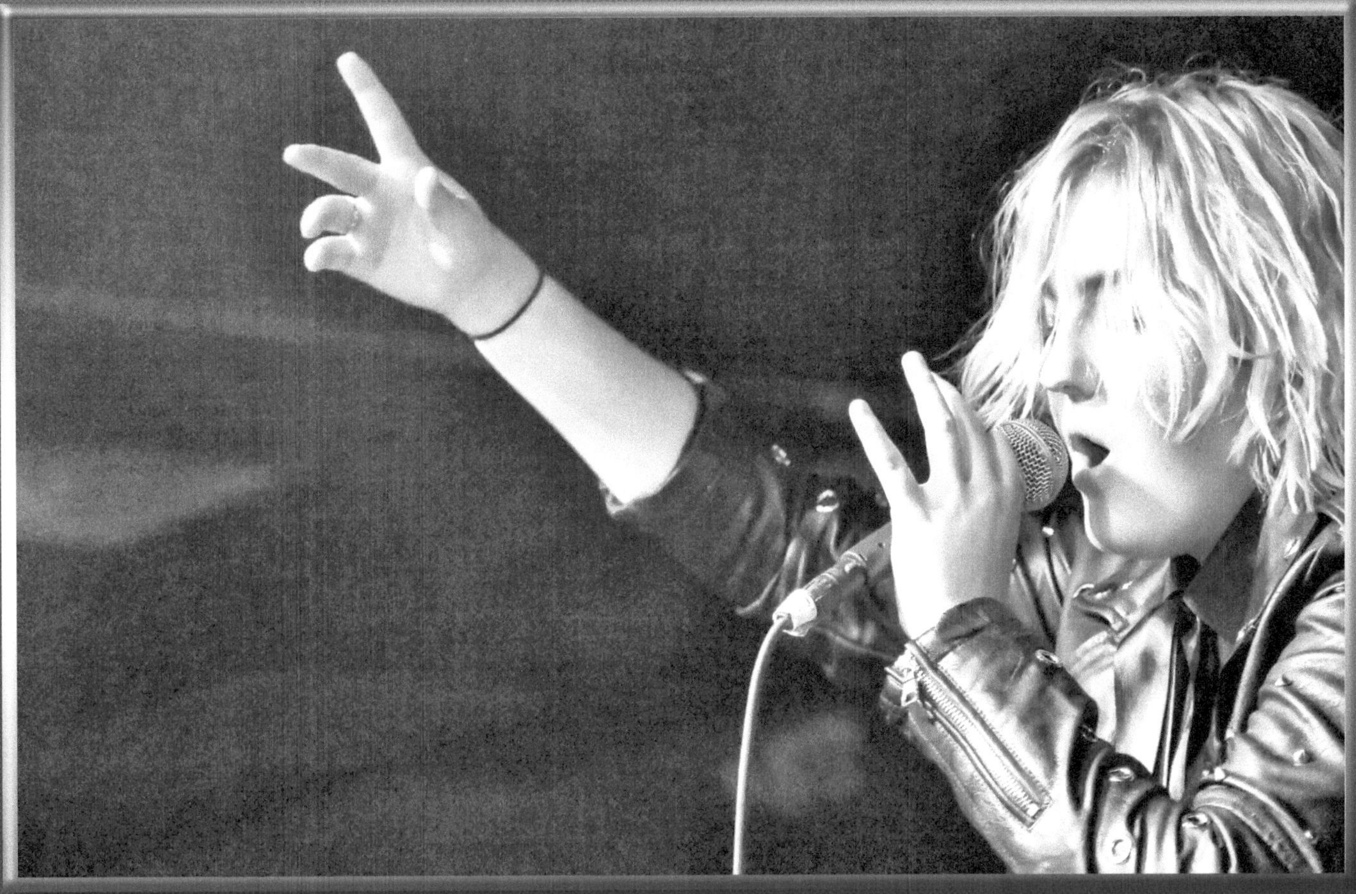

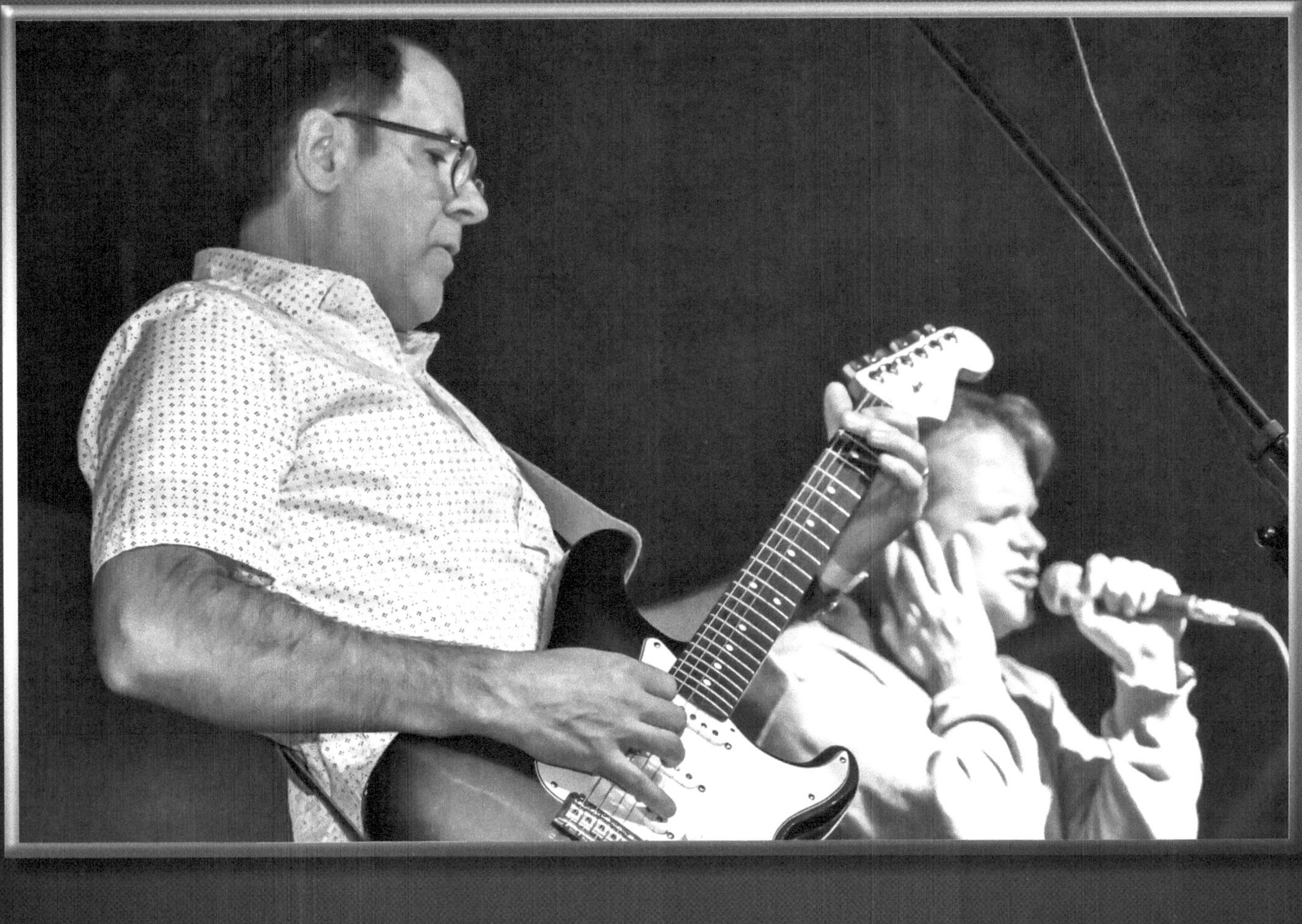

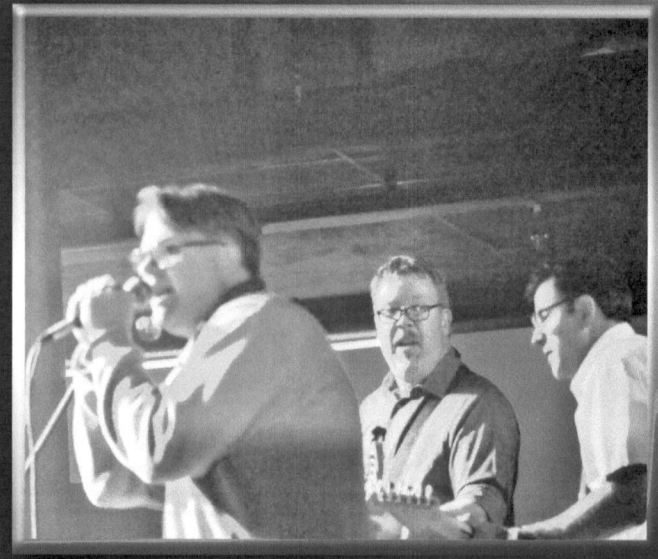
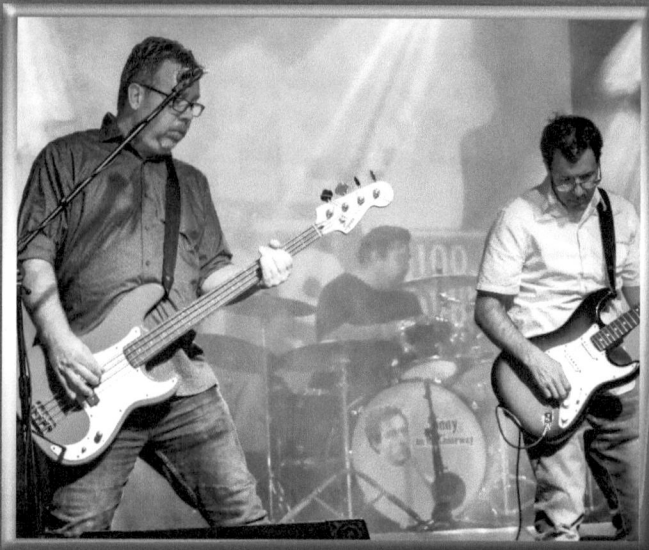
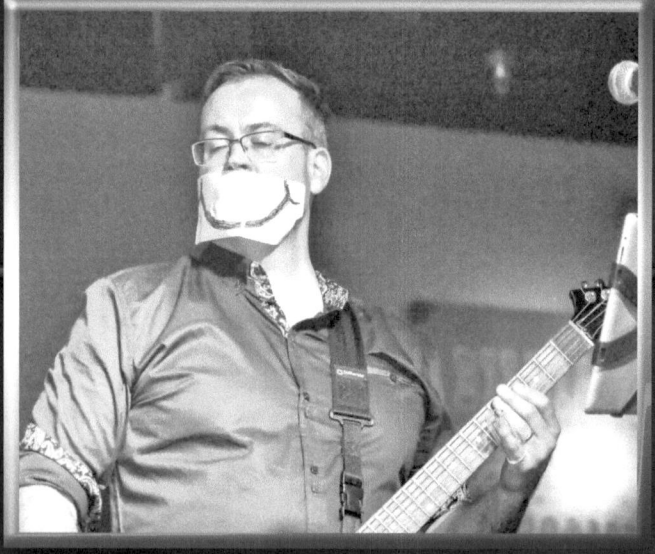
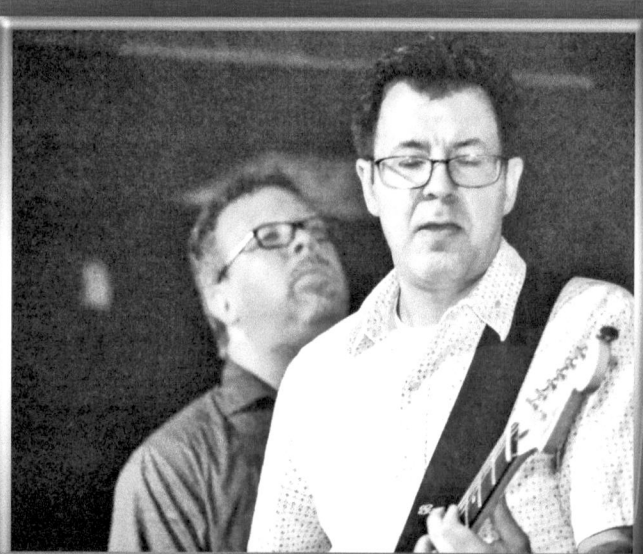
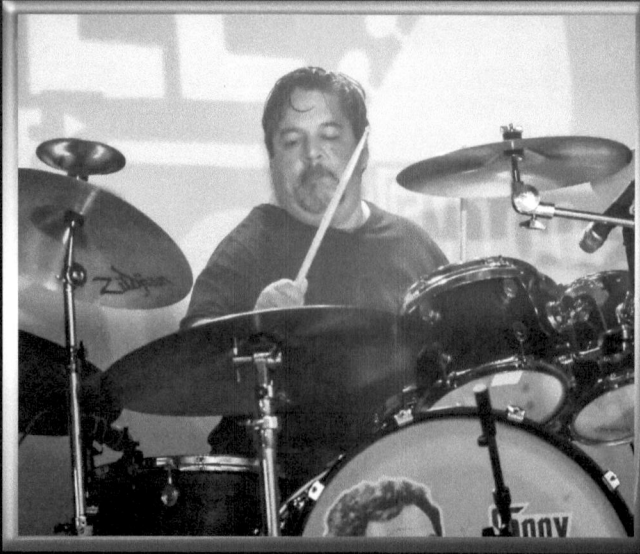
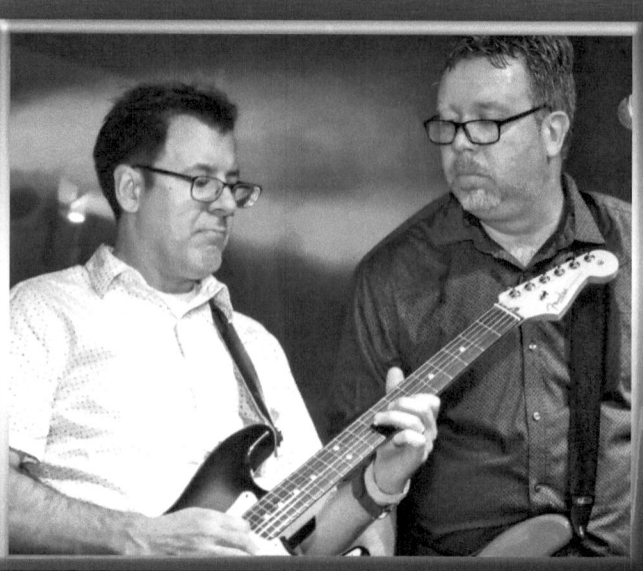

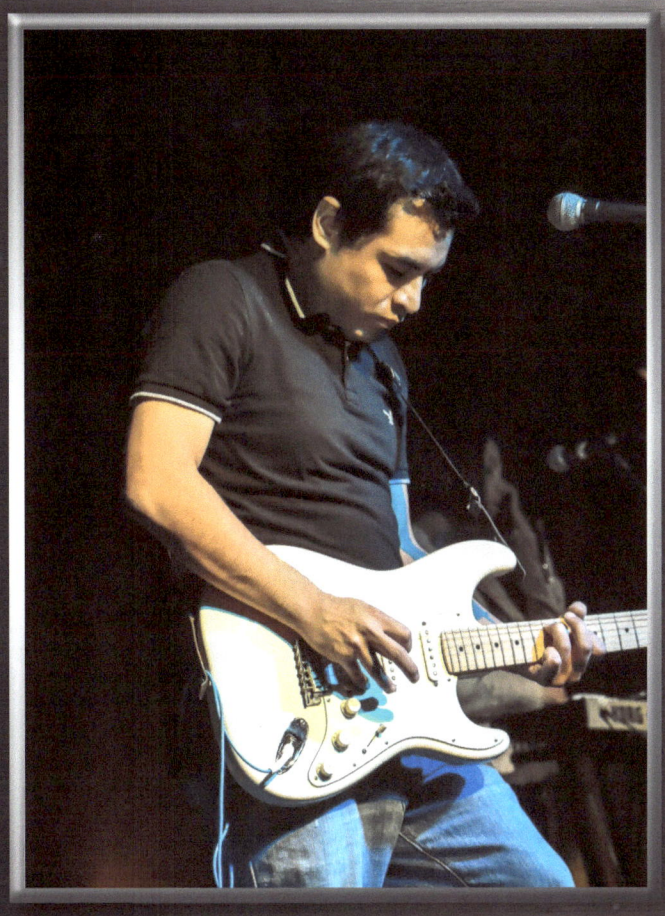
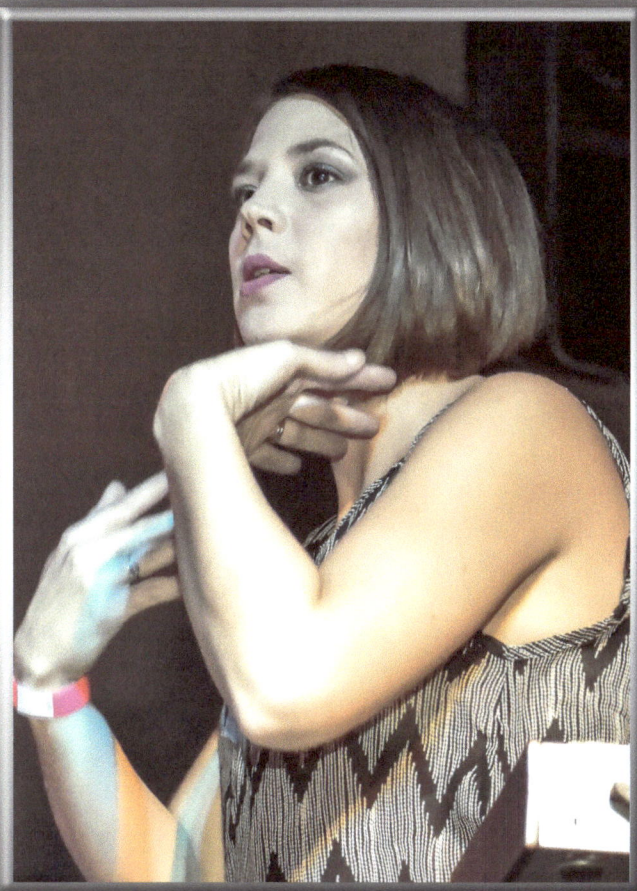
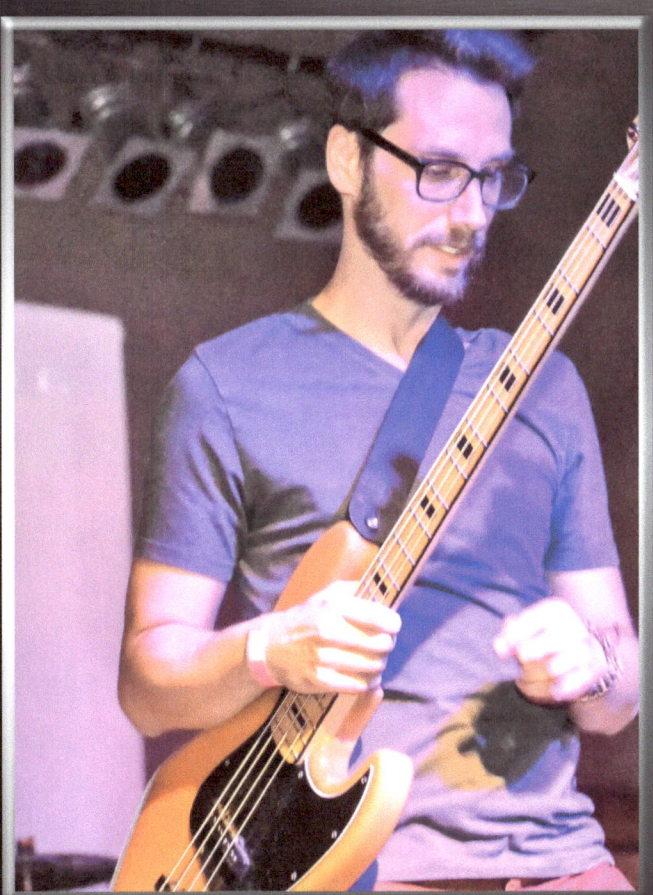
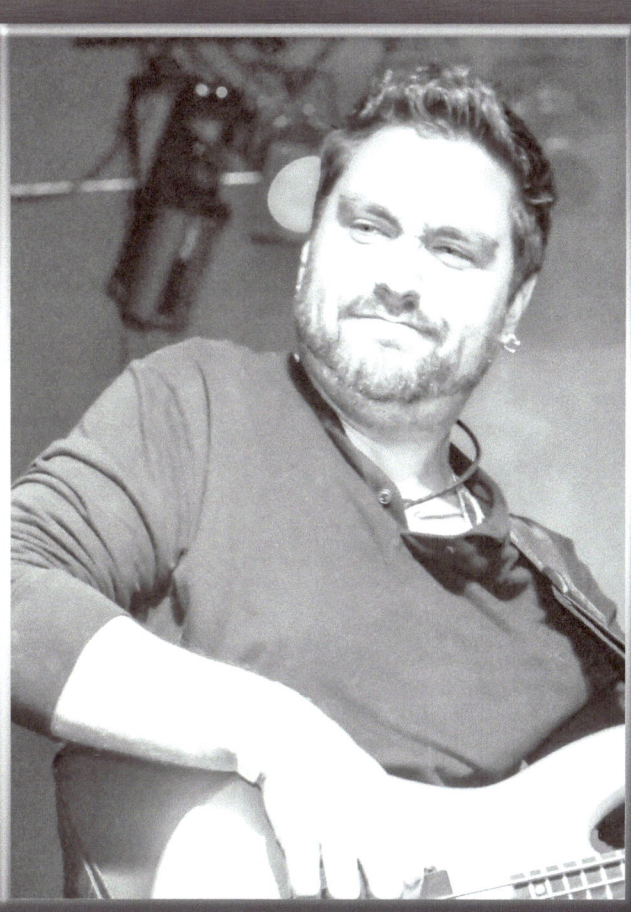

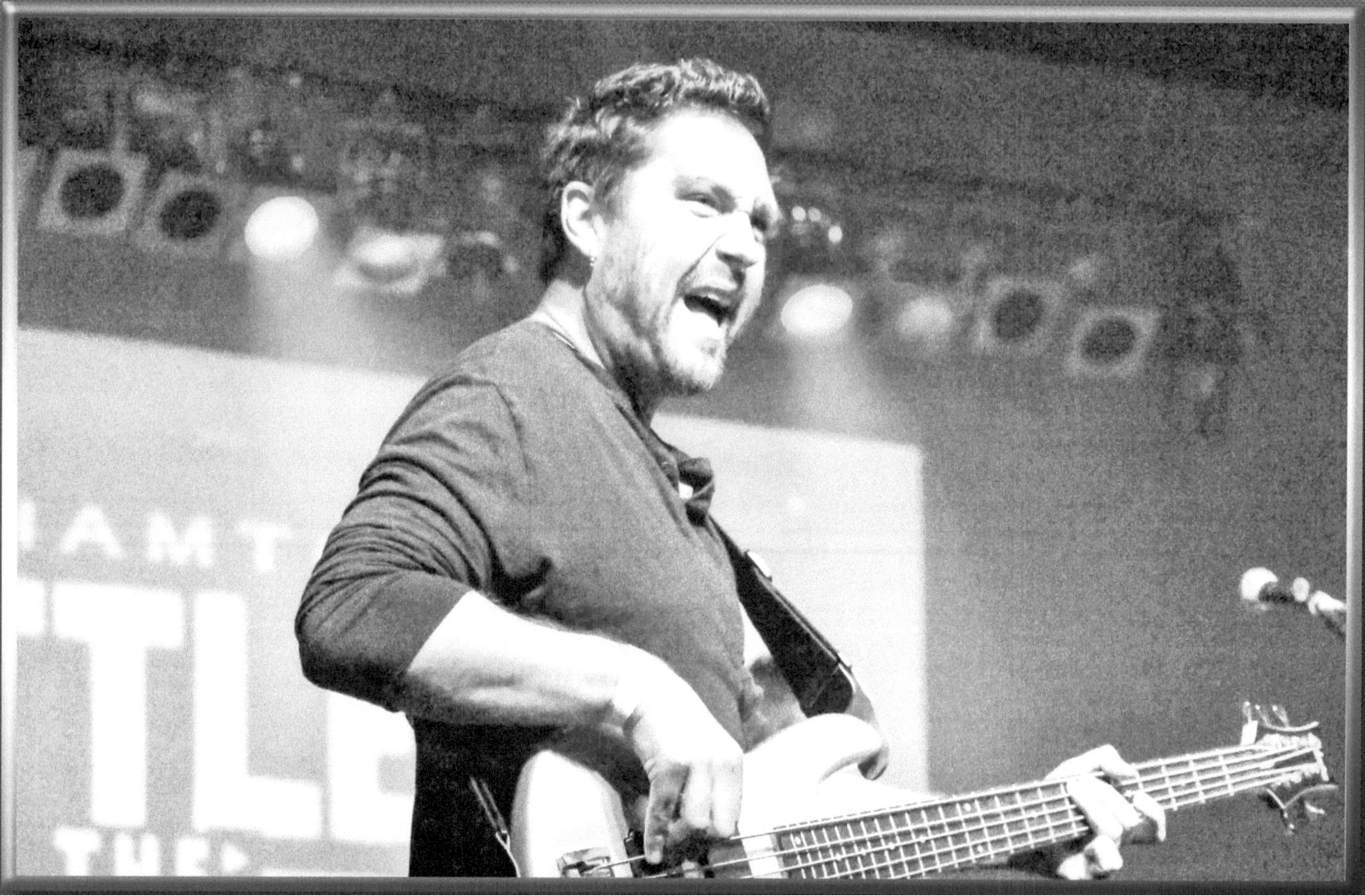

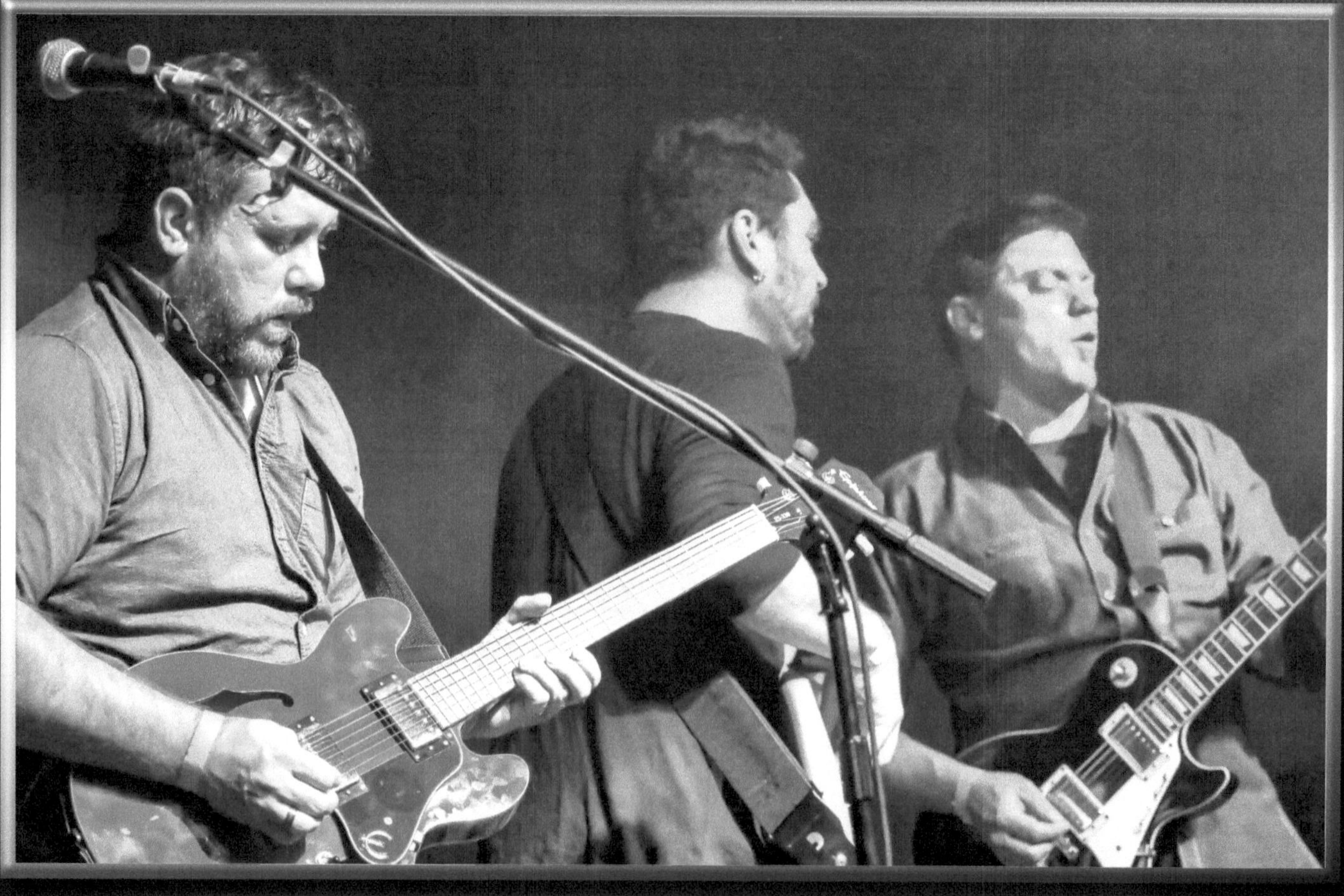

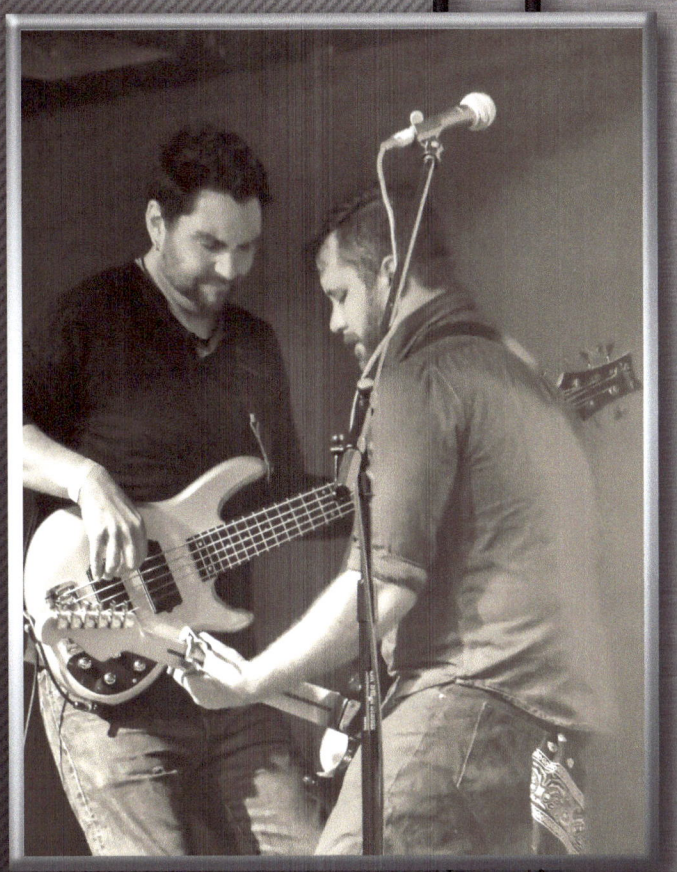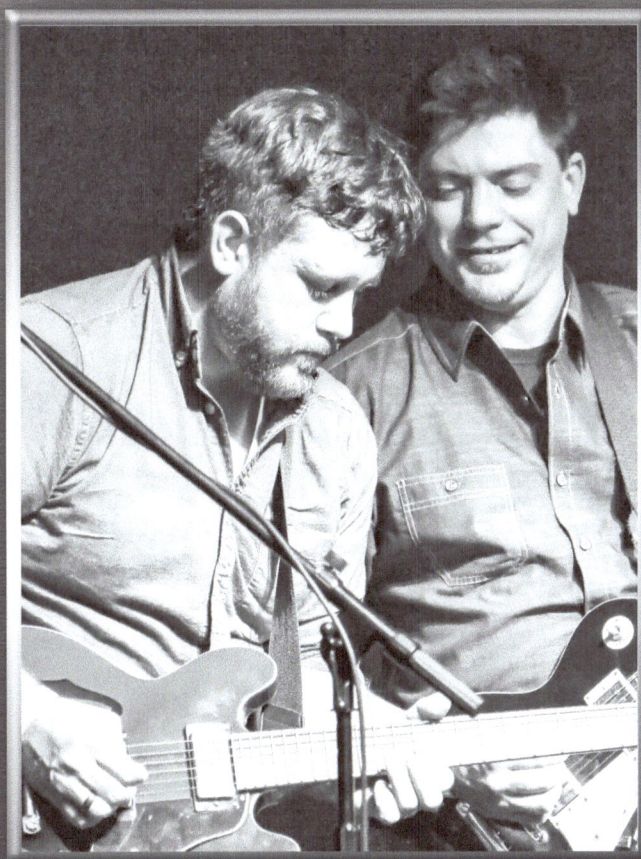

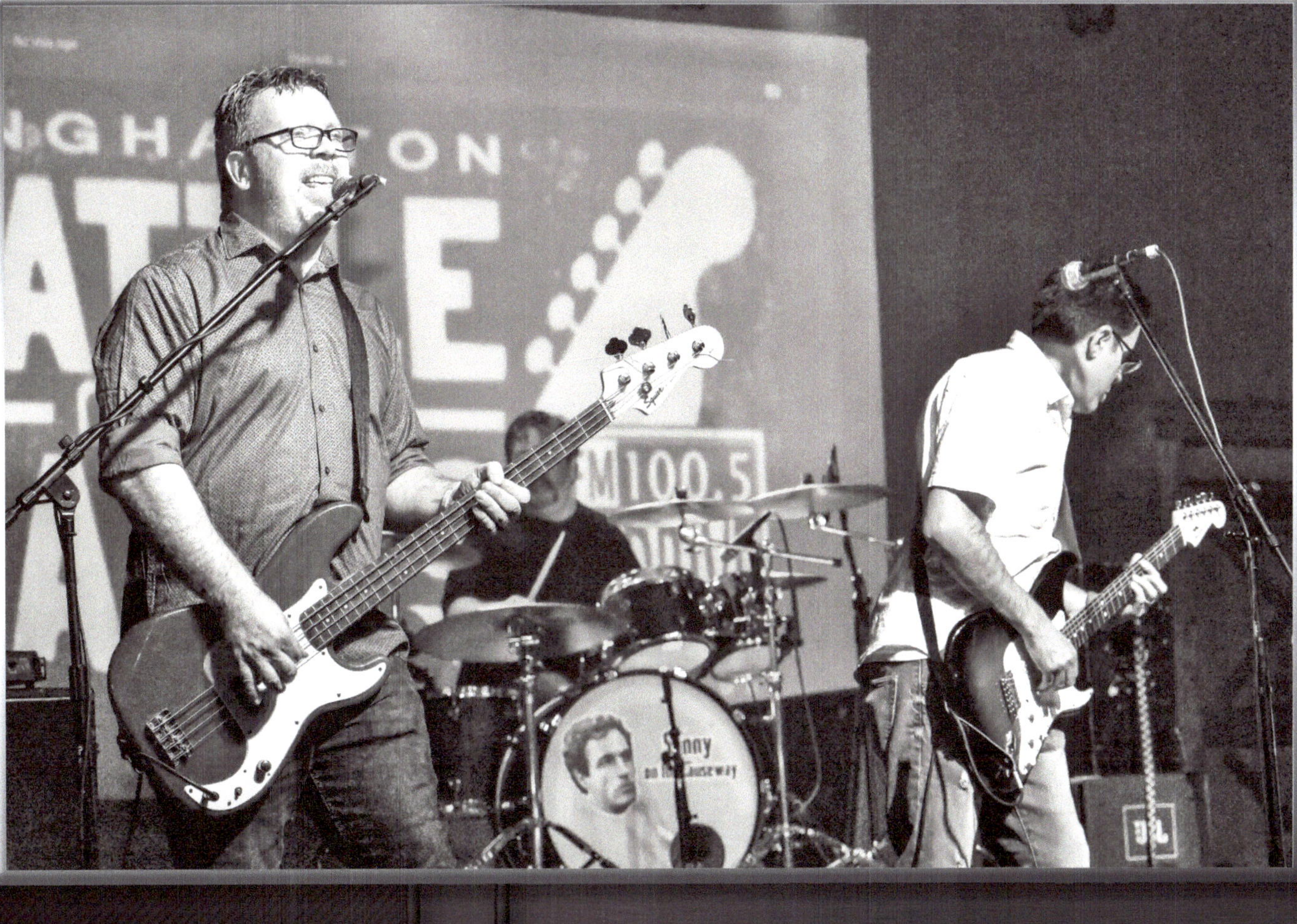

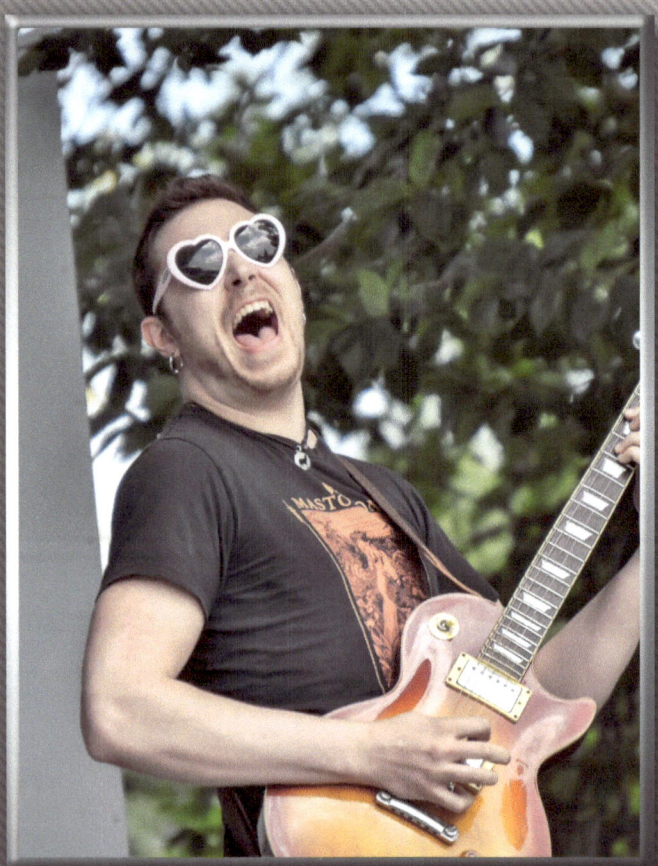
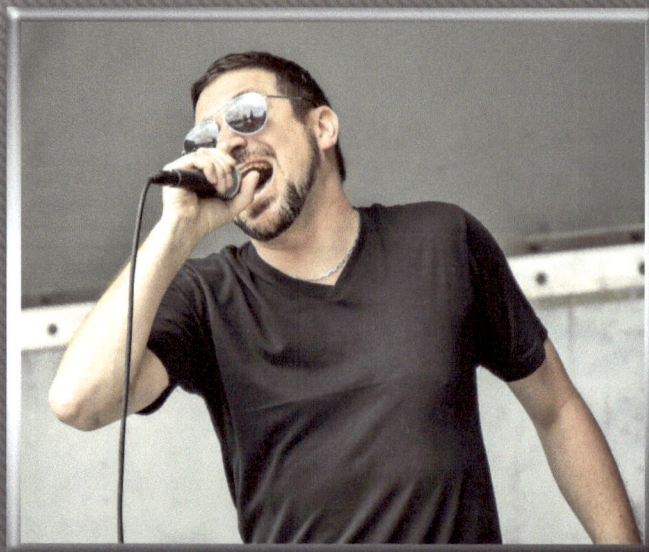

Outdoor festivals and community events are held monthly; and even weekly, during the summer. You would be hard pressed to not find local musicians performing during these at area parks, in the middle of busy city intersections, on porches or on a bridge.

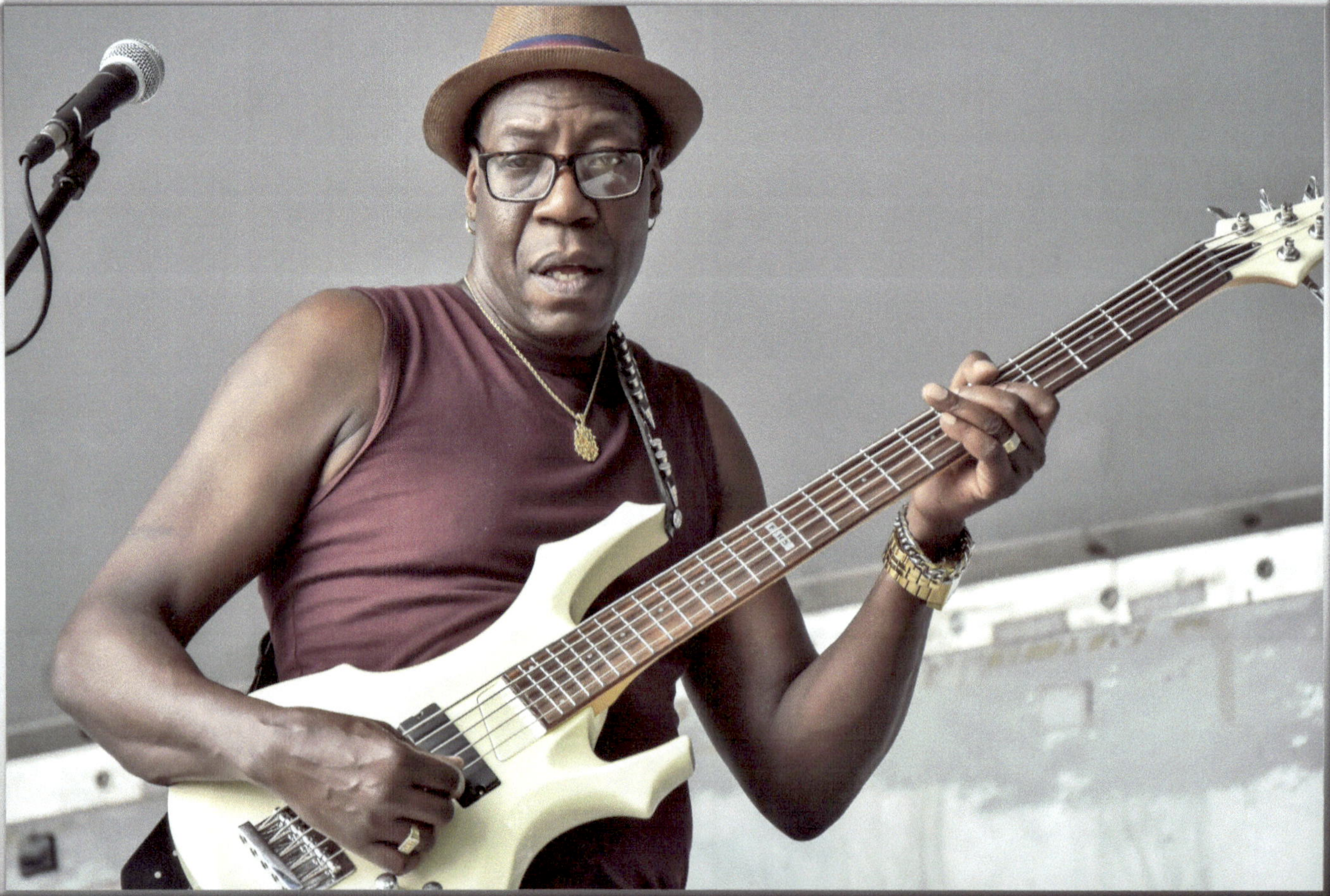

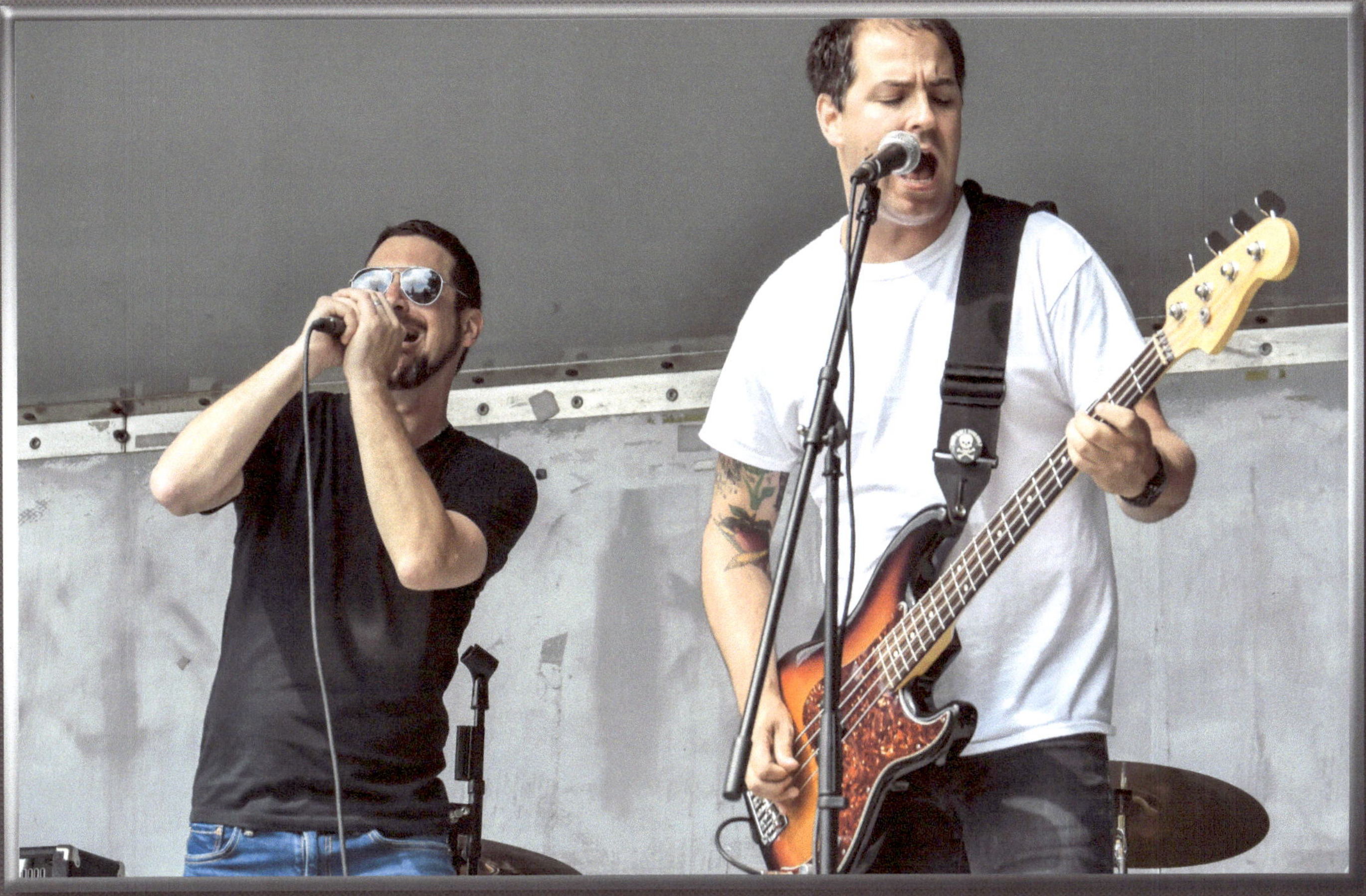

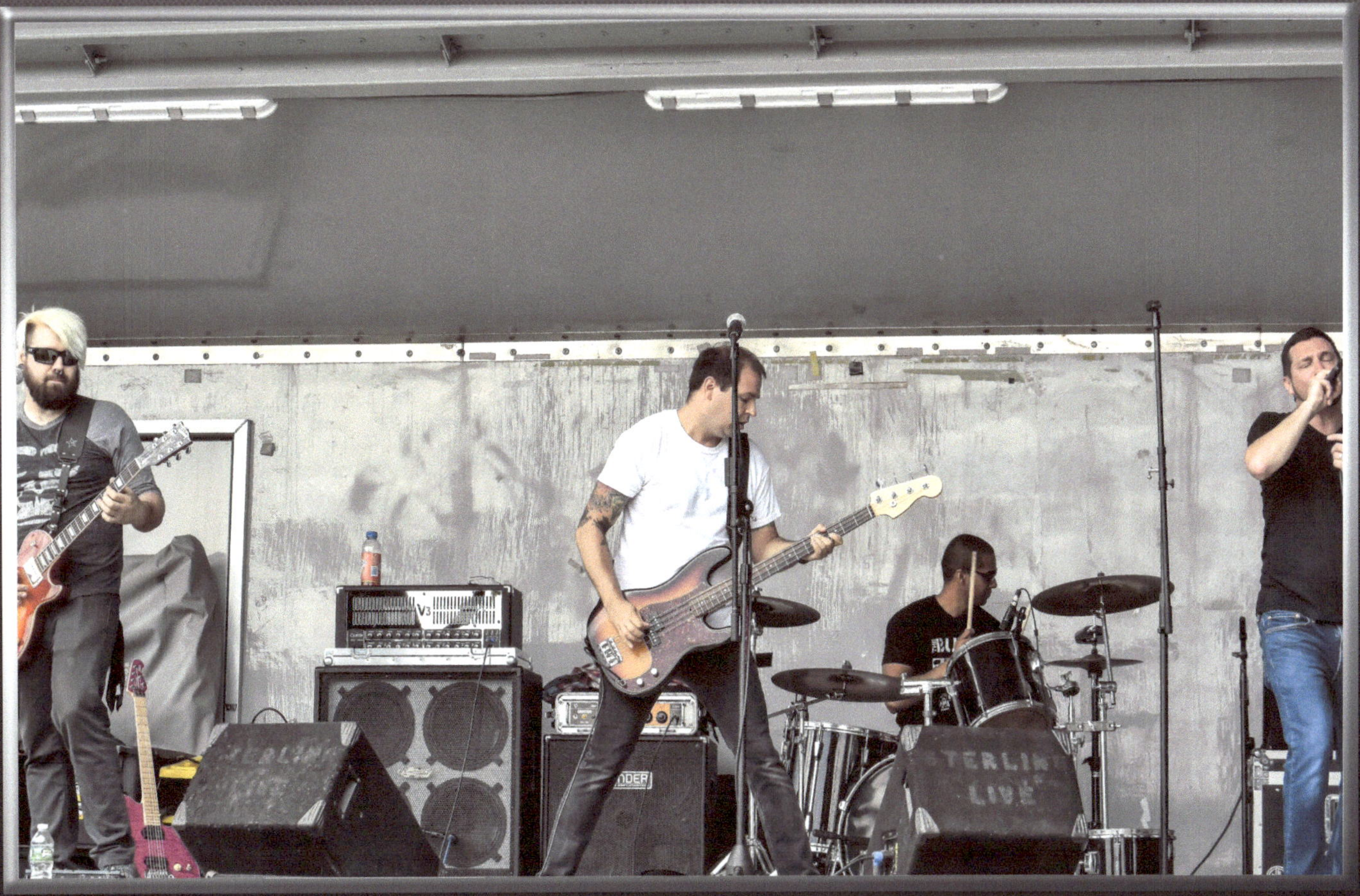

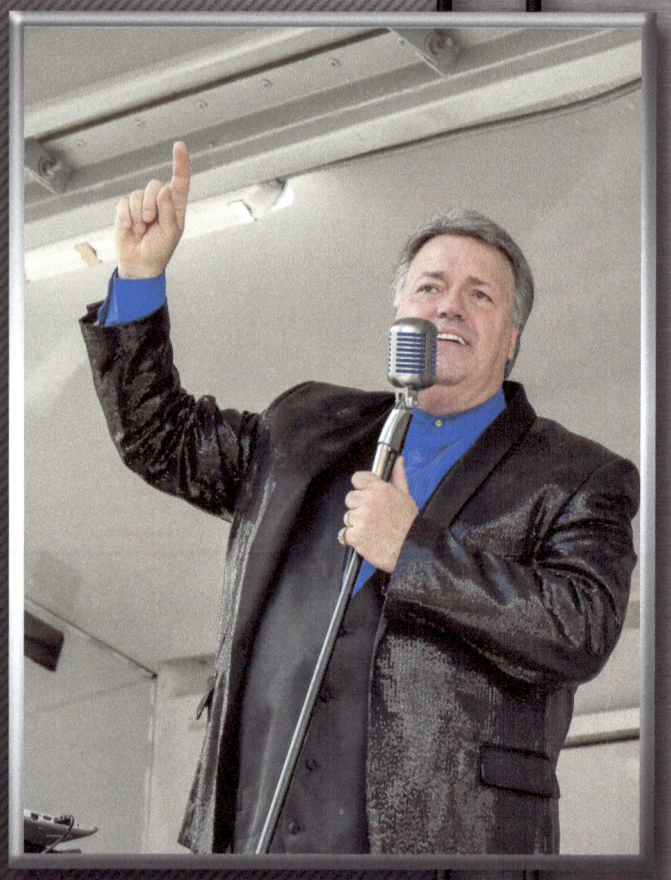
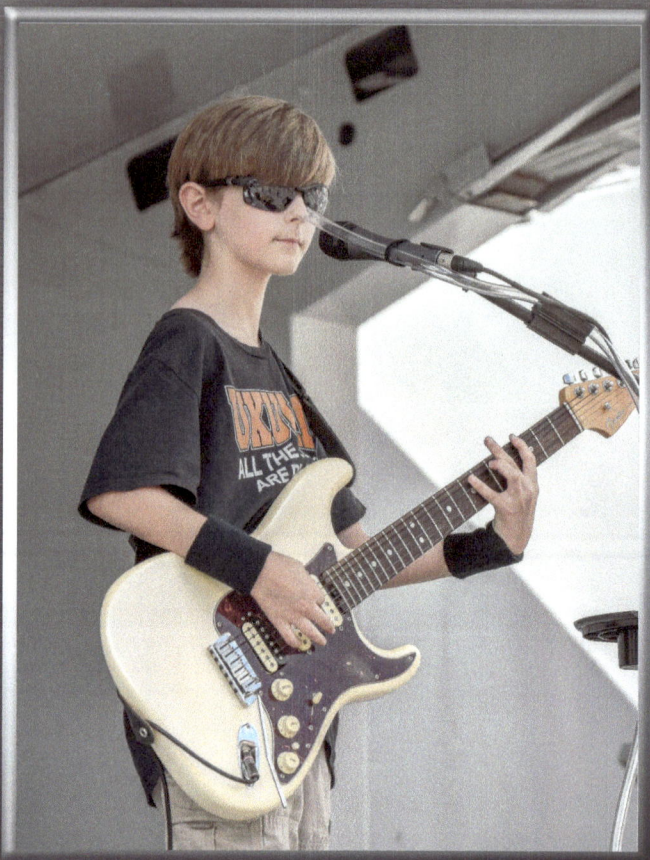

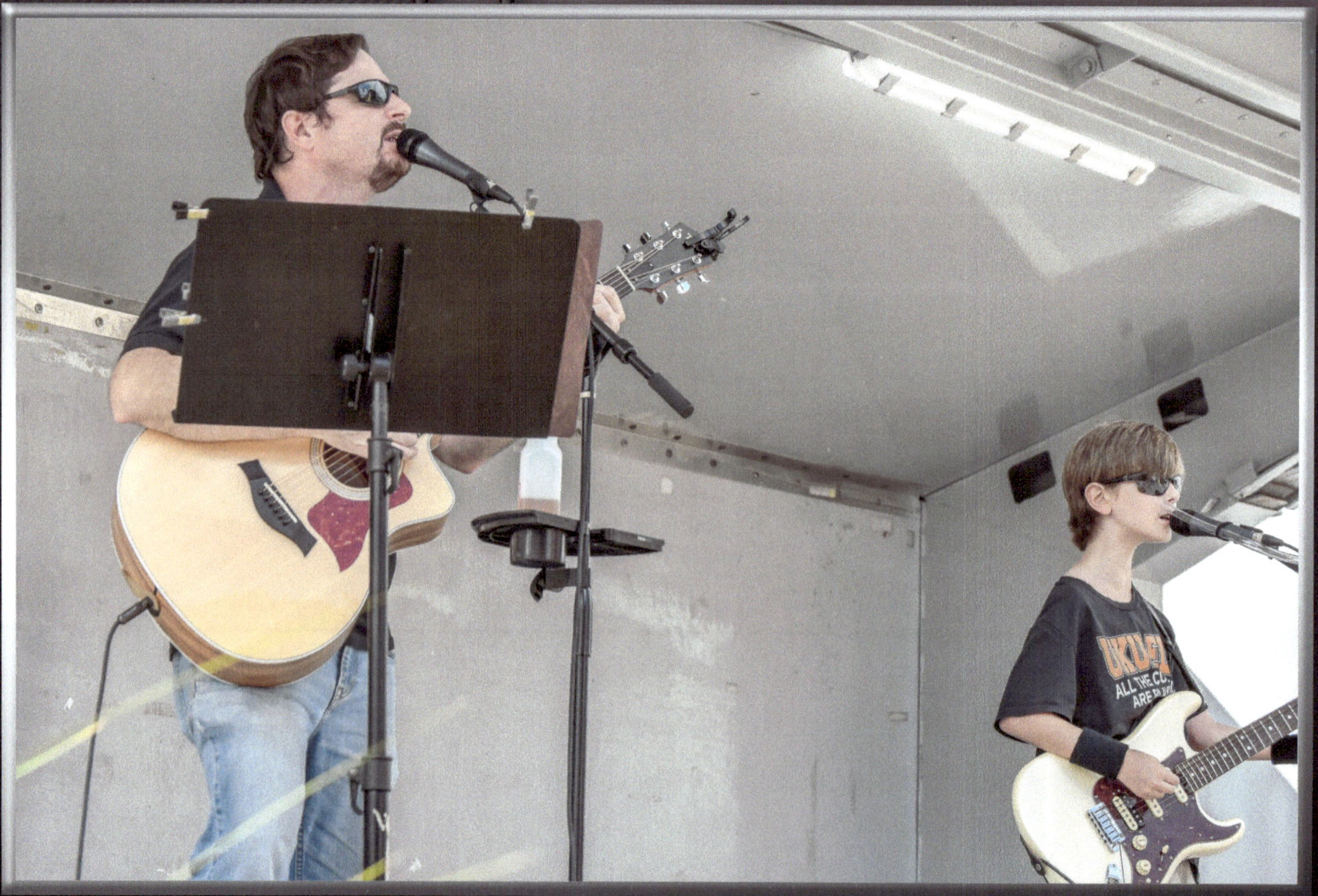

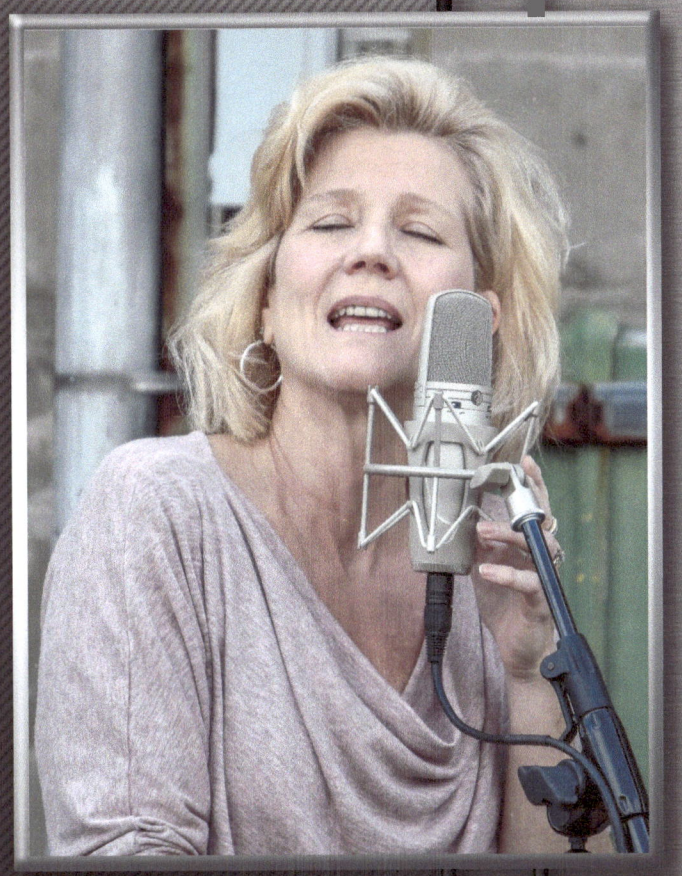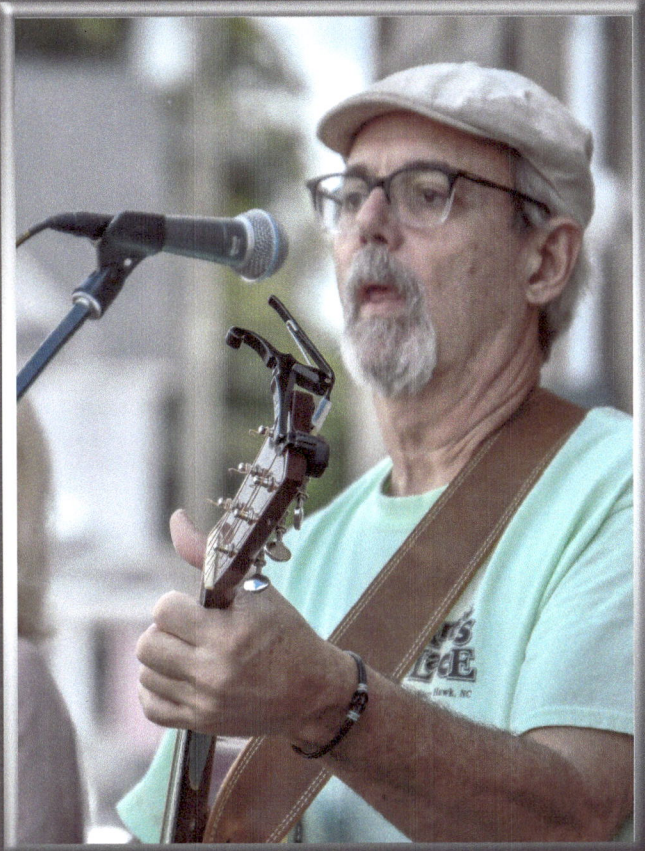

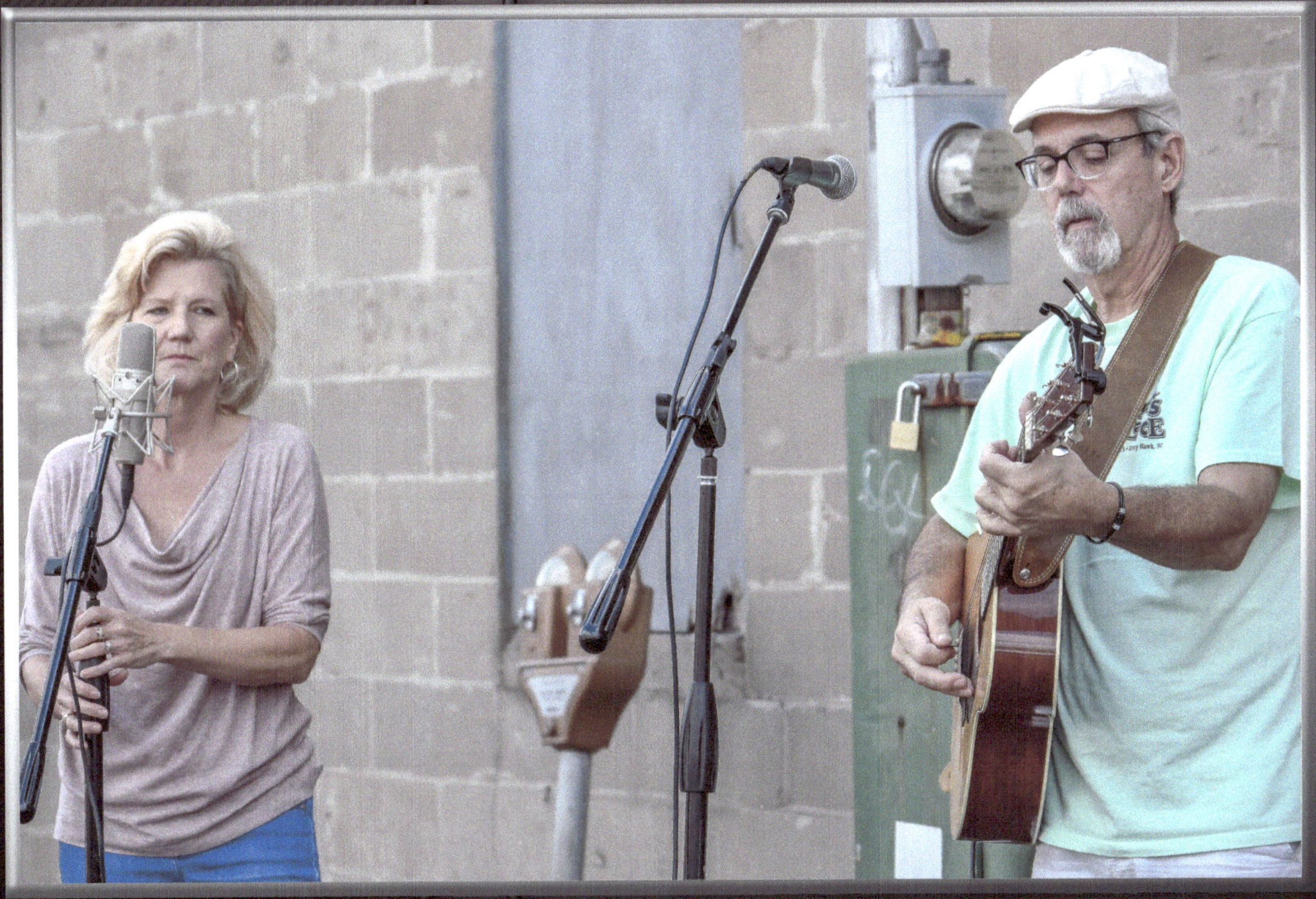

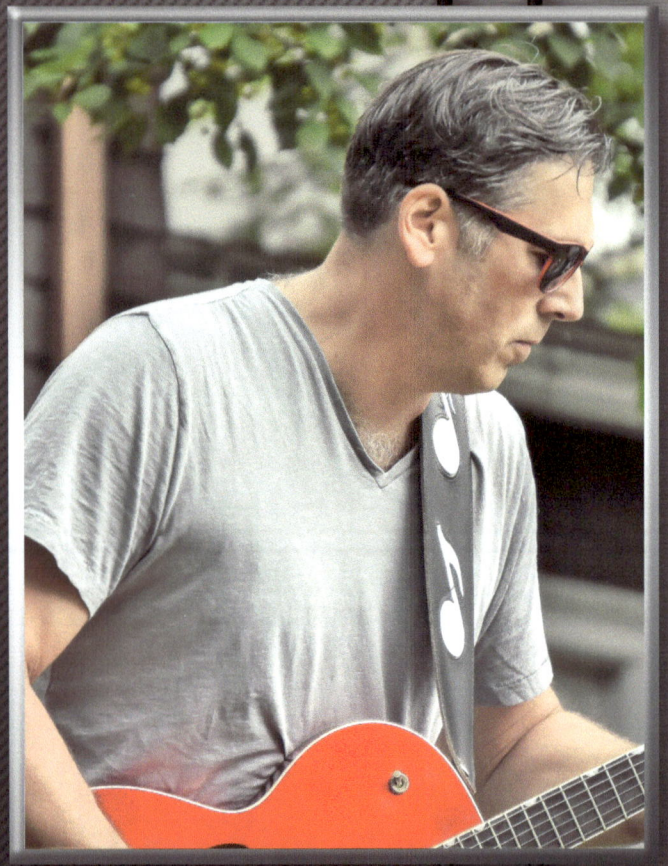
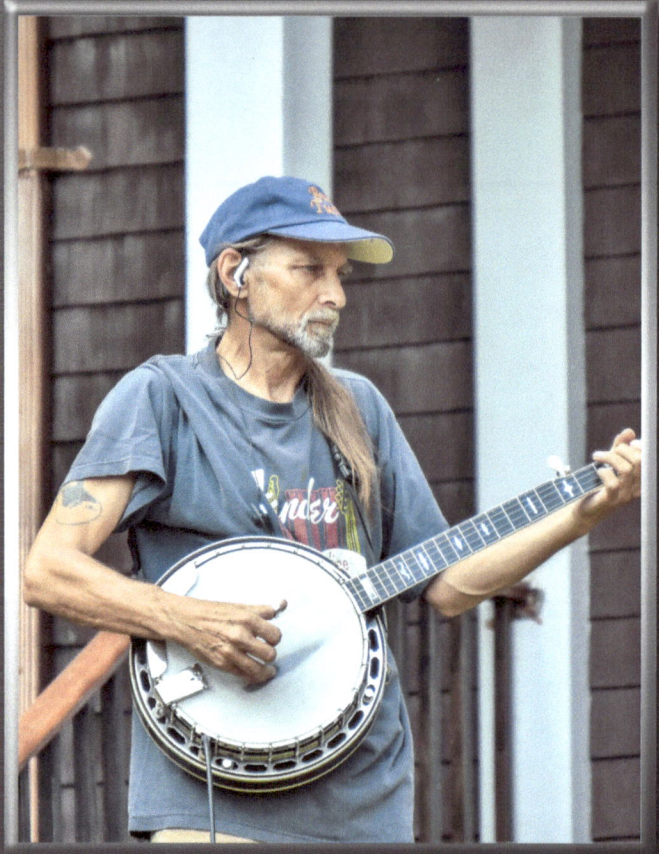

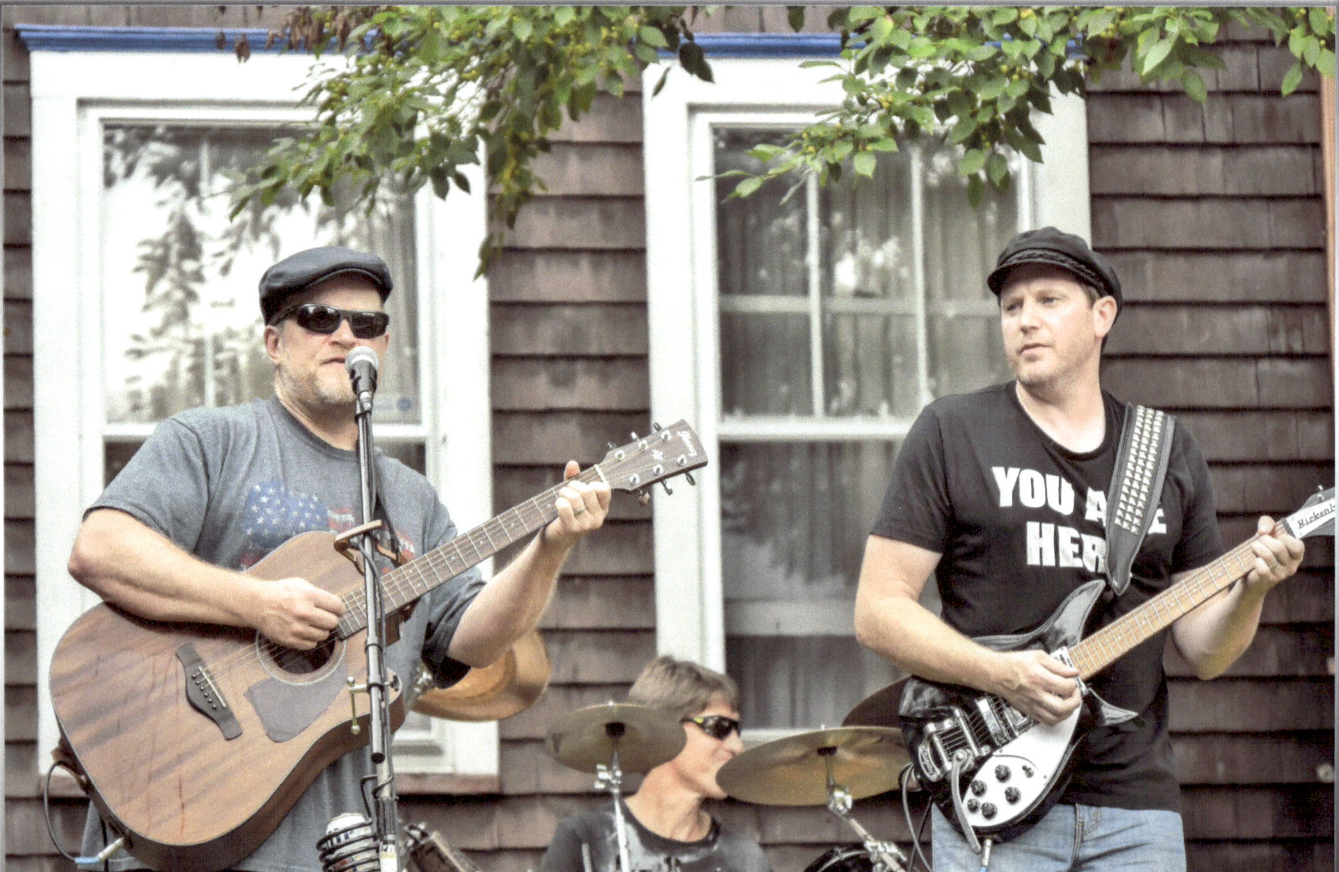

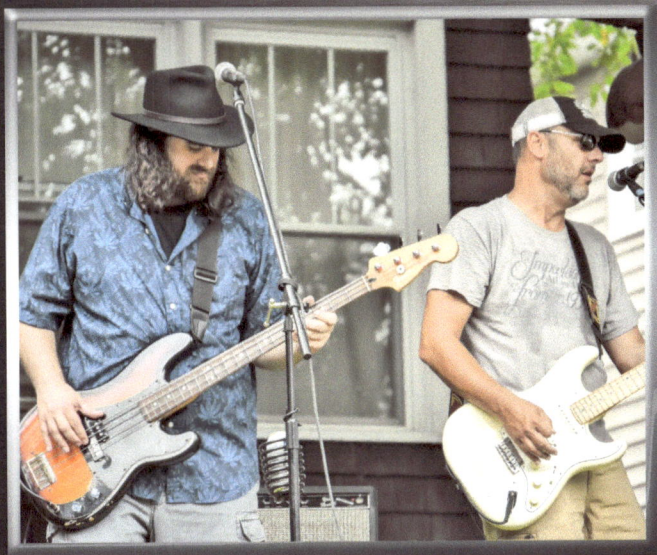
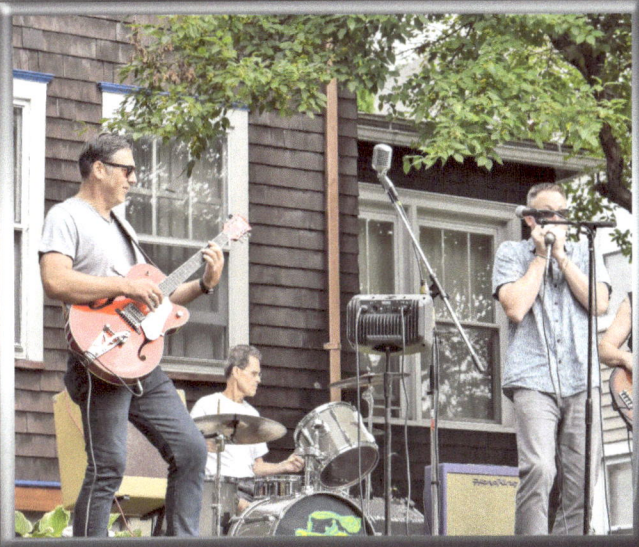
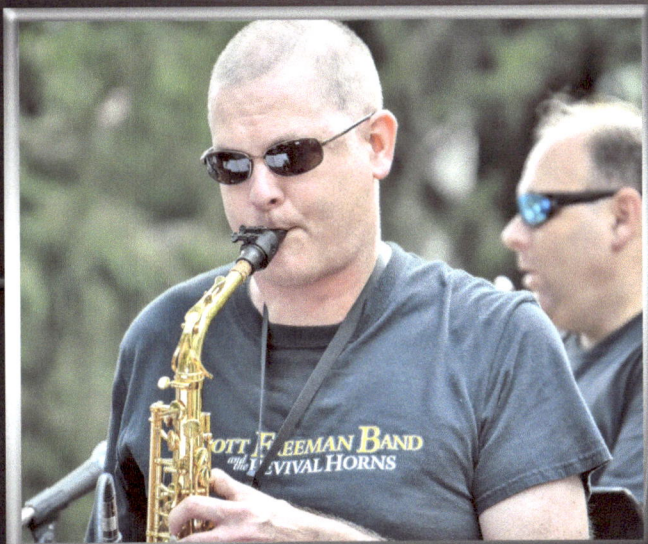
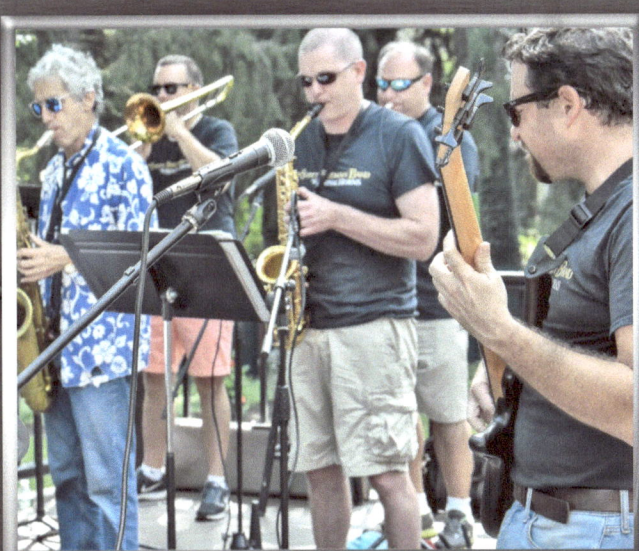
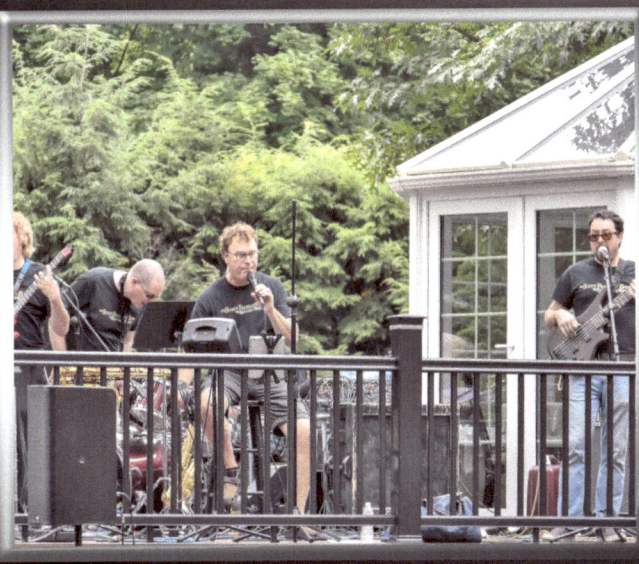
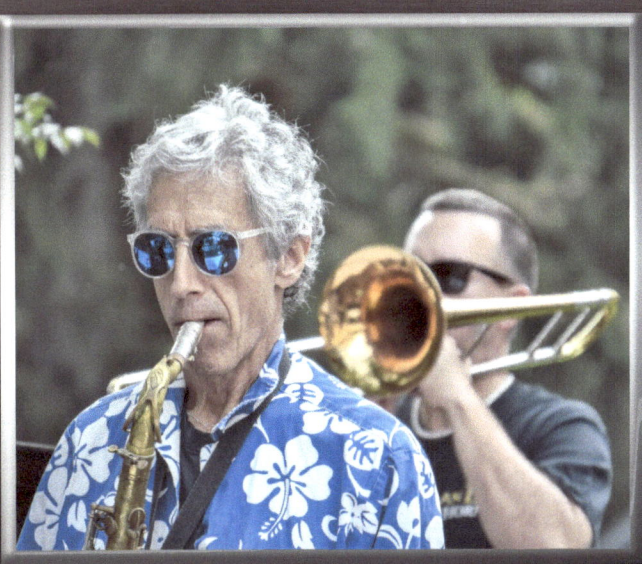

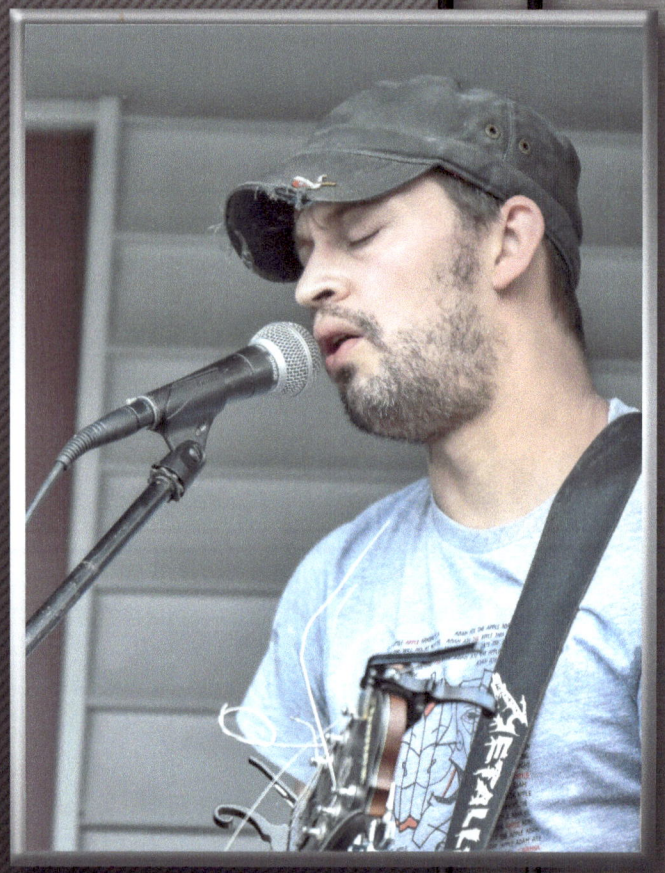
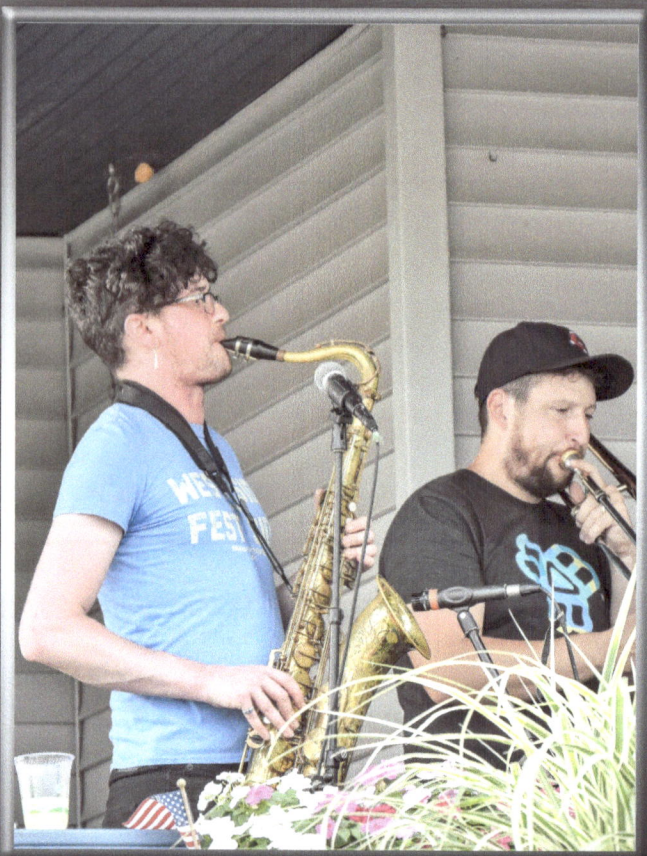

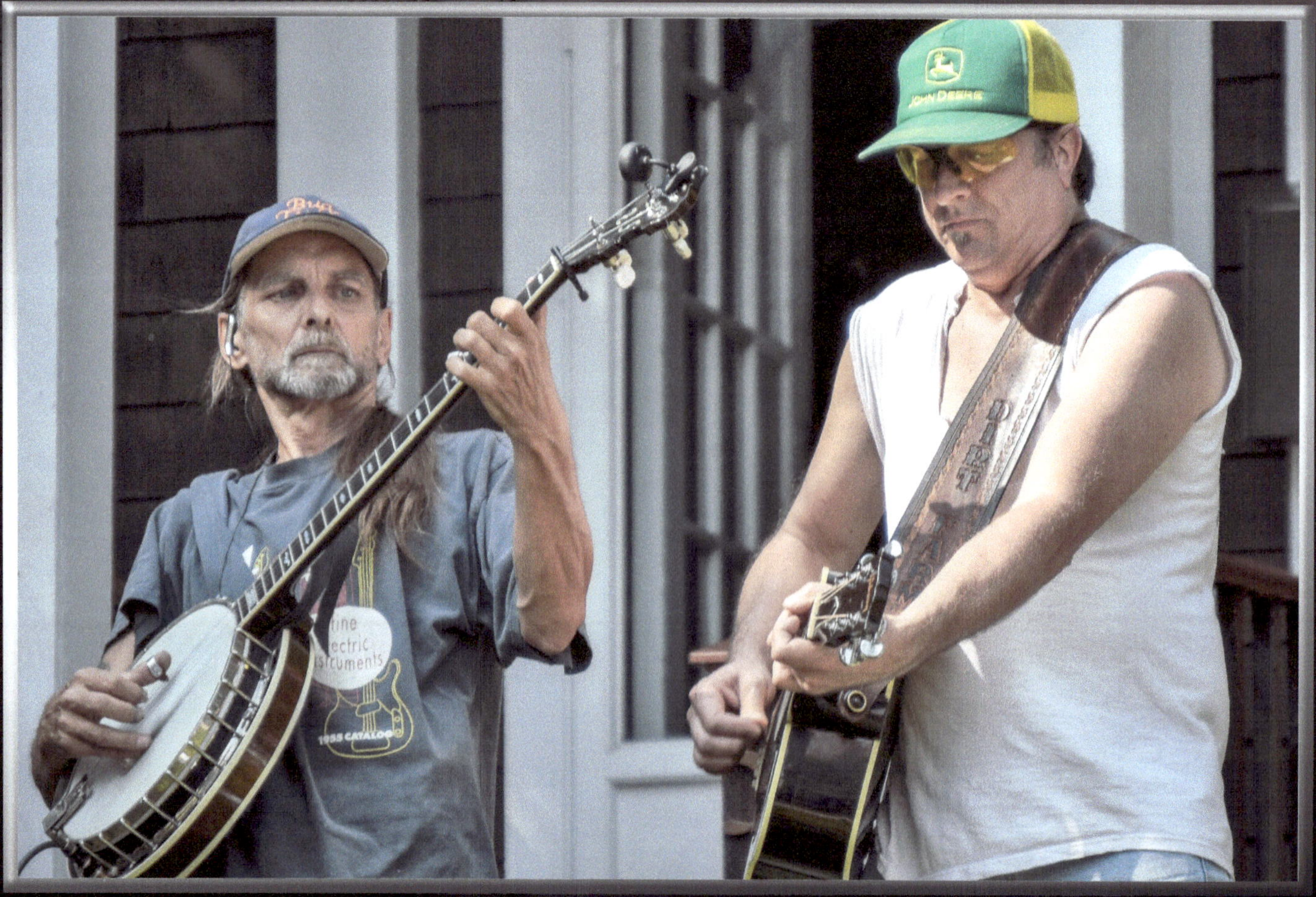

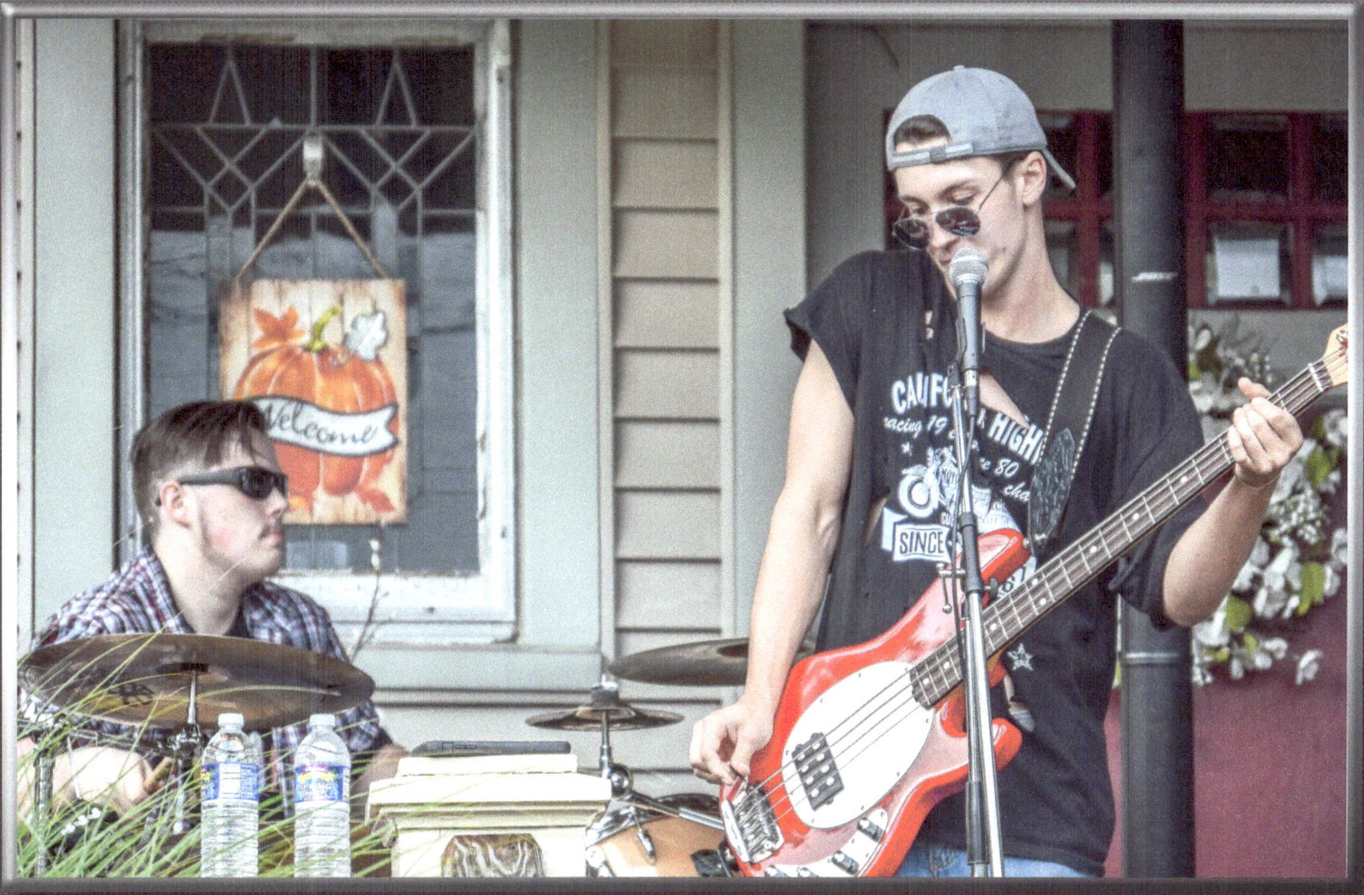

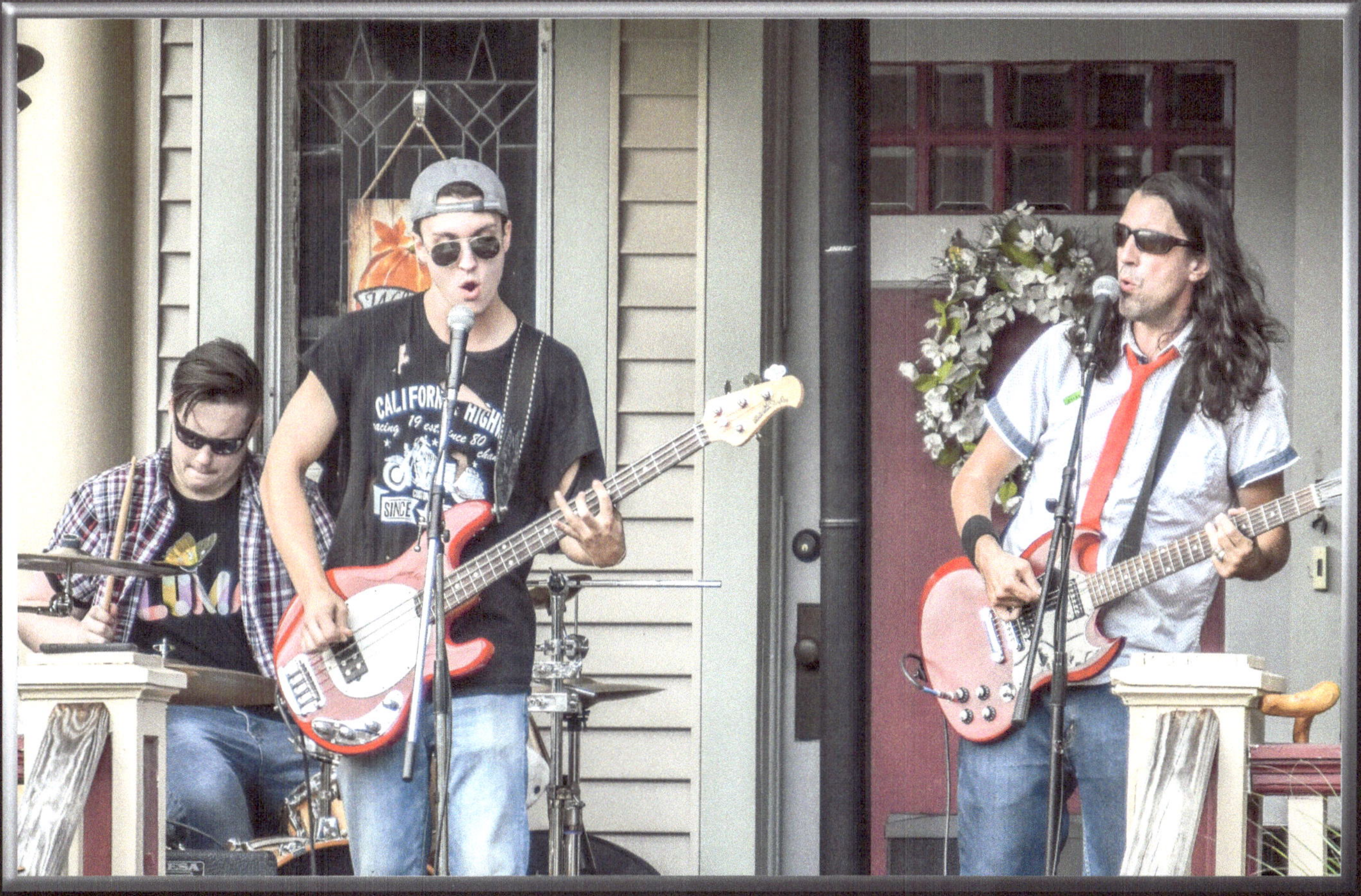

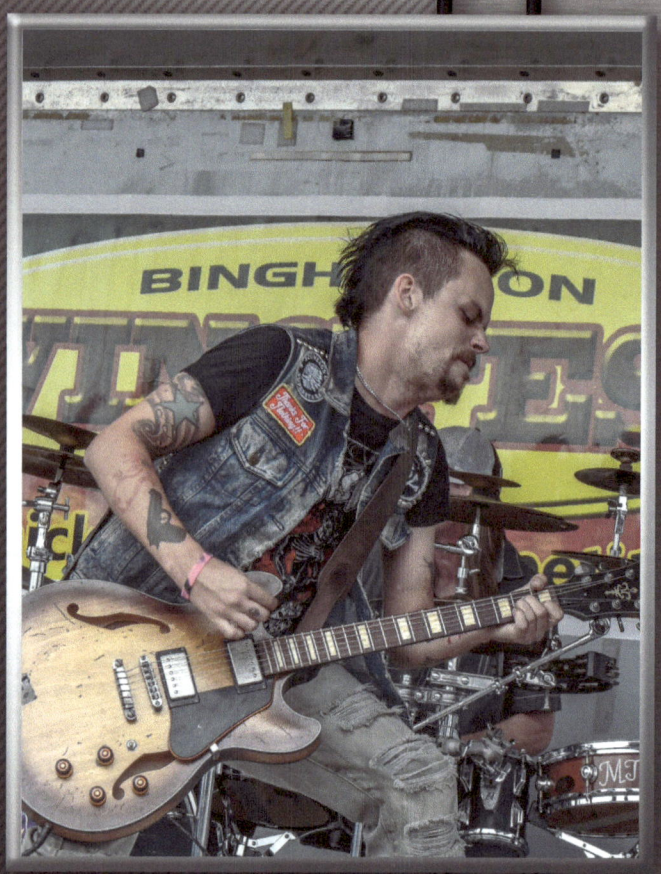
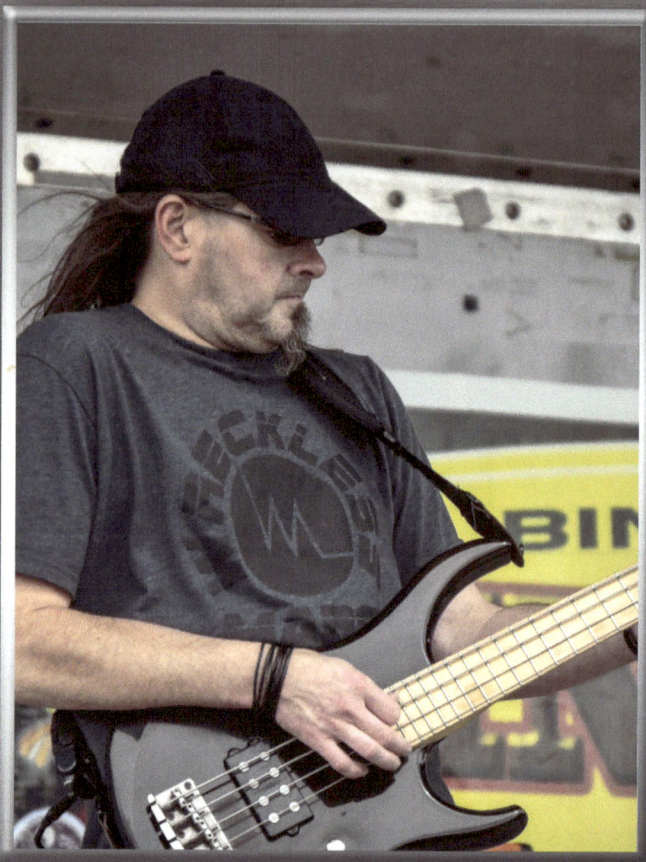

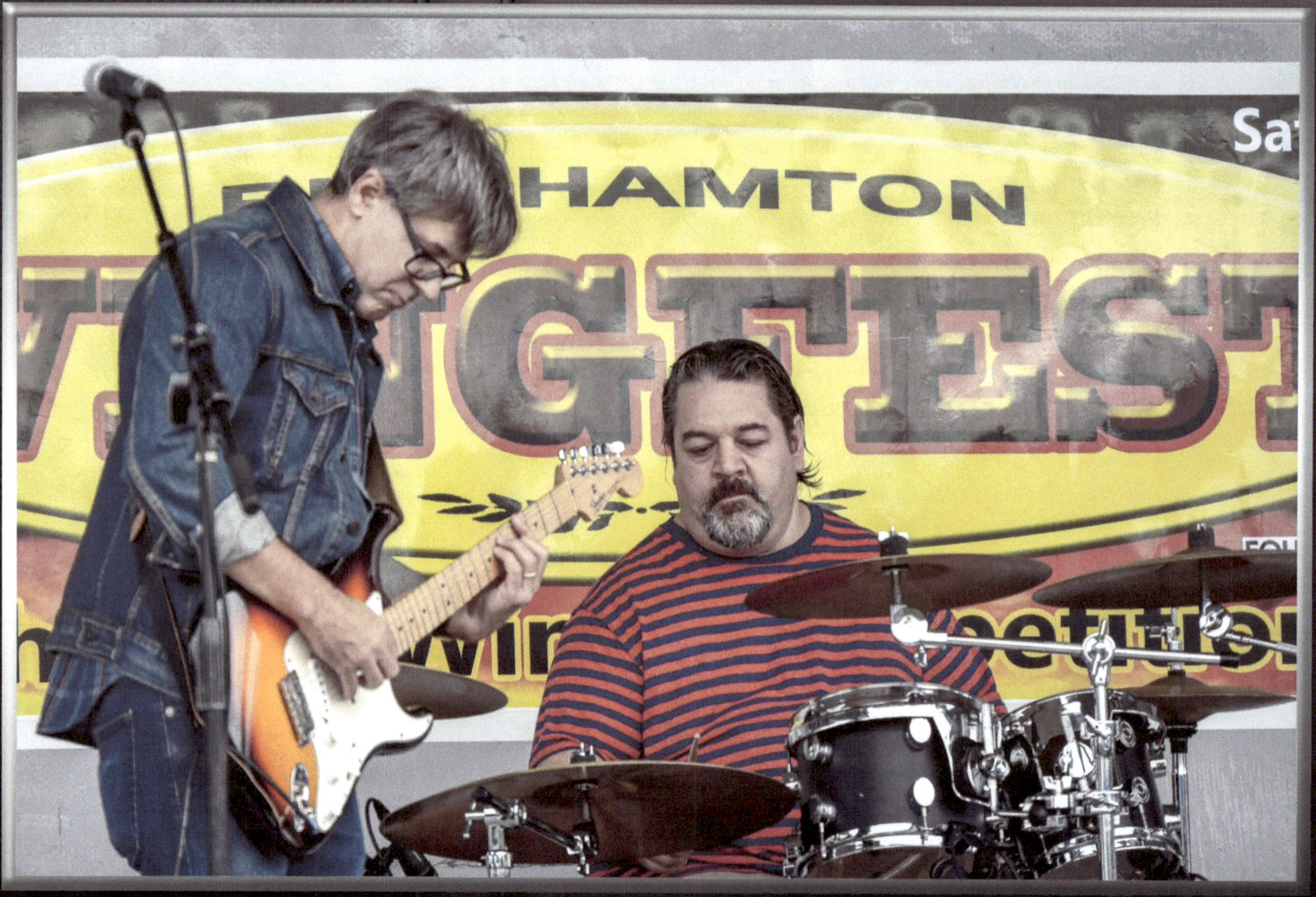

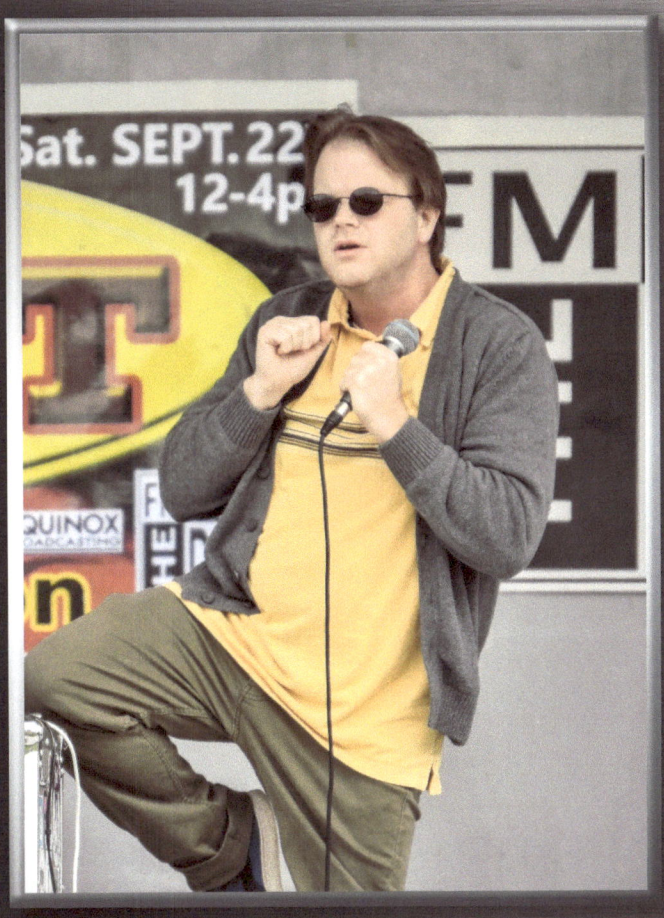
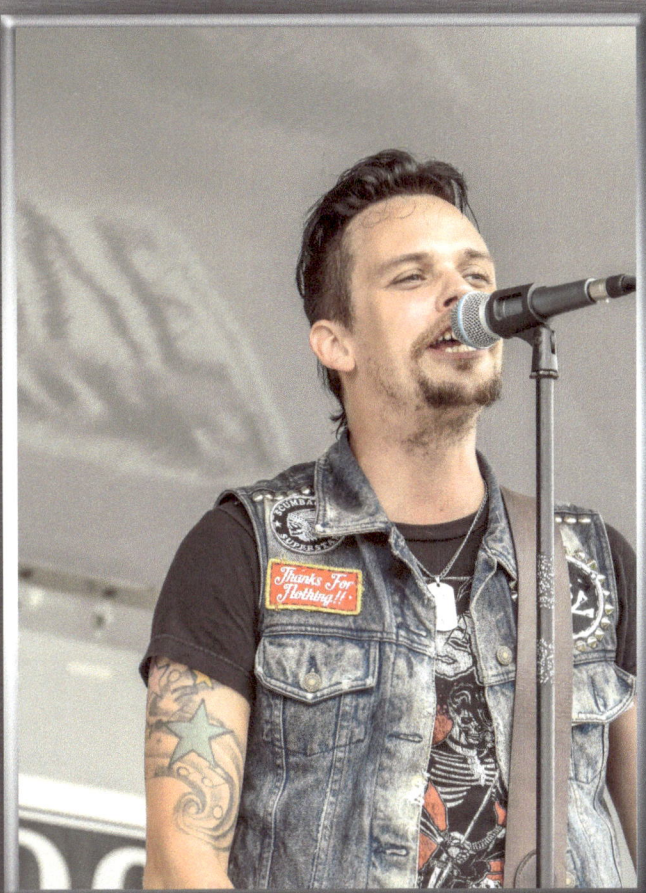
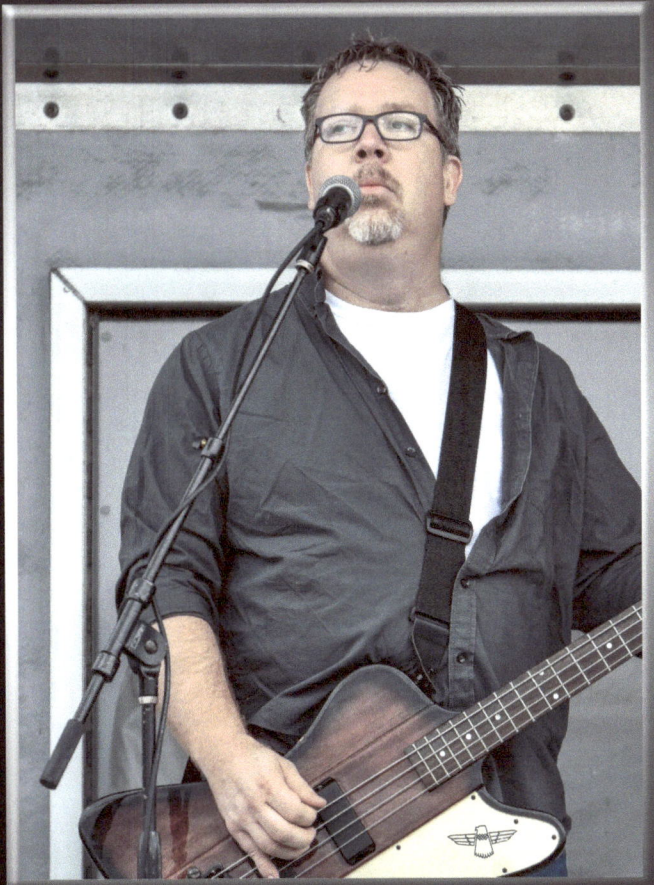
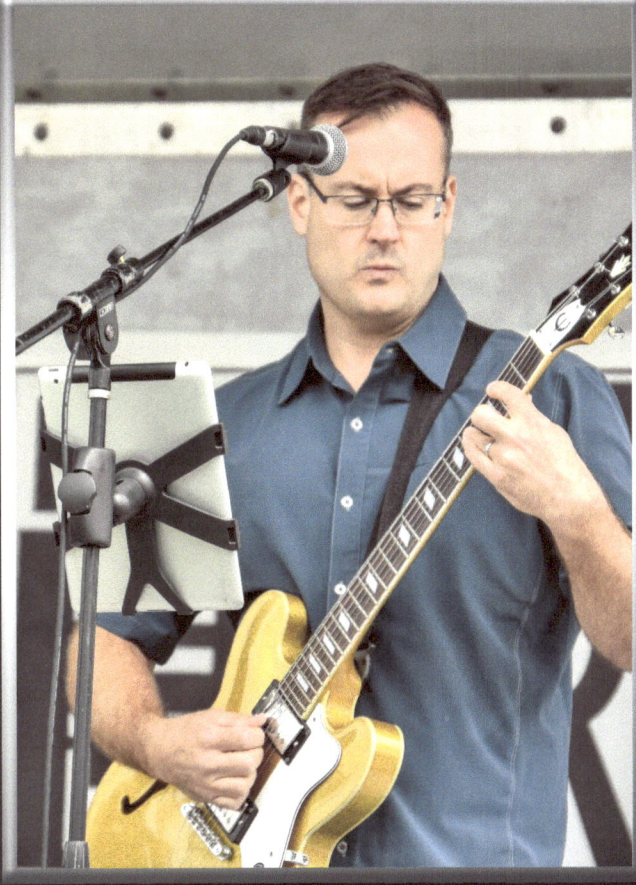

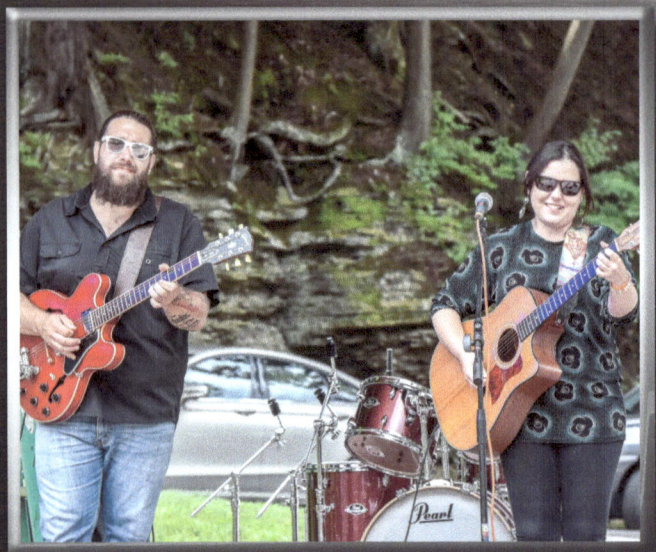
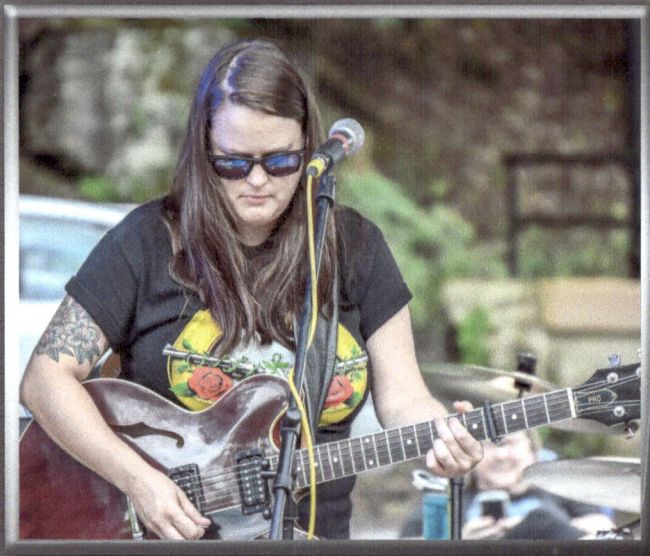
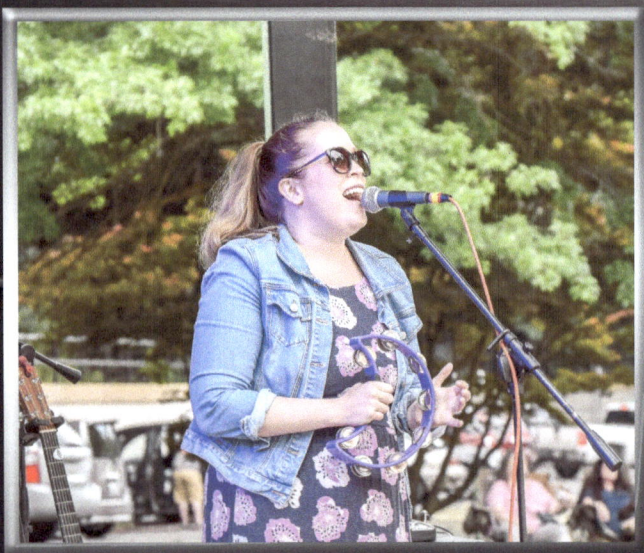
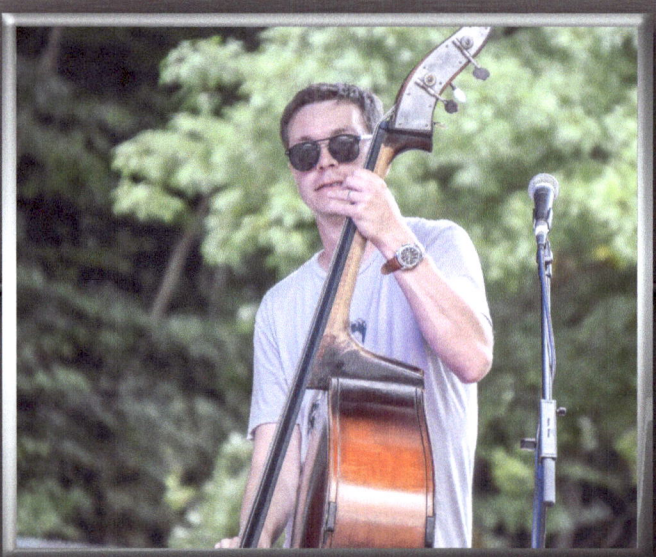
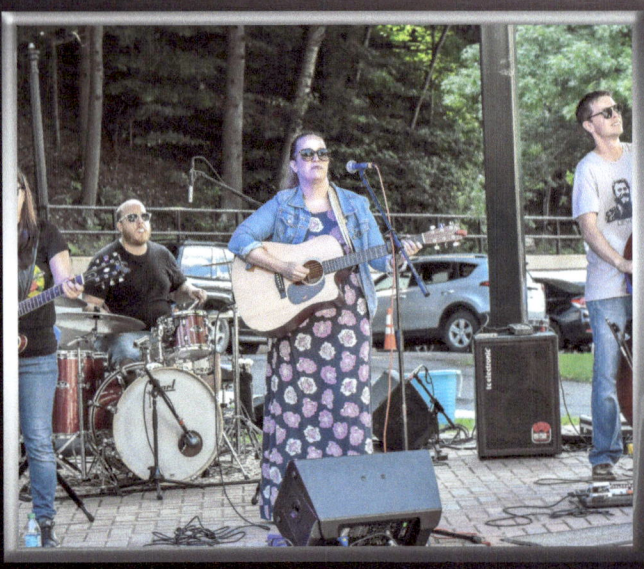
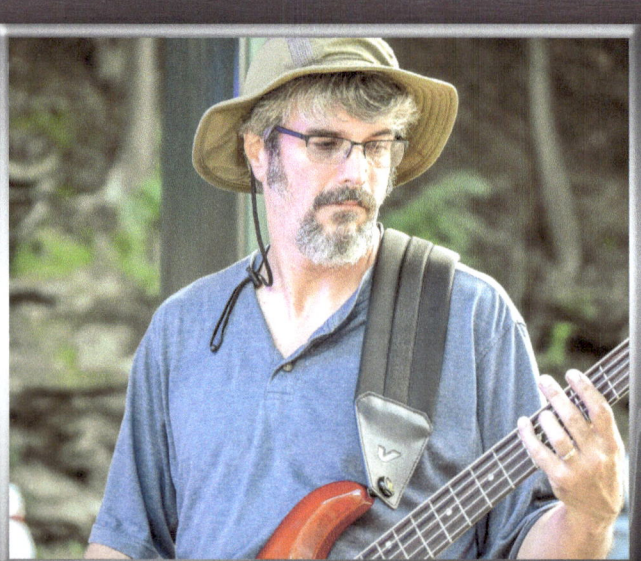

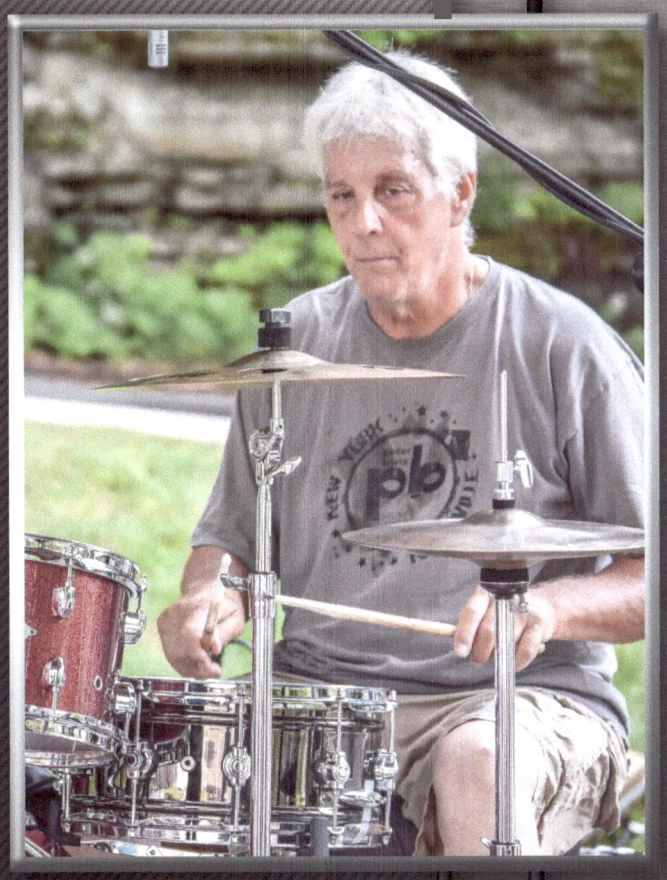
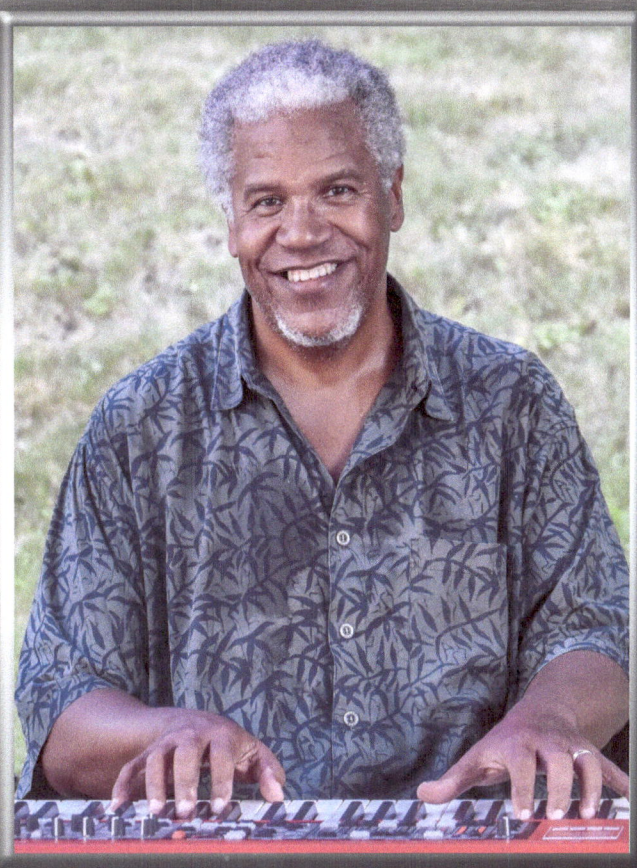

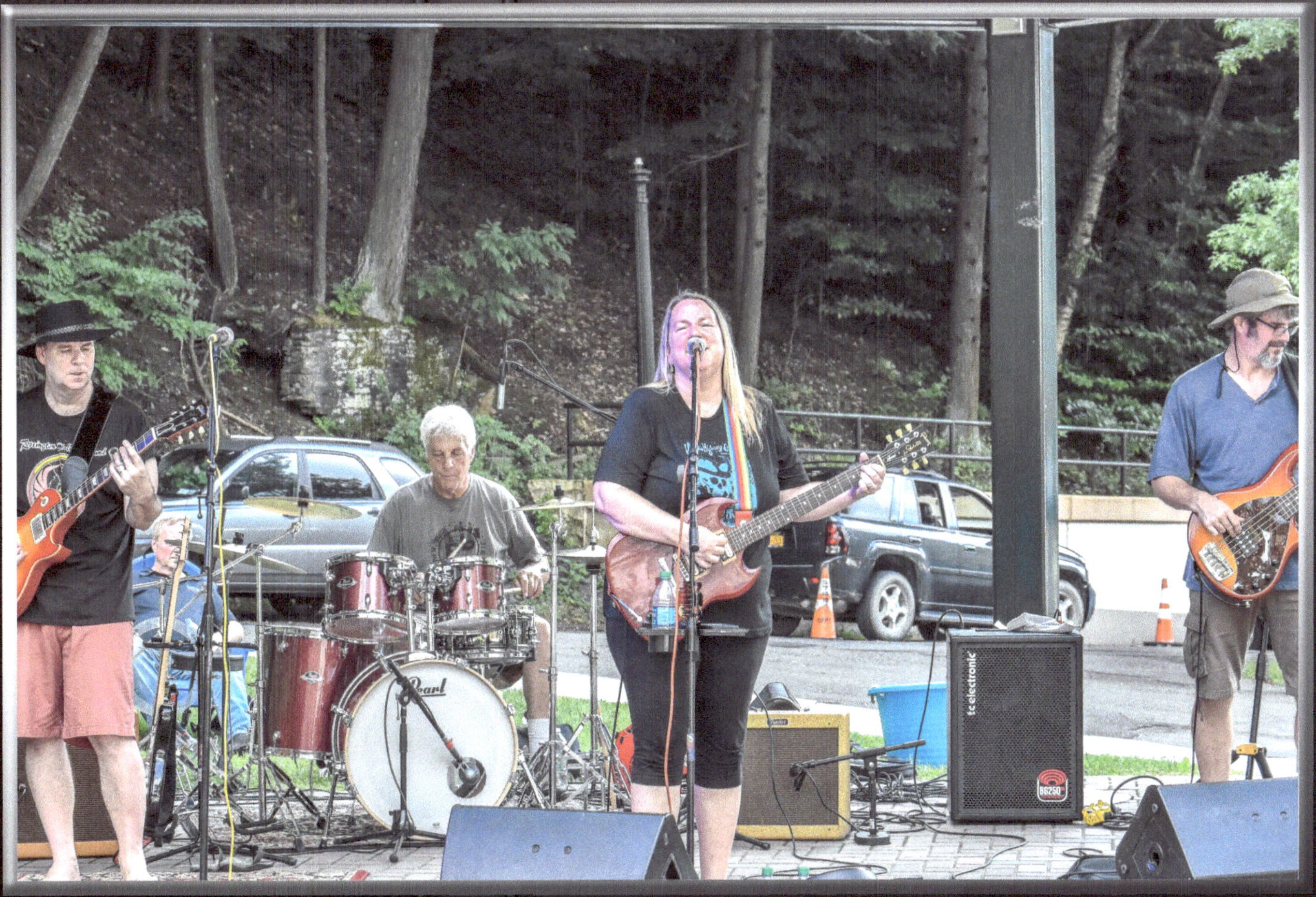

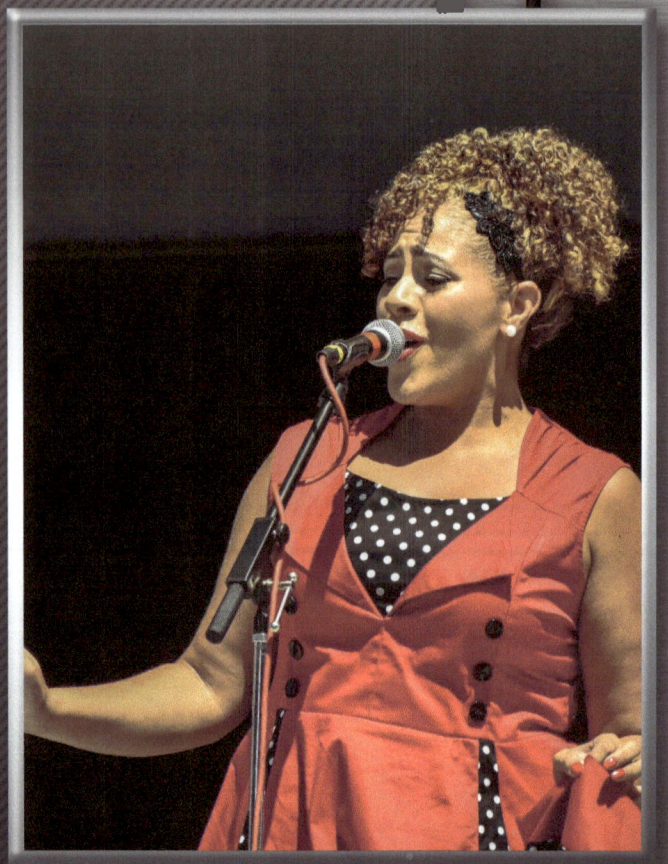
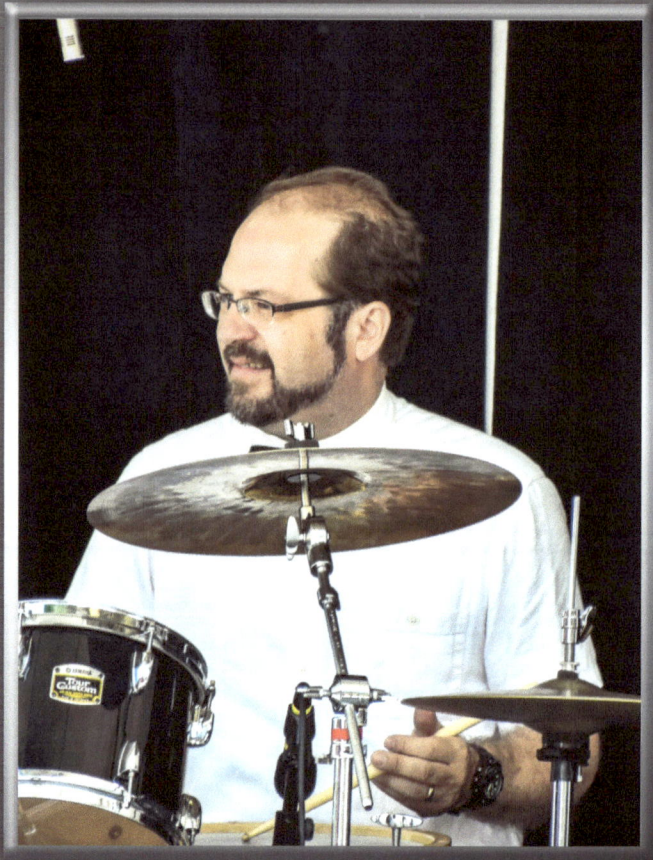

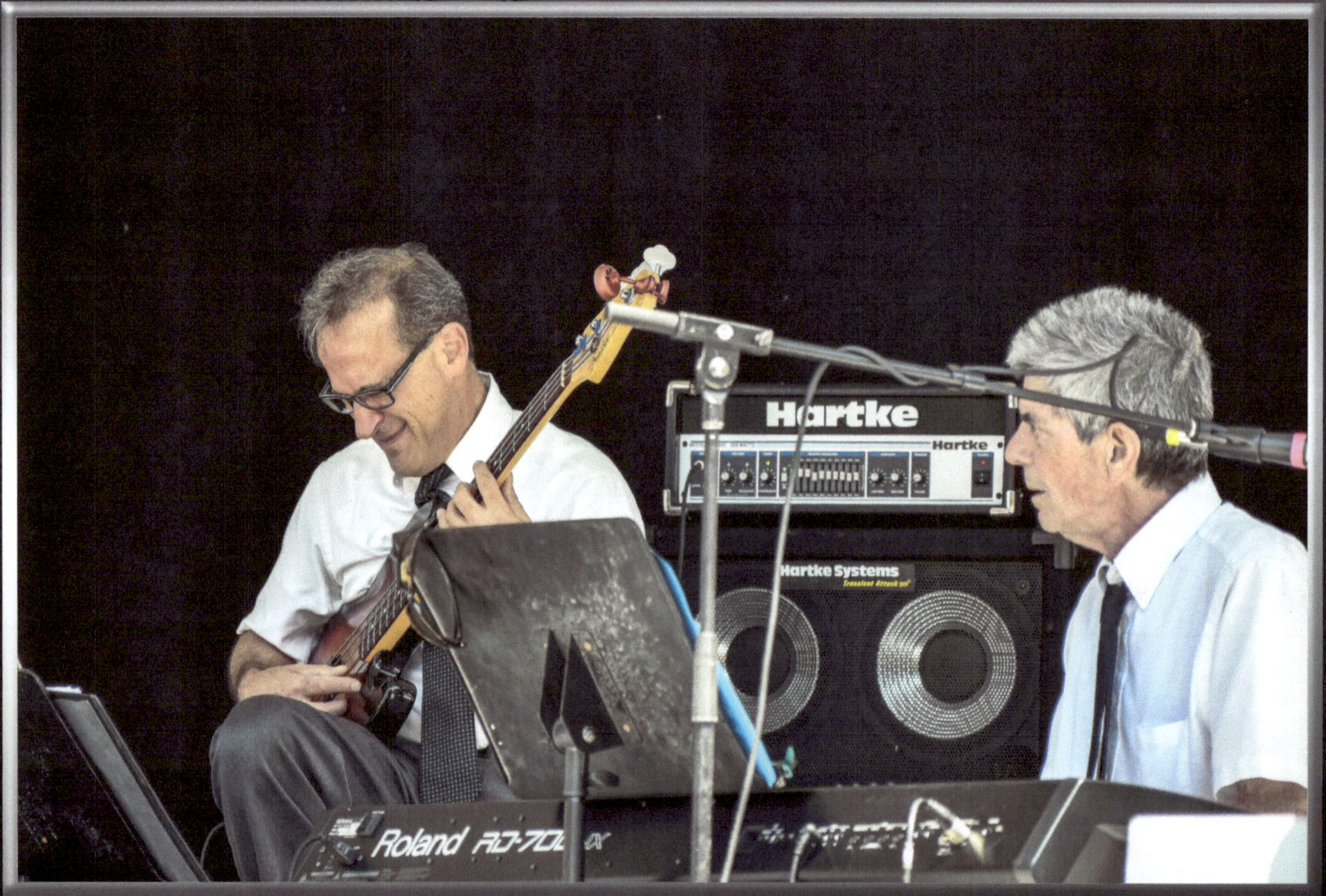

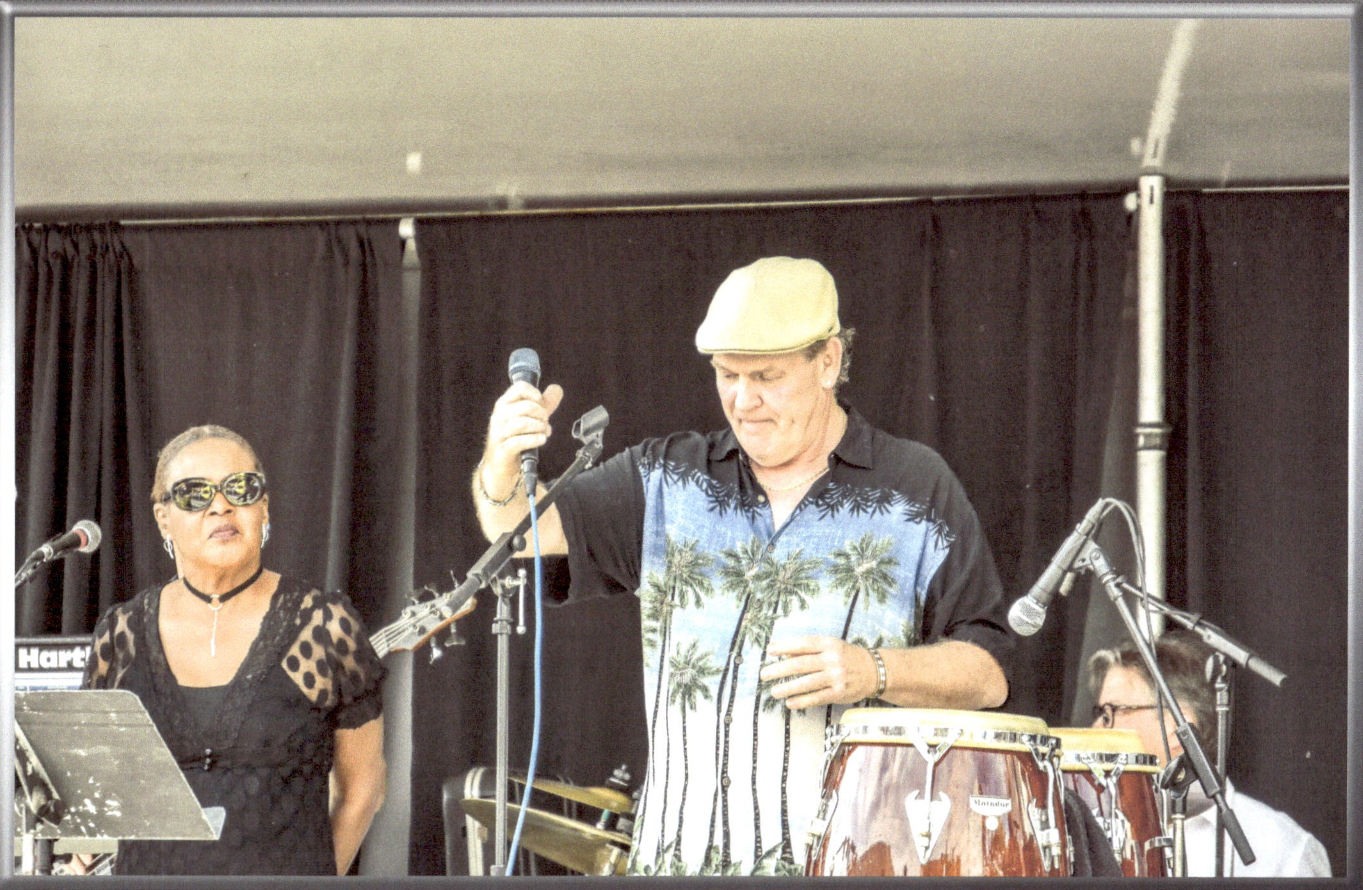

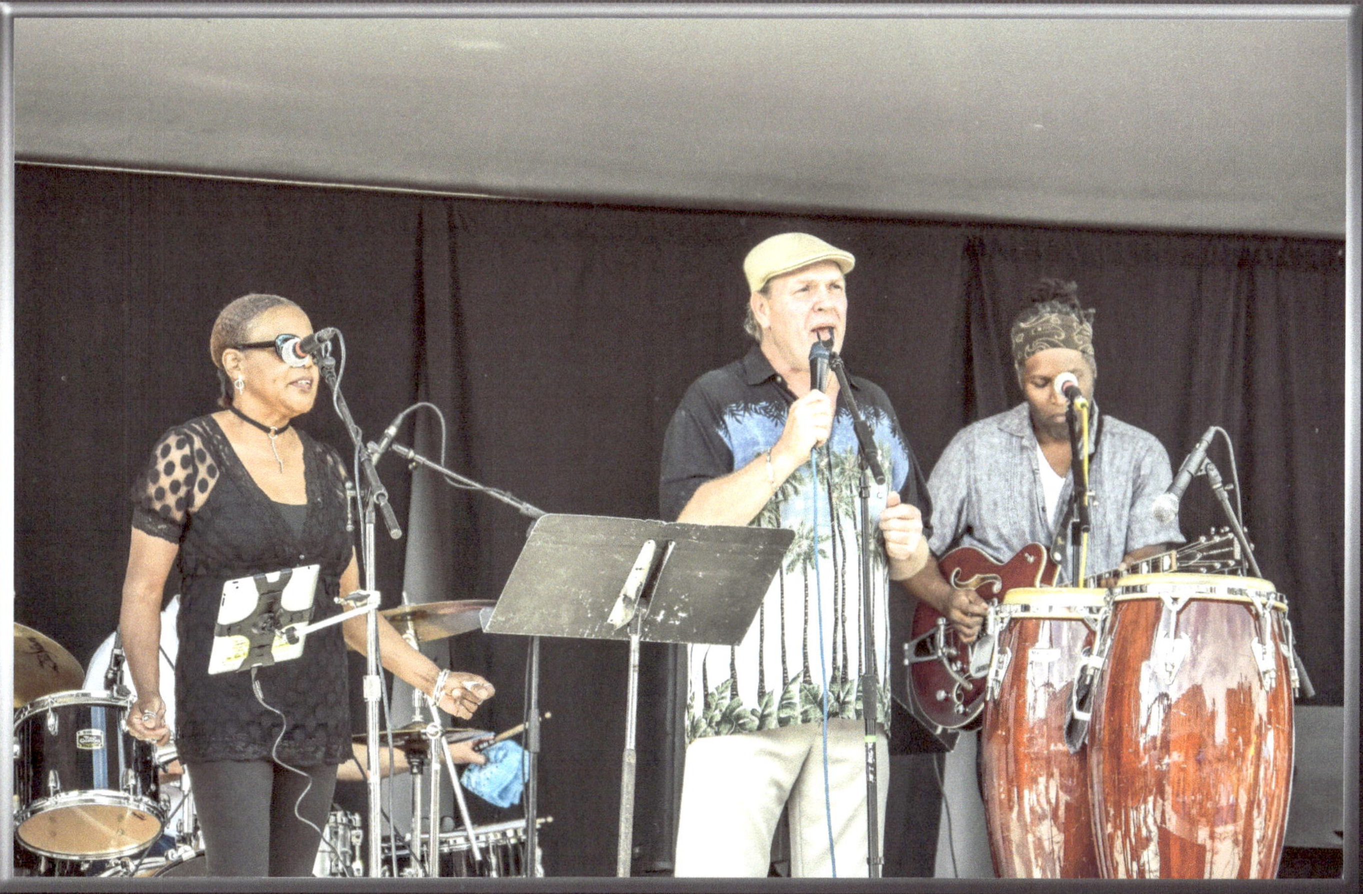

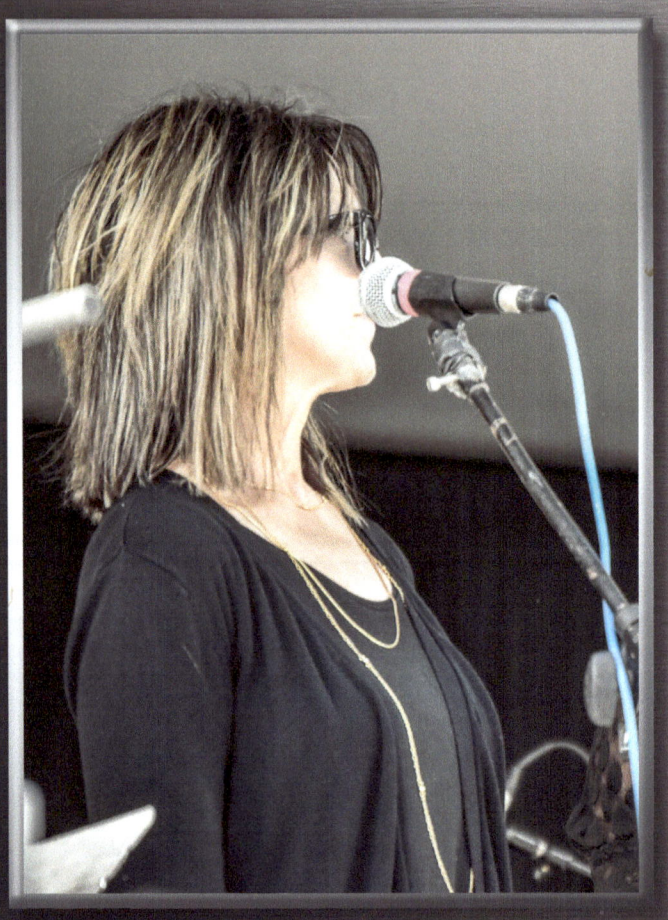
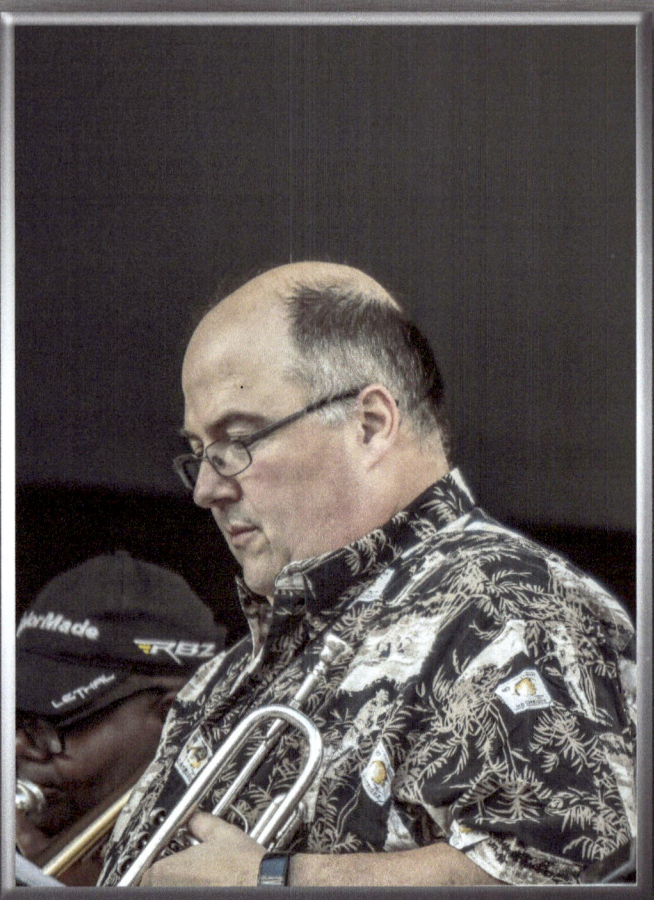
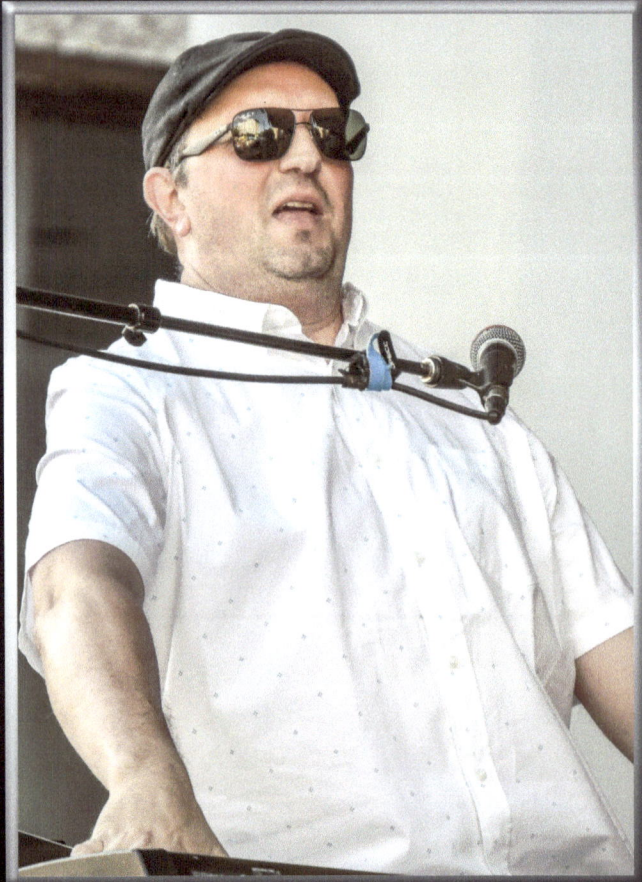
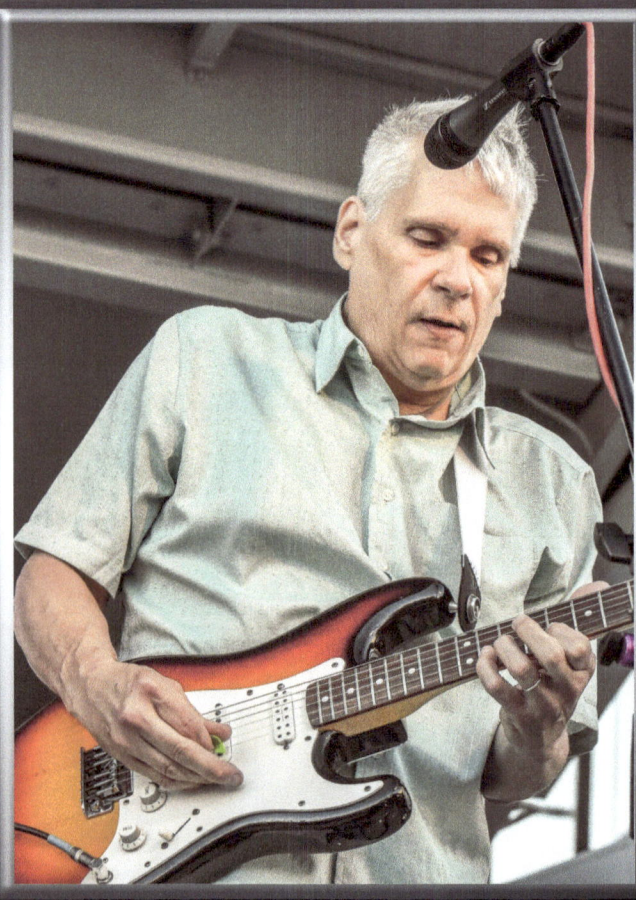

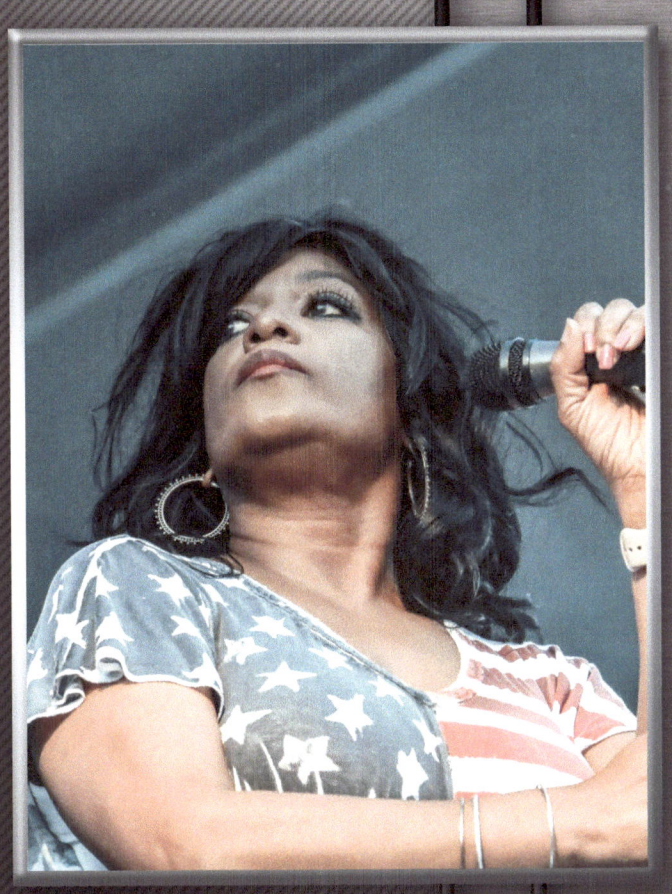
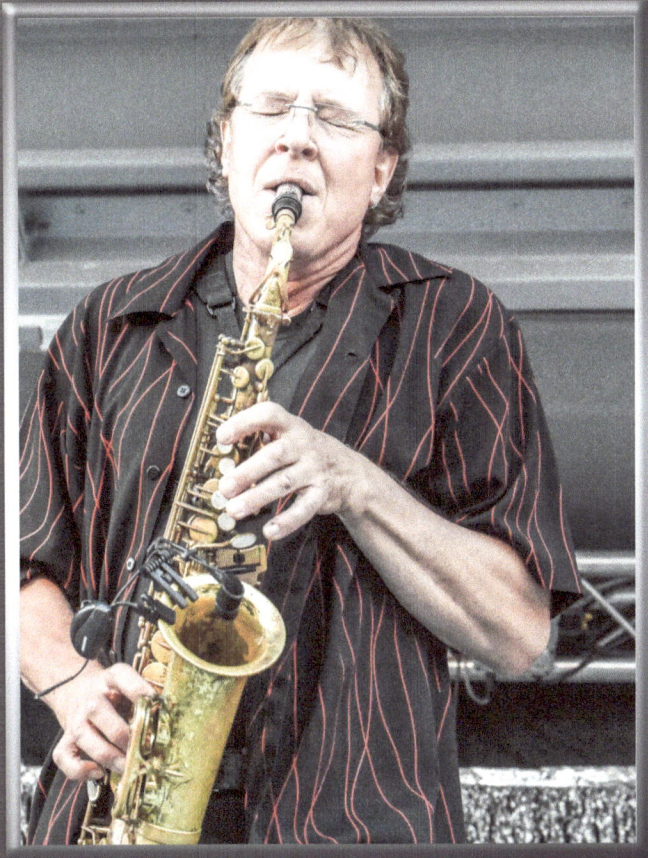

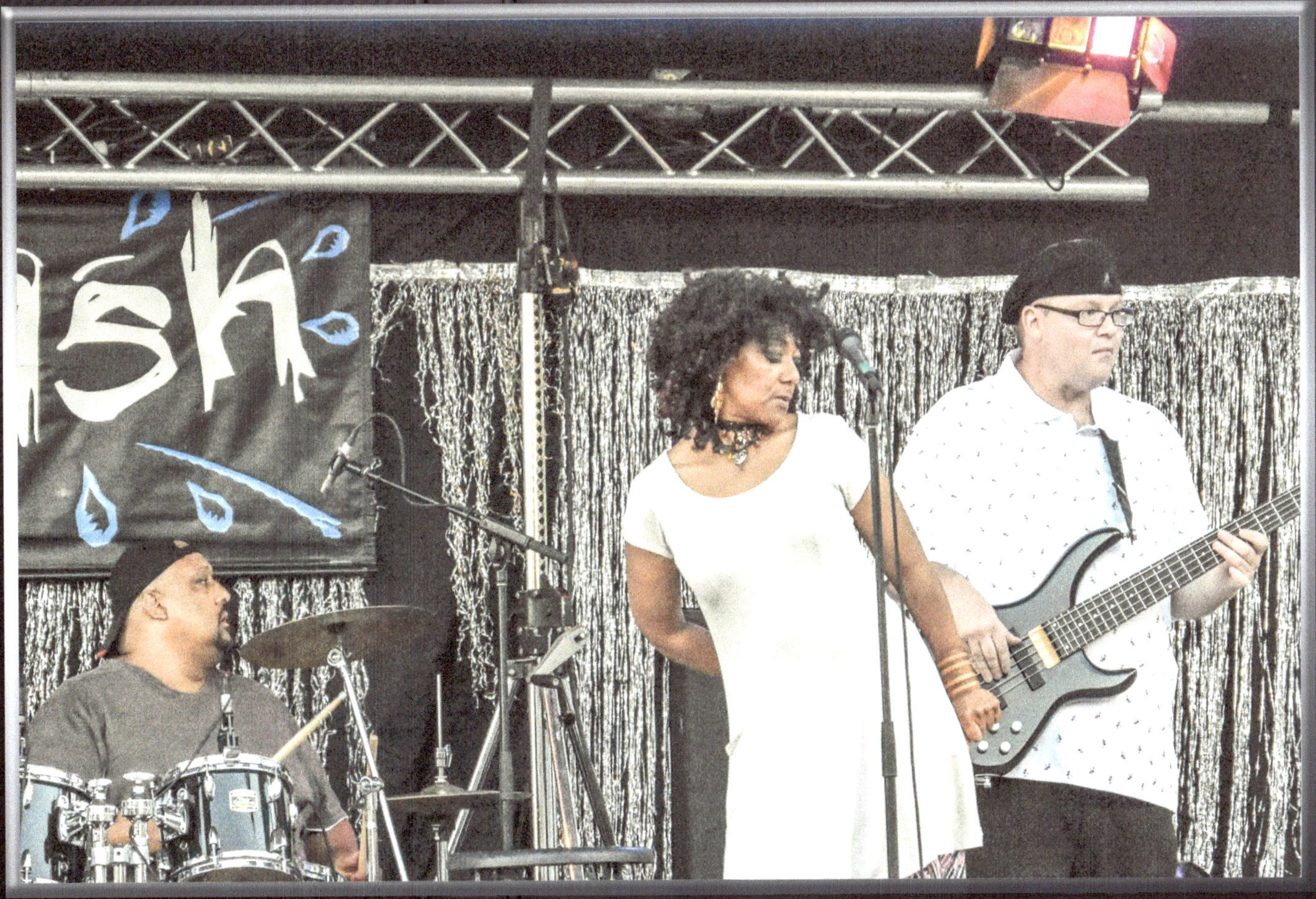

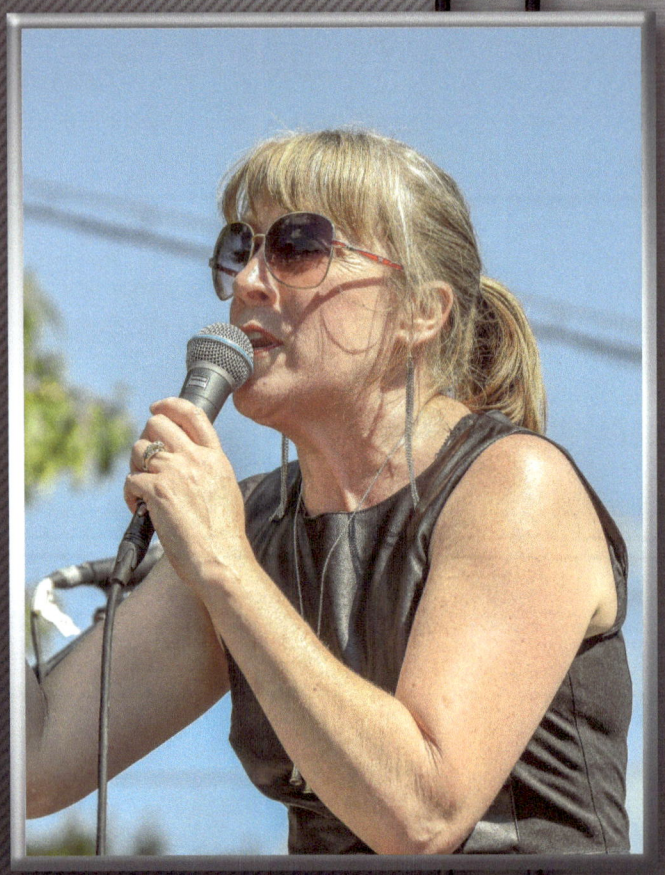
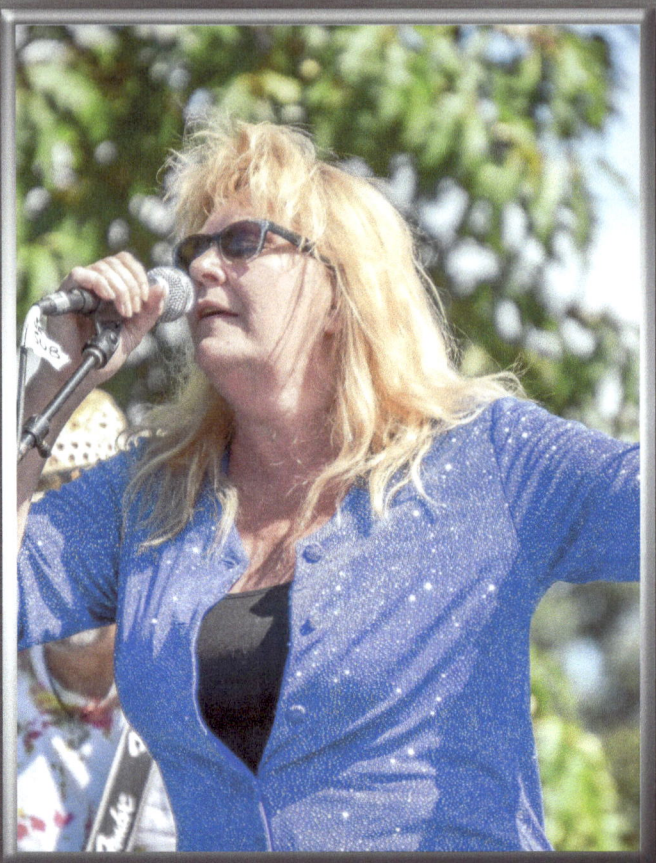

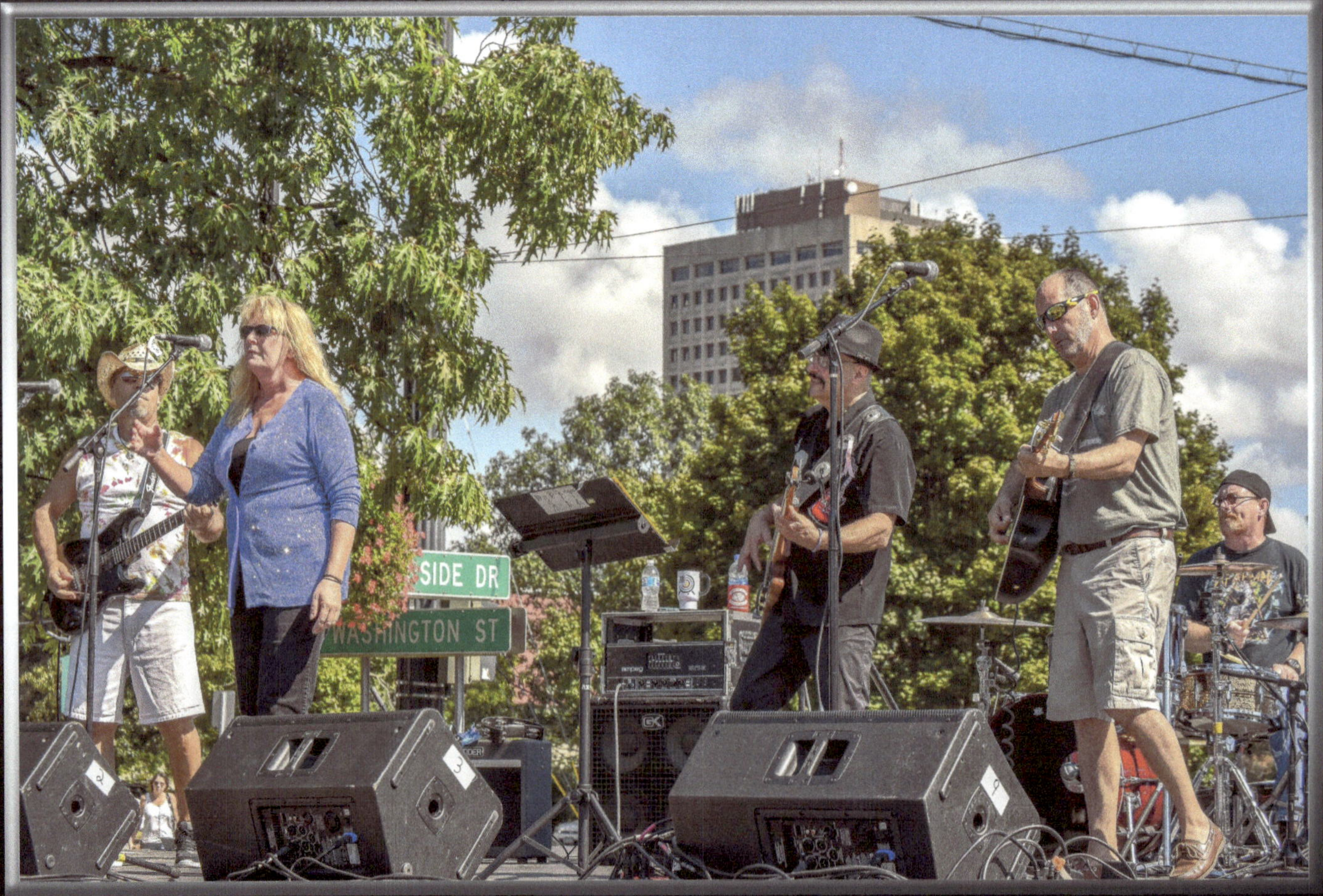

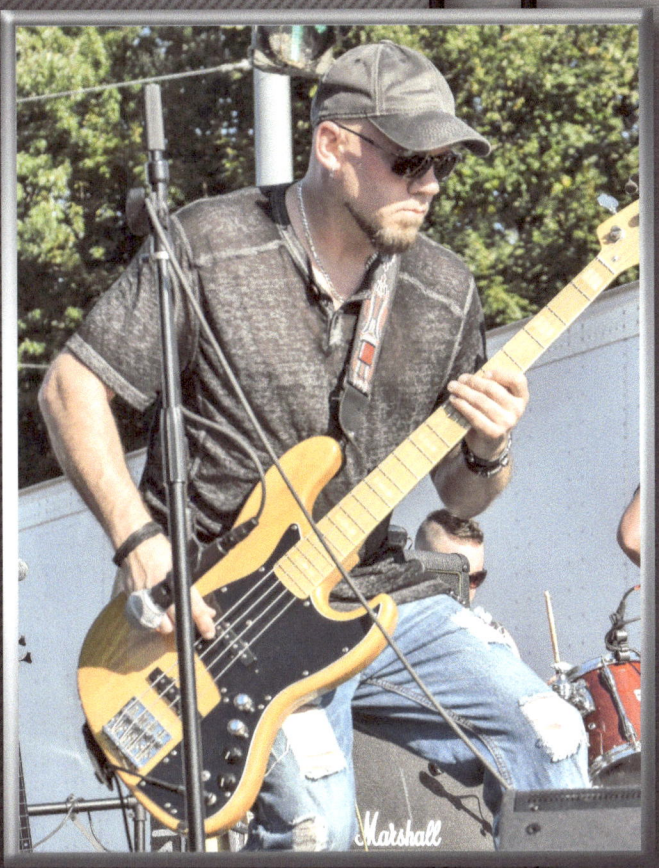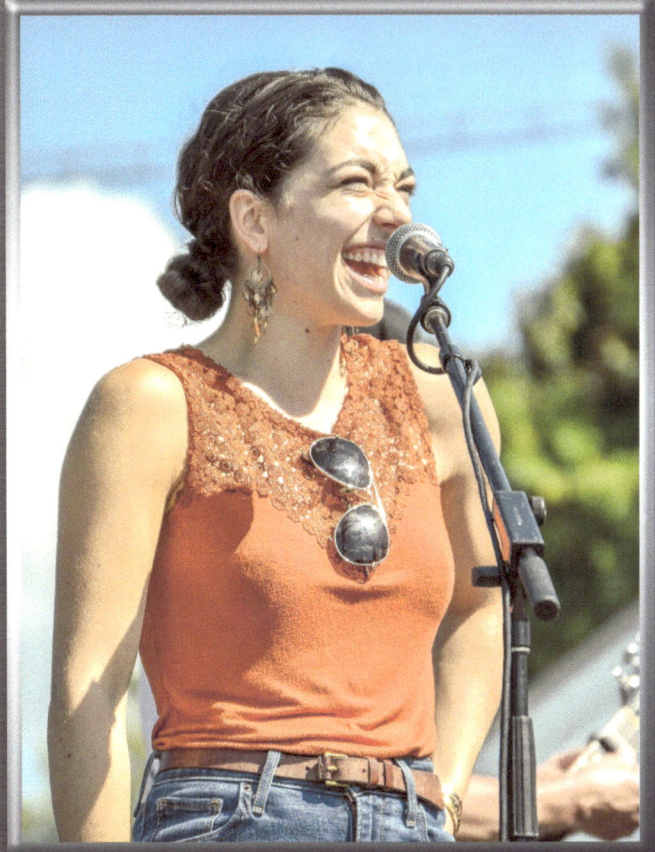

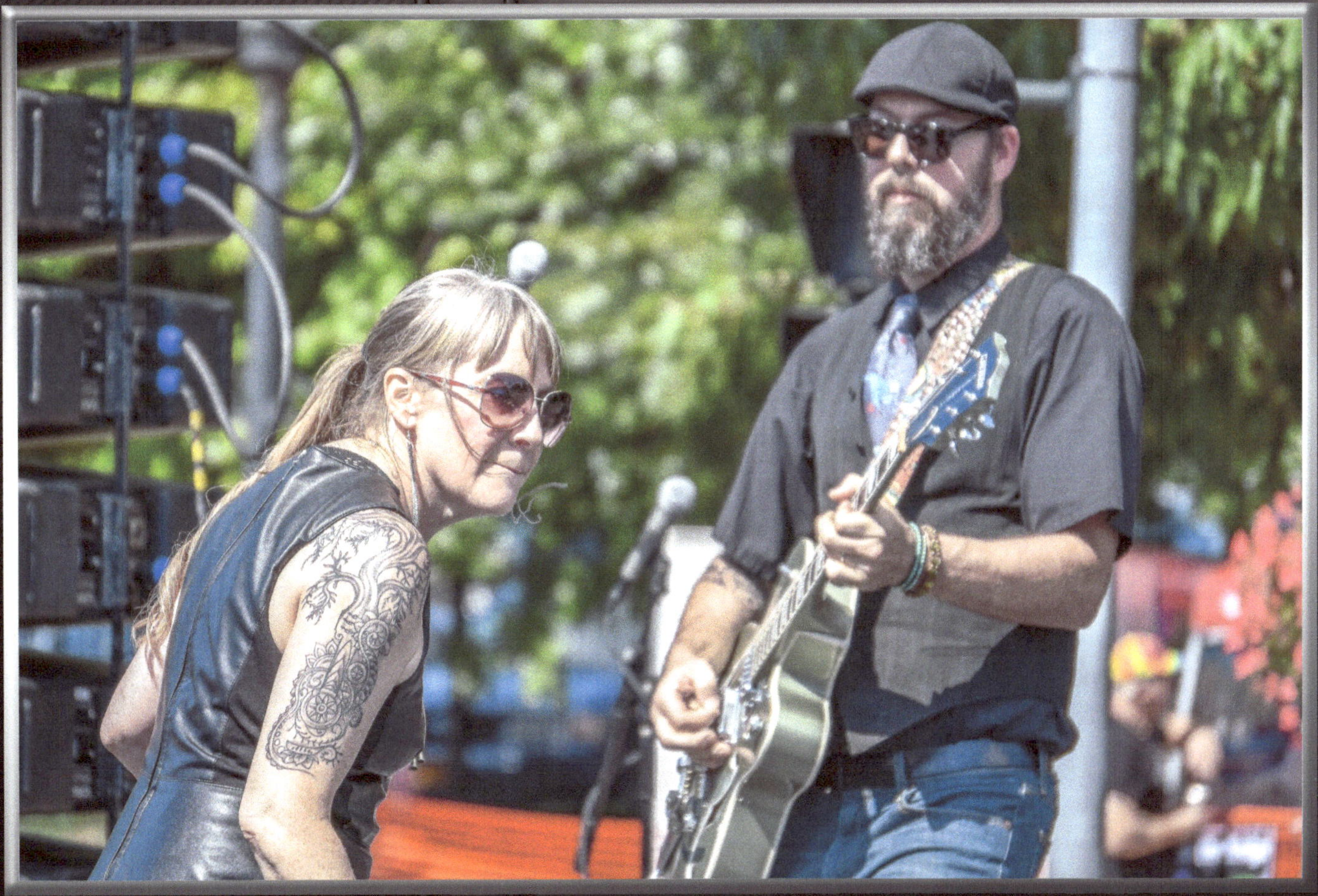

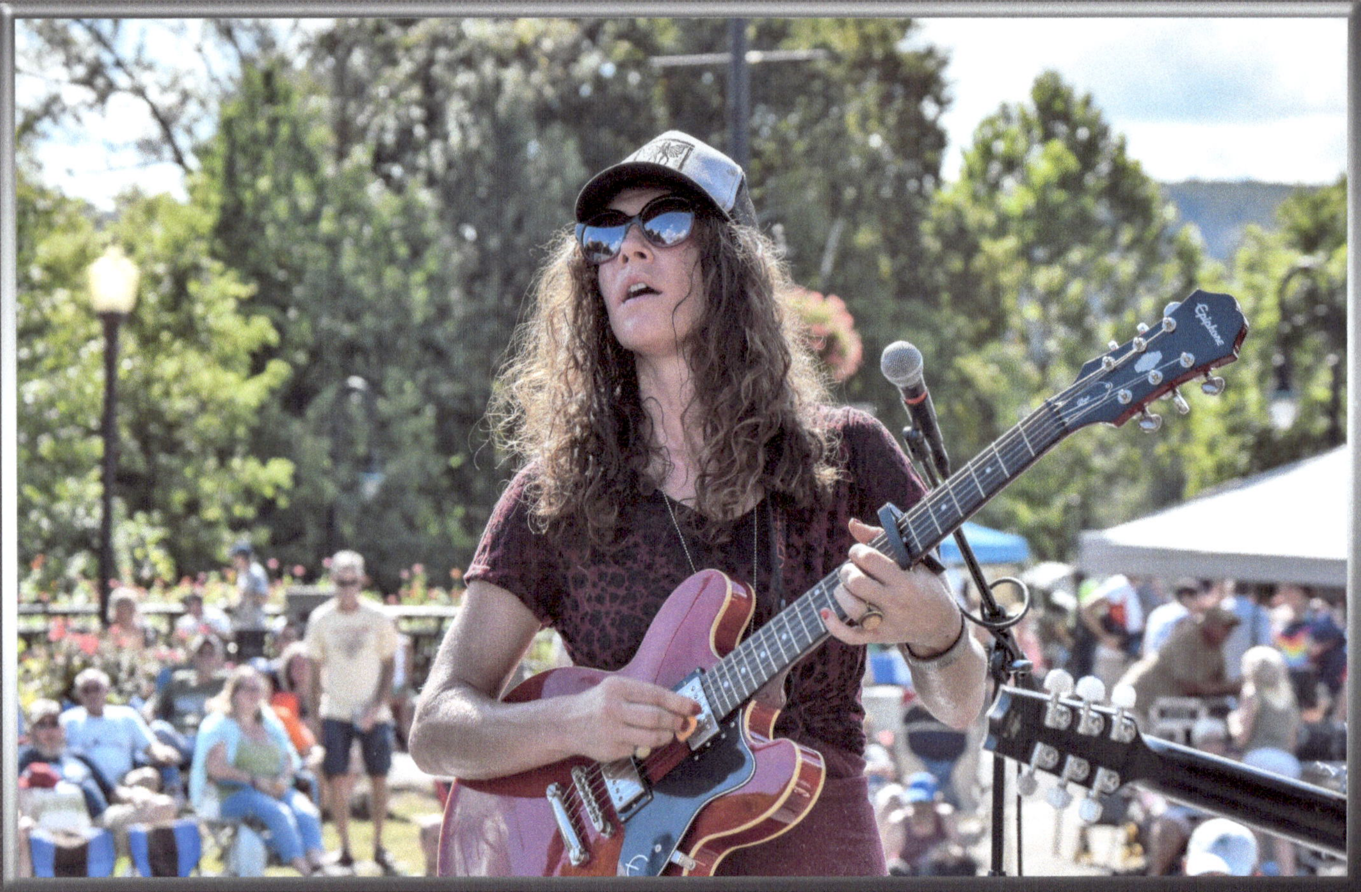

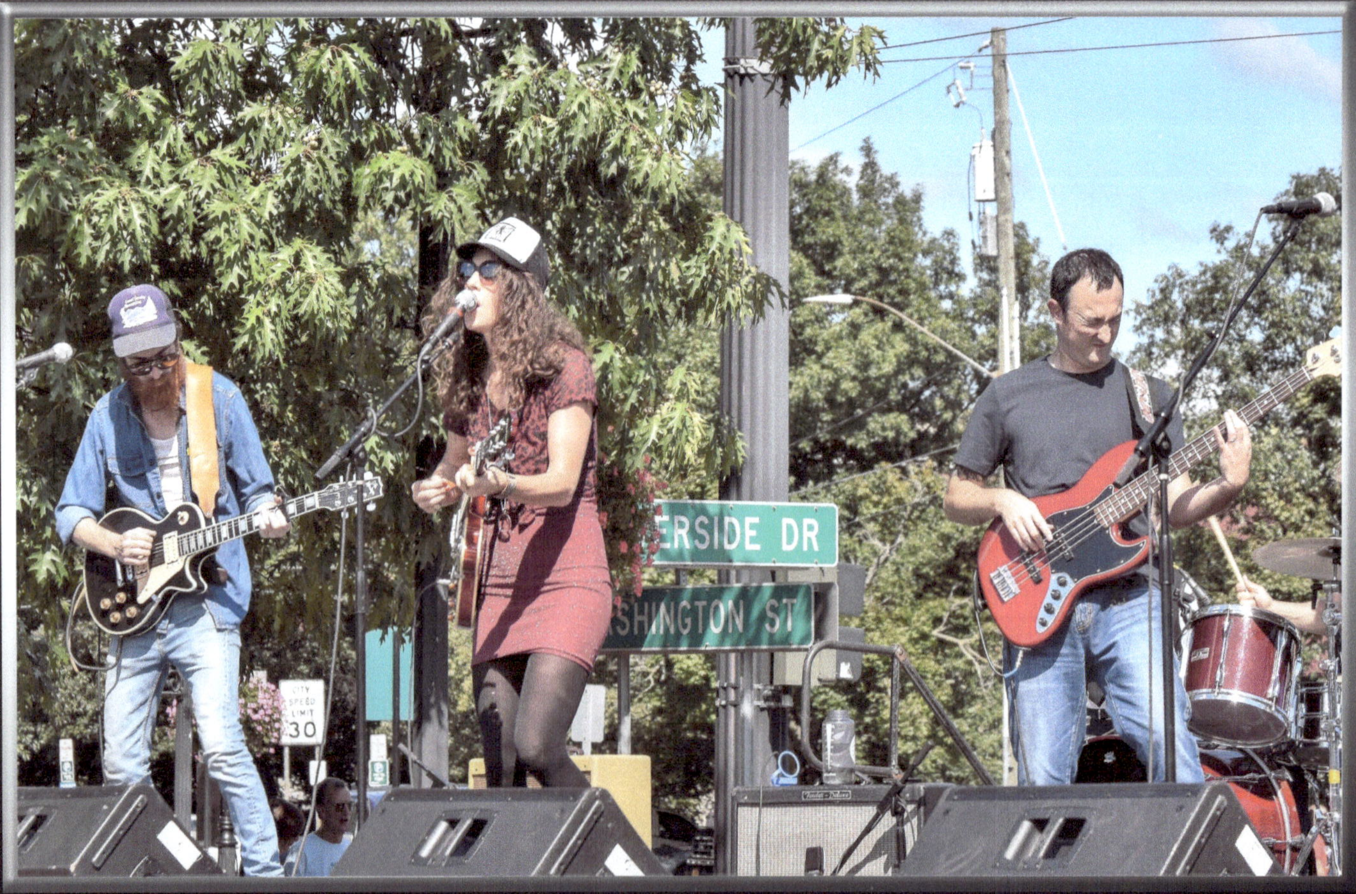

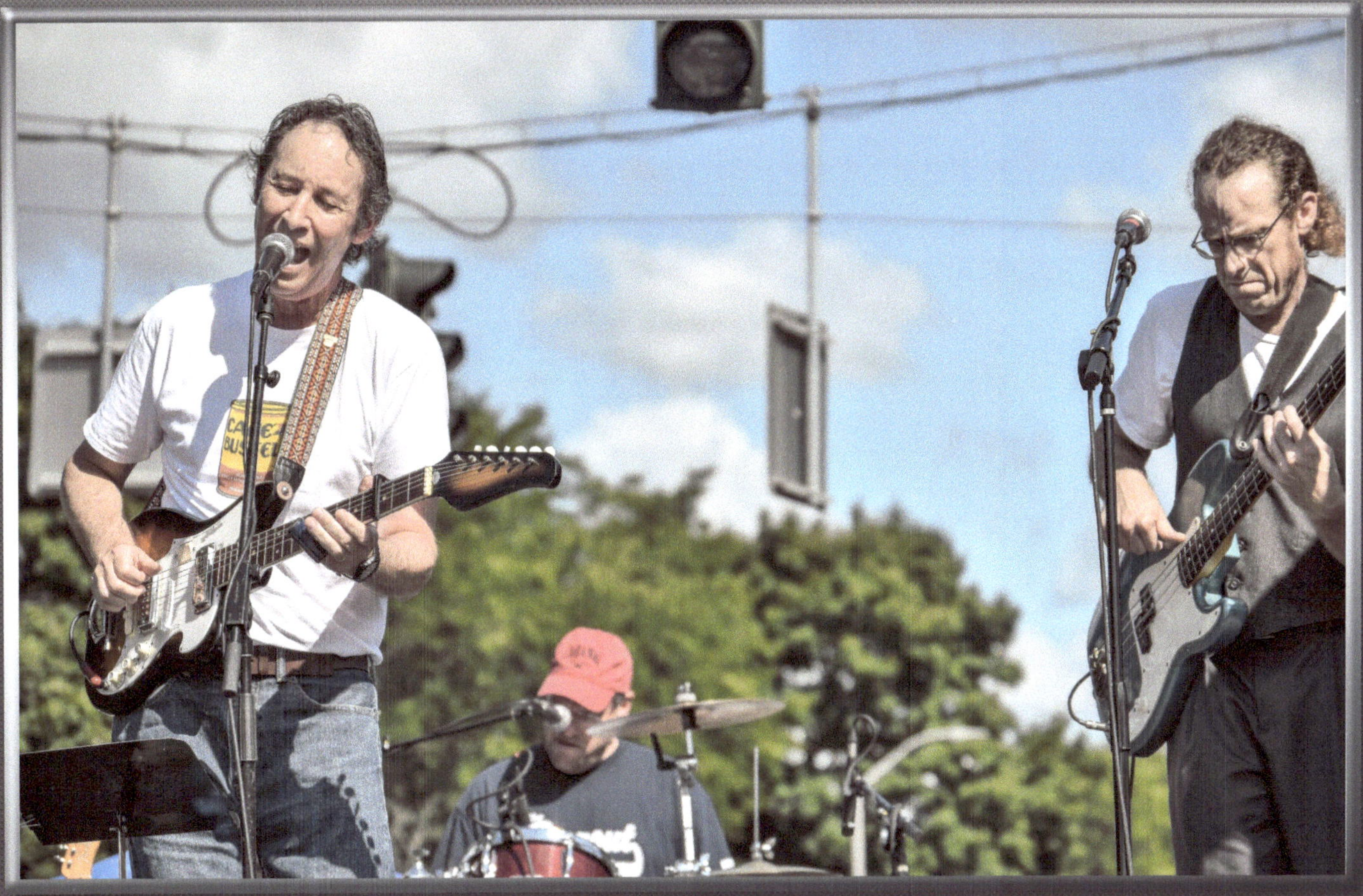

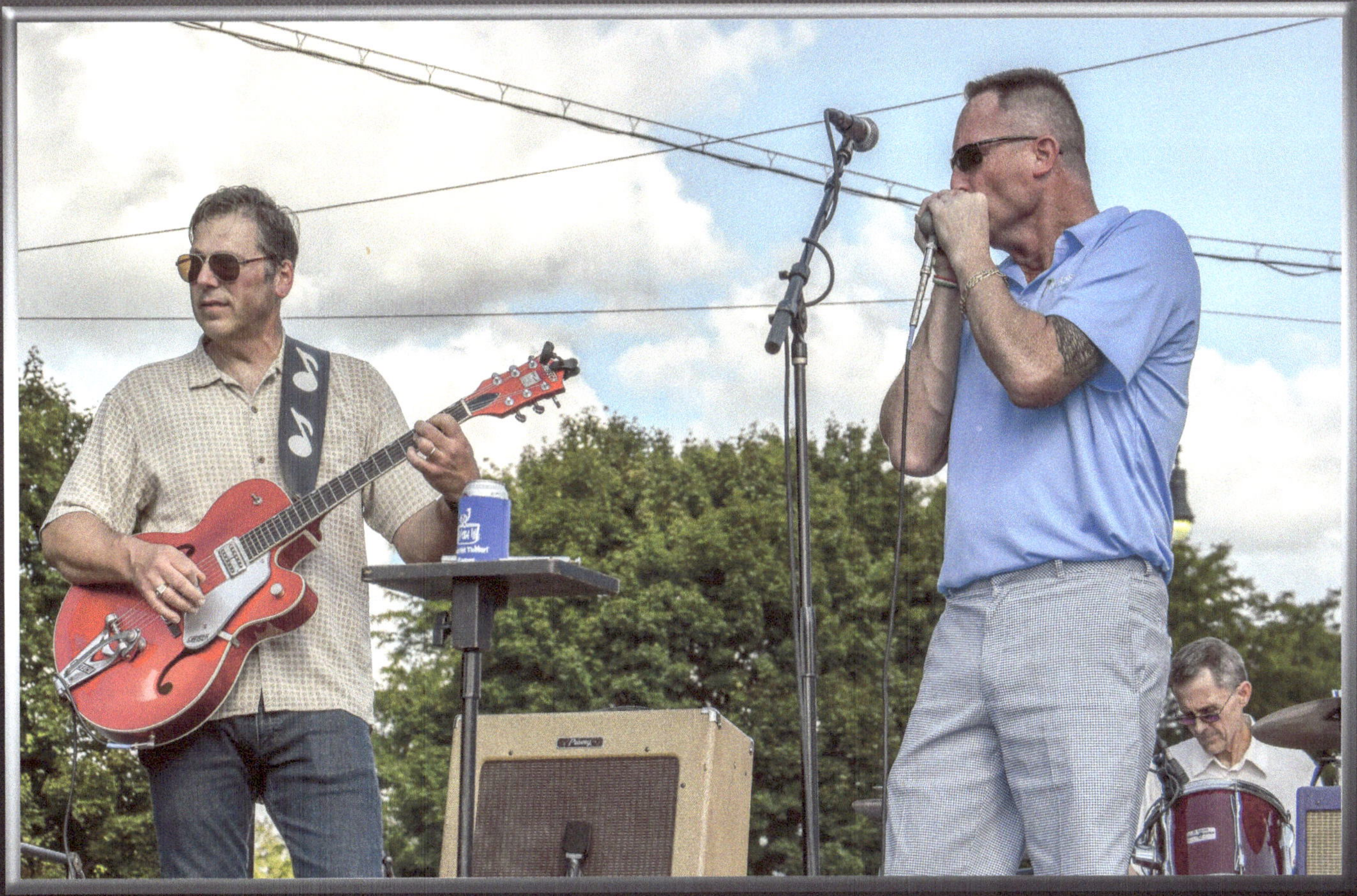

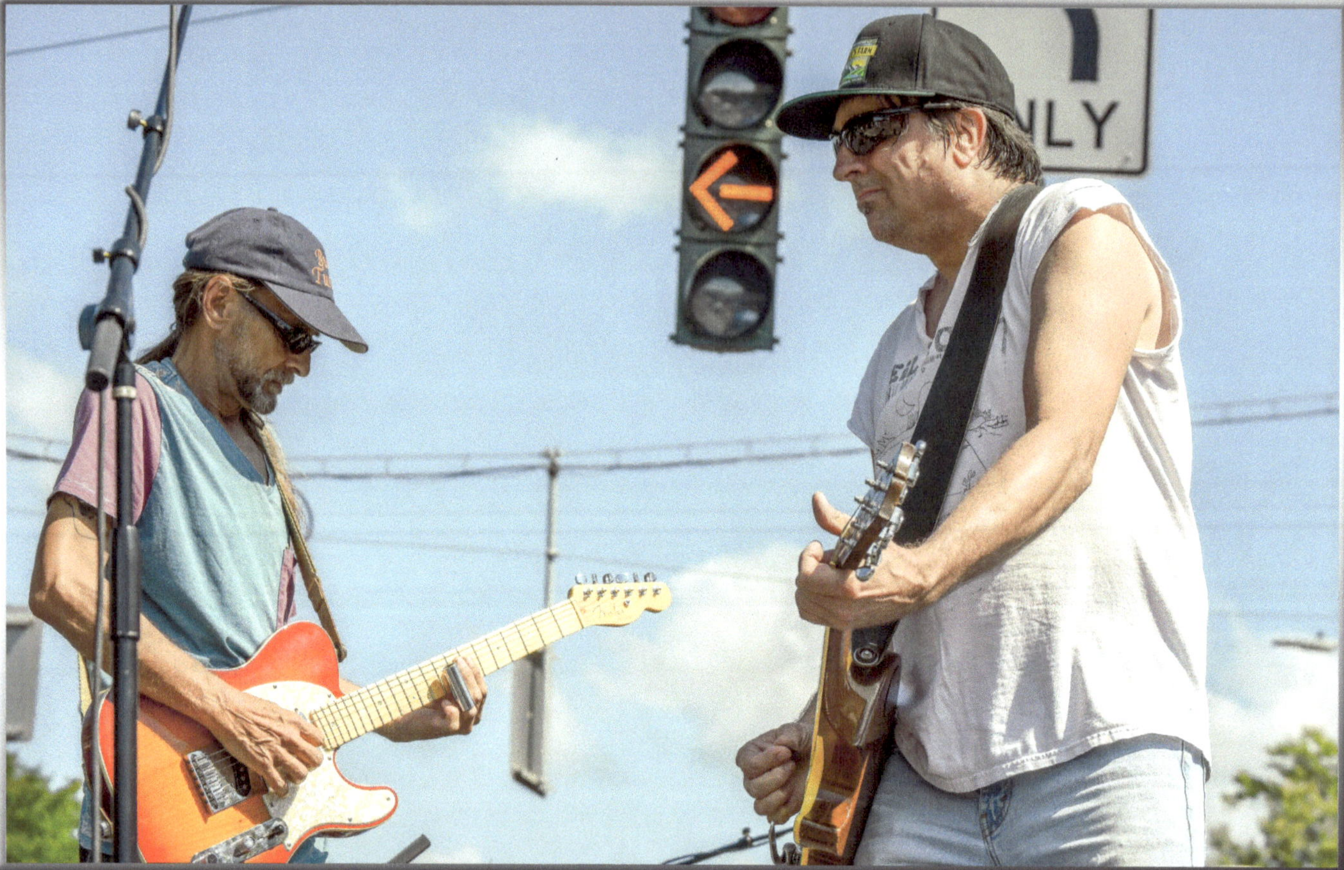

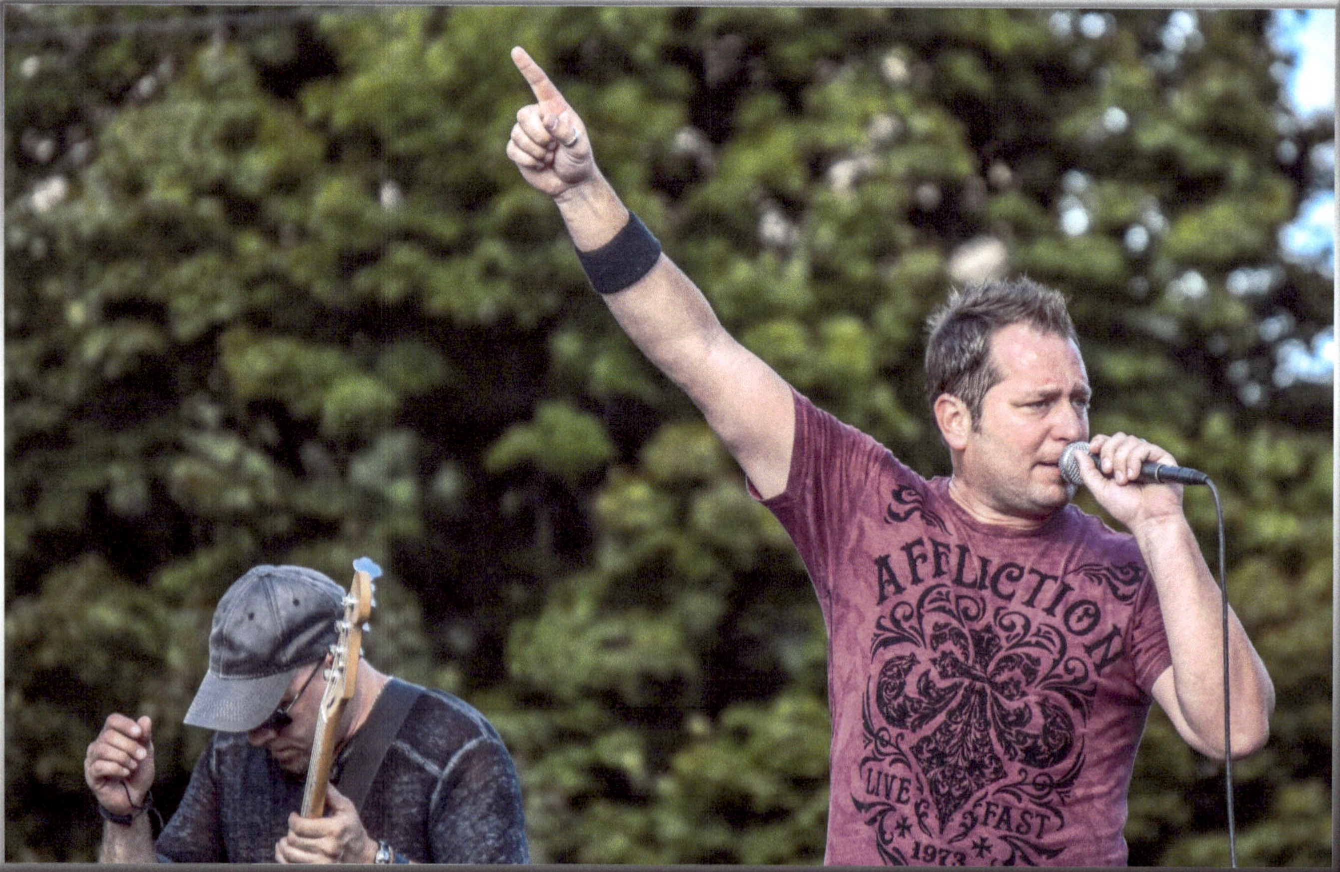

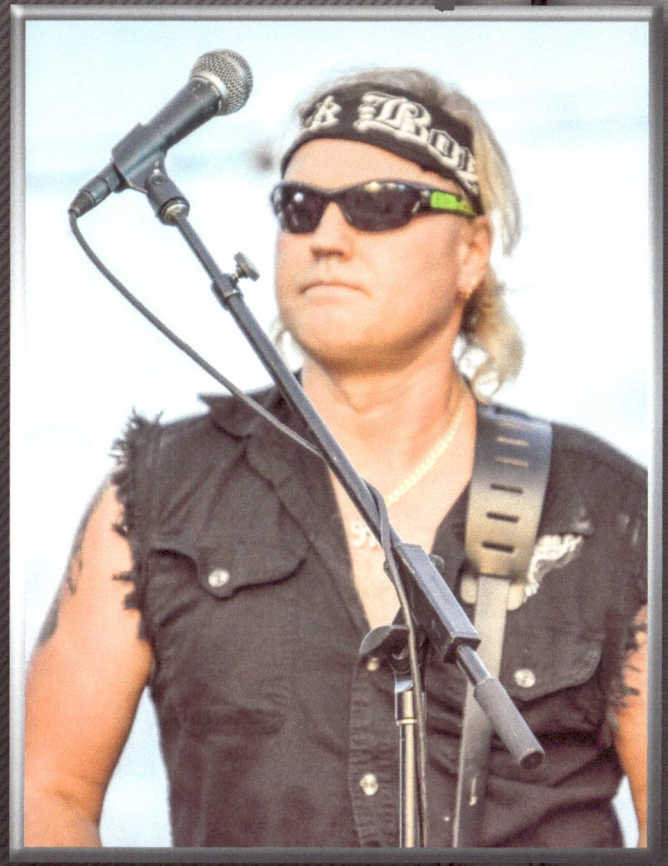
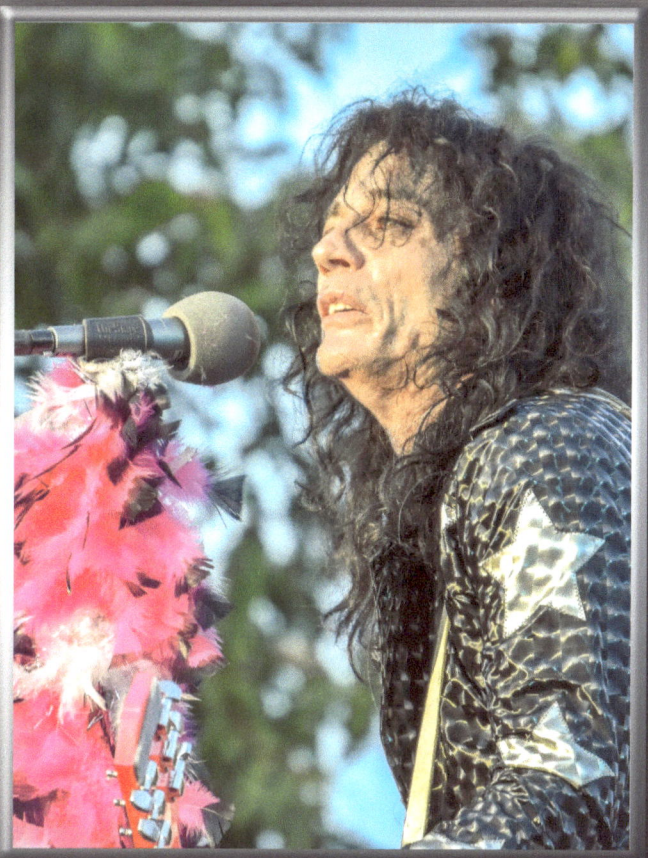

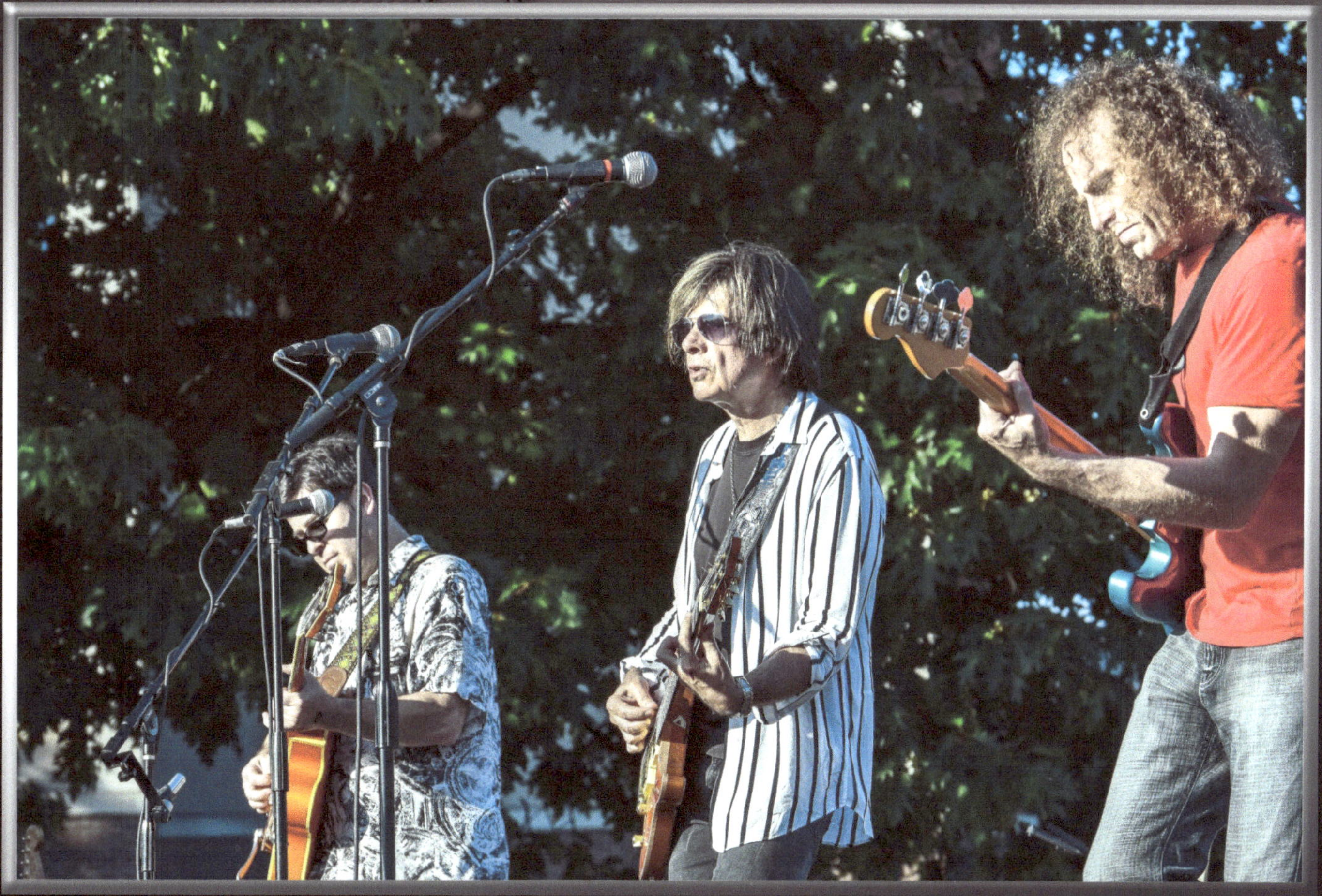

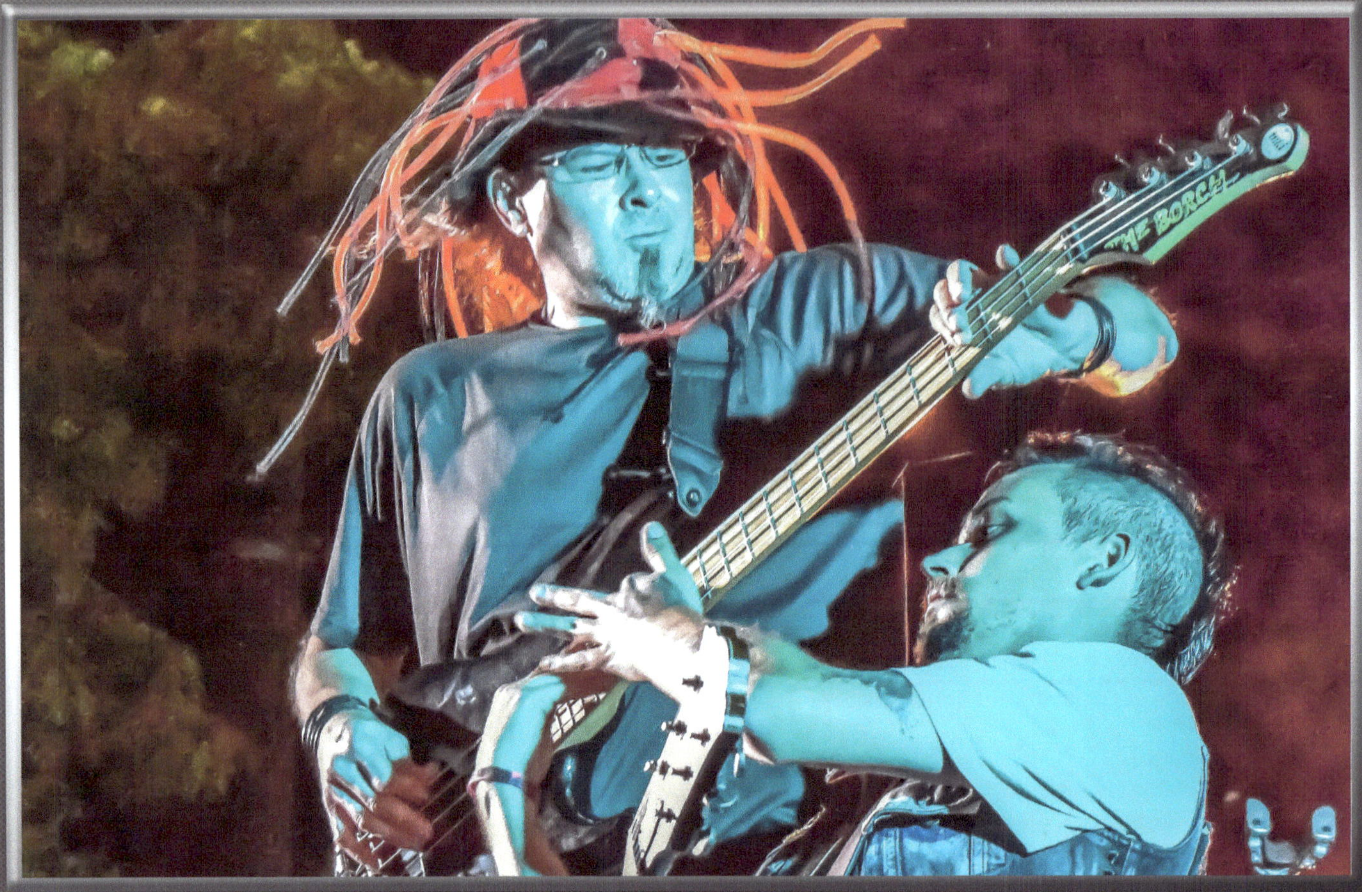

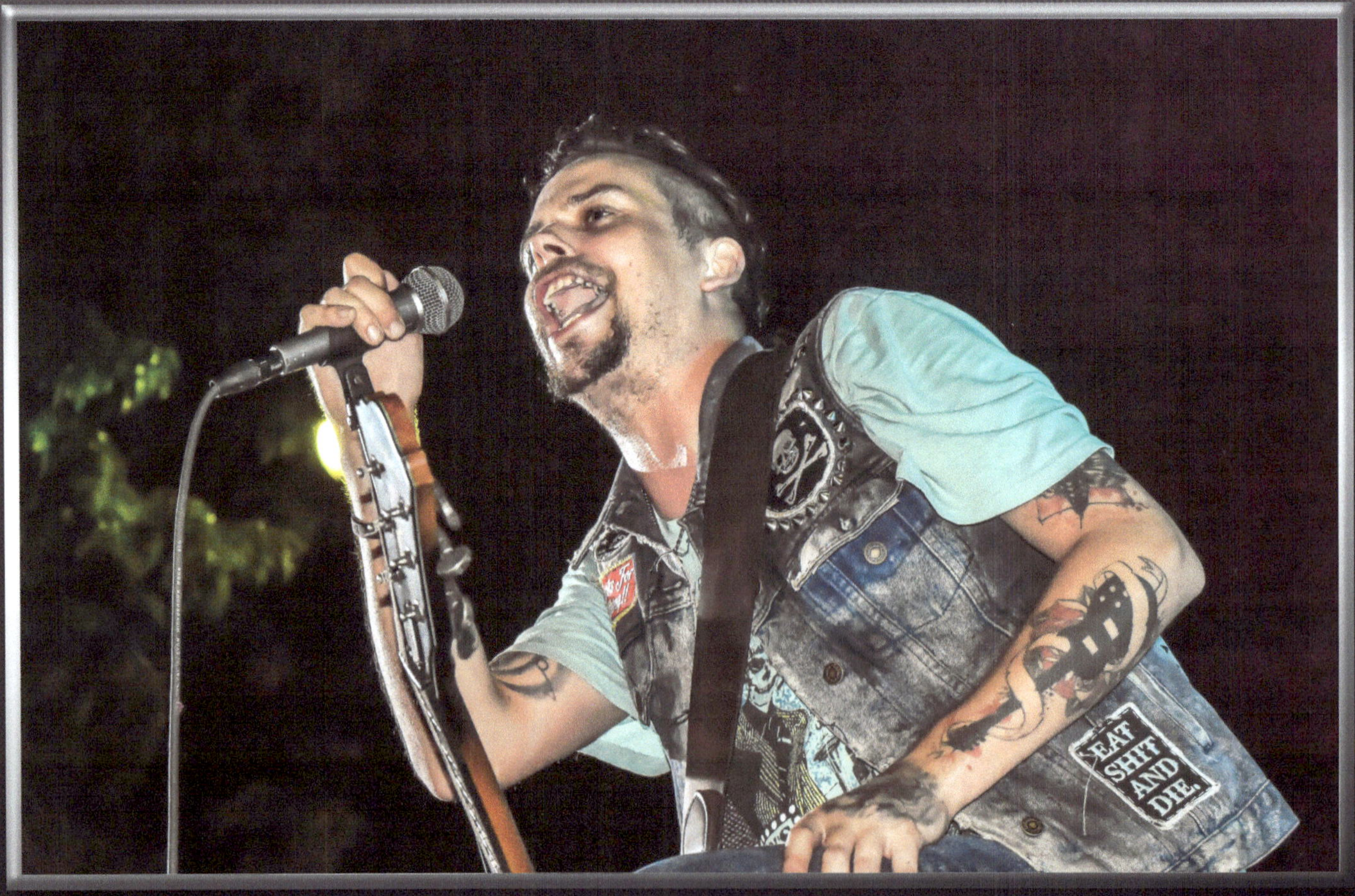

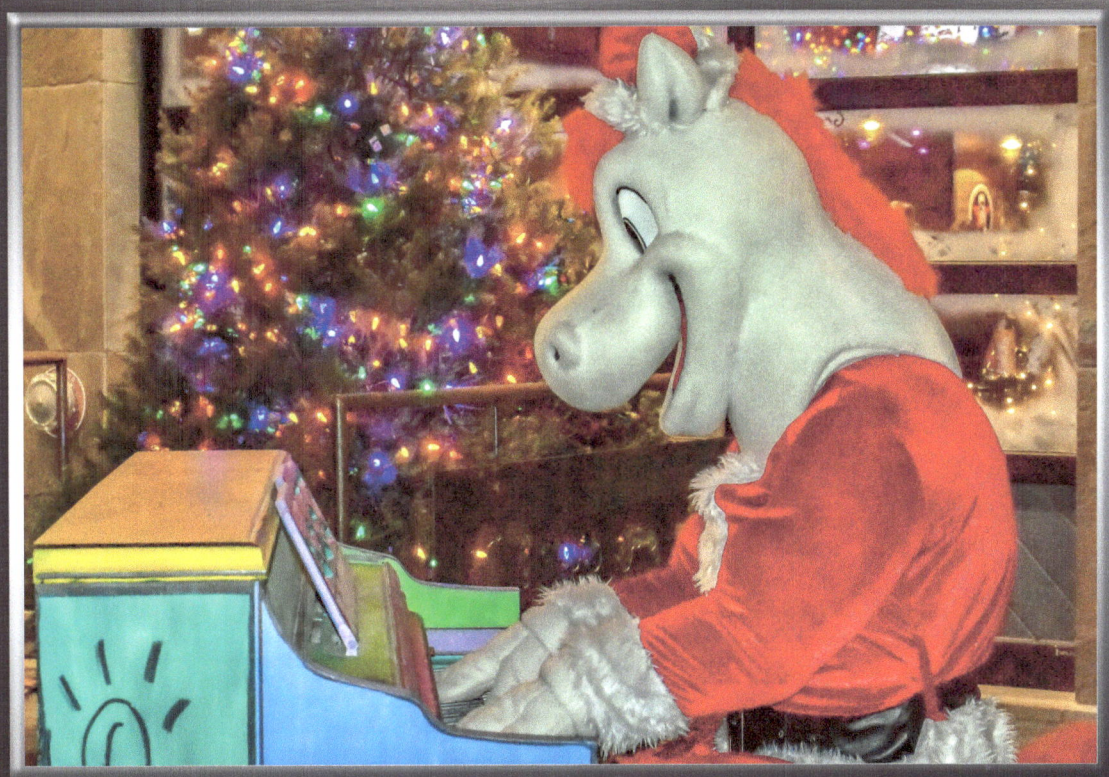

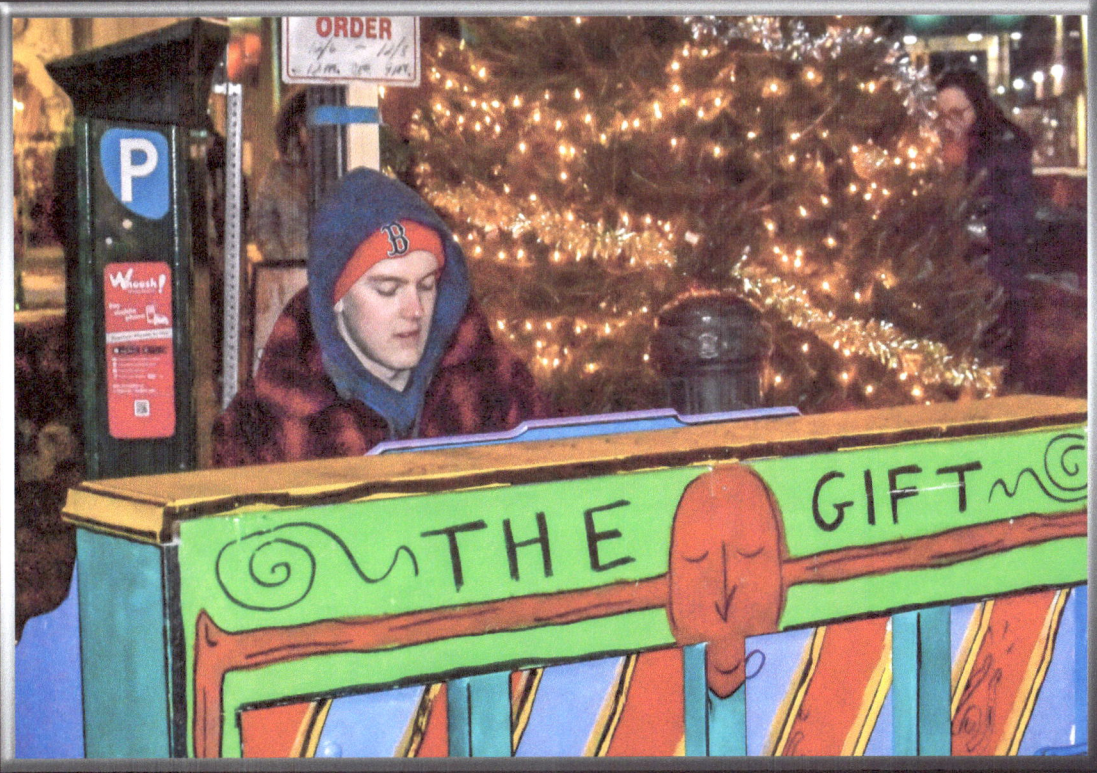

Summer is not the only time of year that you will hear the sounds of music playing outside.

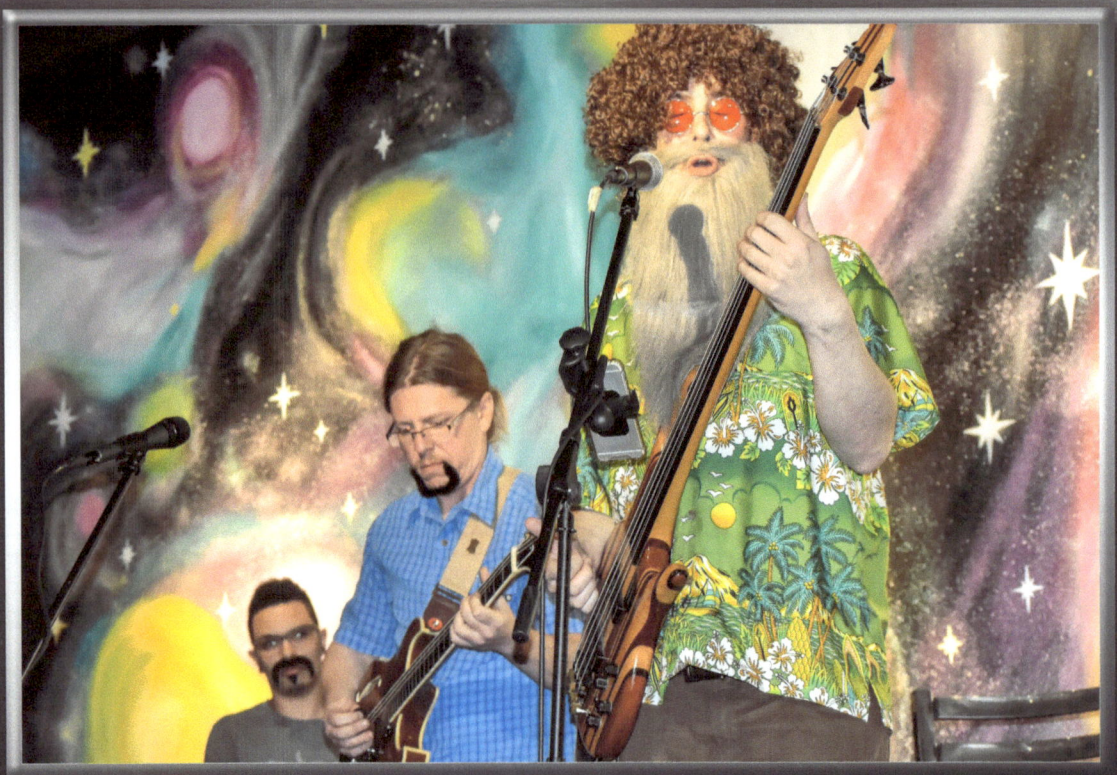
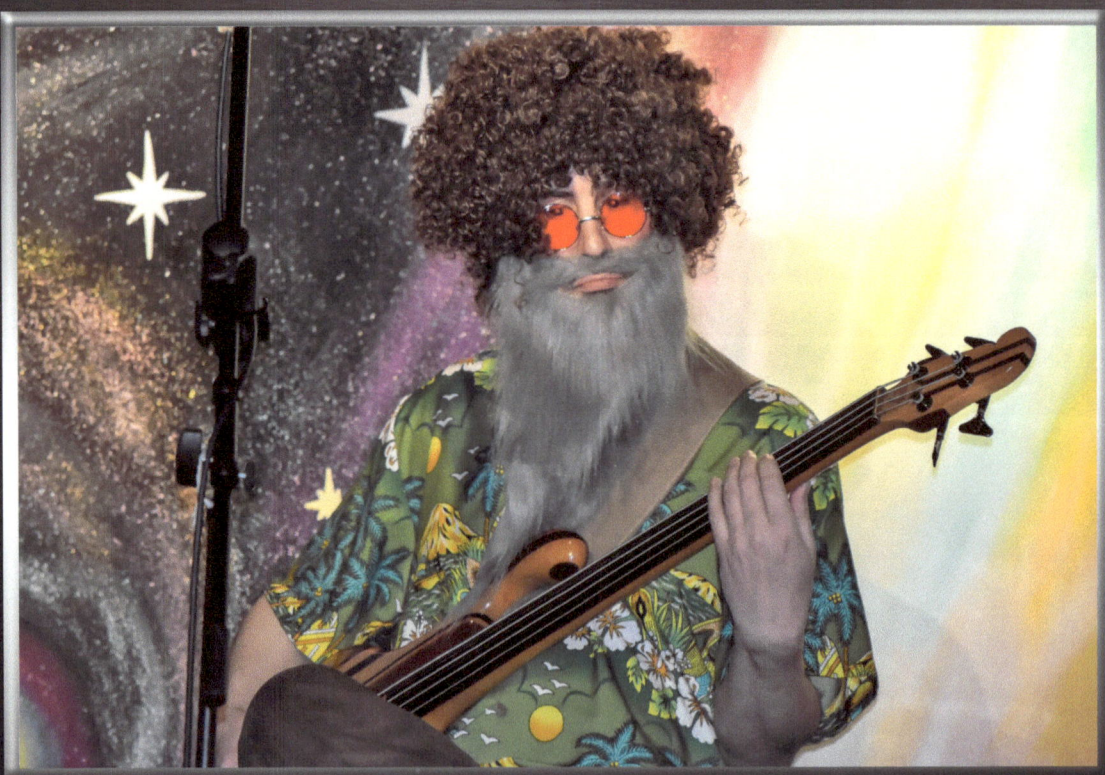

Of course, you will never fail to find one of your favorite local bands playing in one of the area bars.

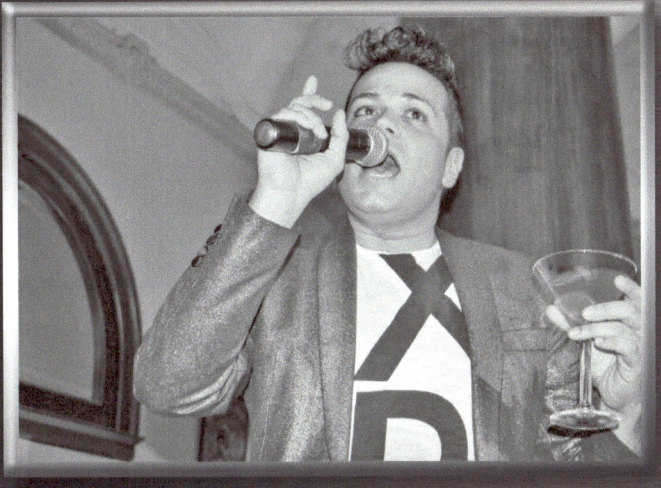
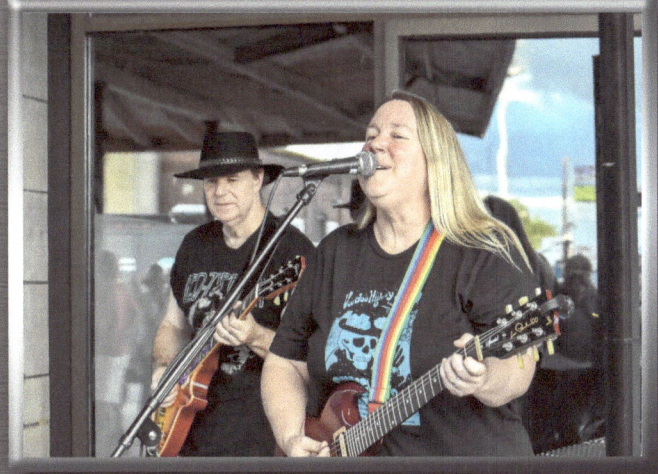
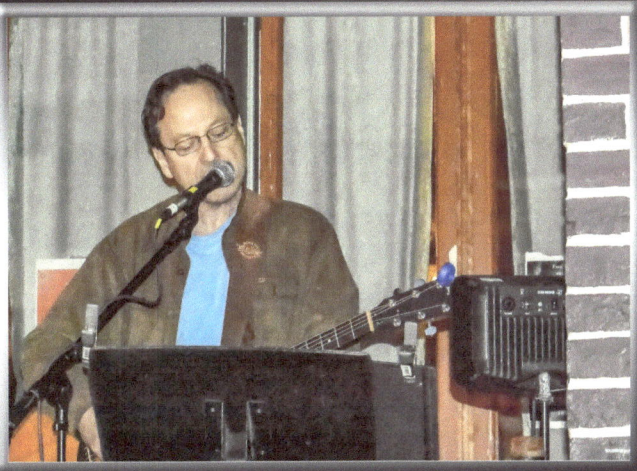
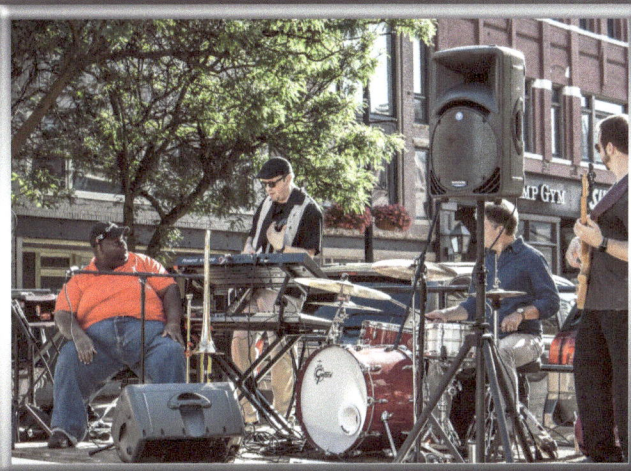
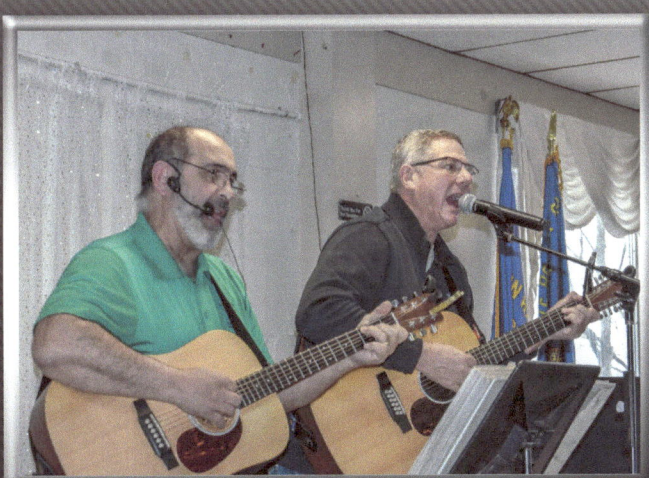
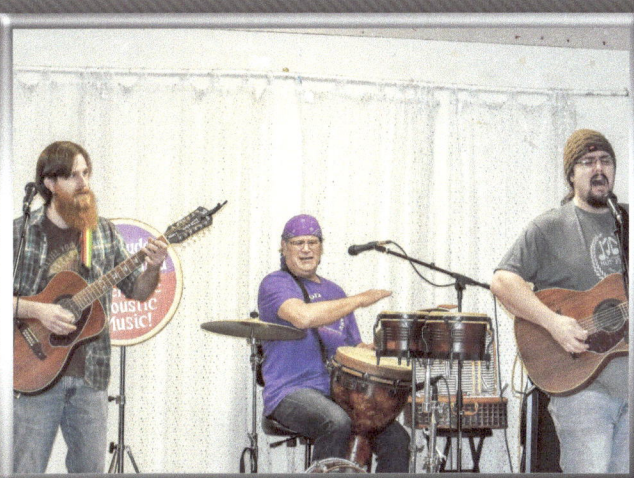

No matter the venue or genre, local music is live and well in the Southern Tier.

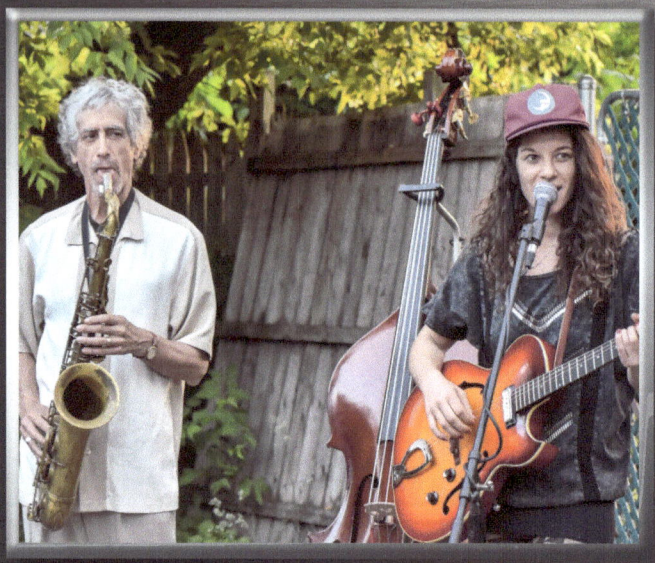
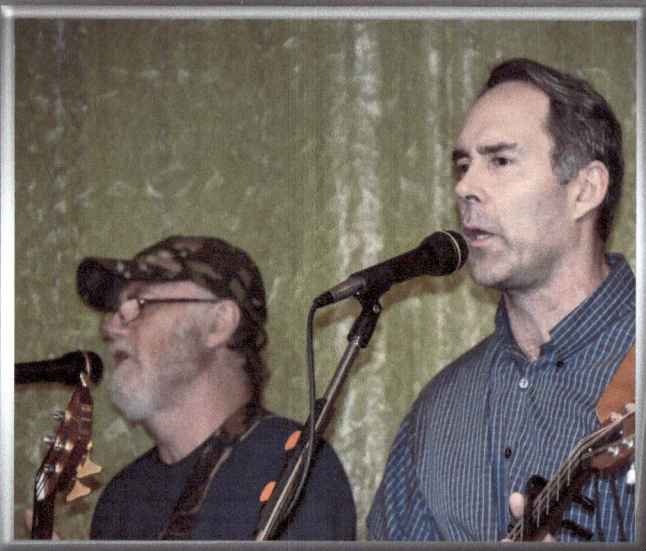
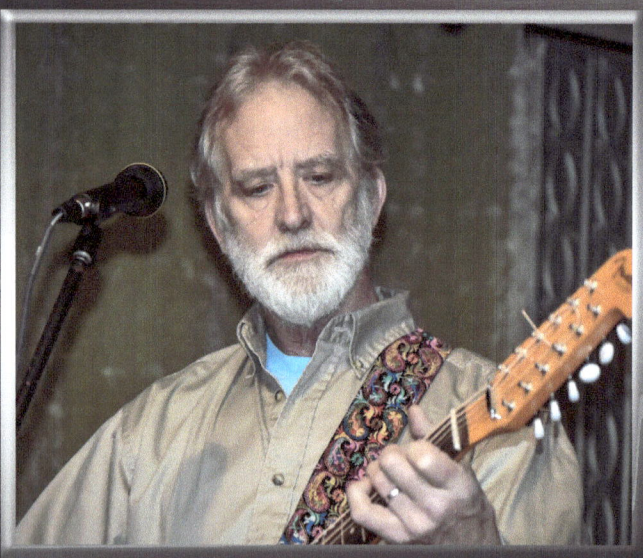
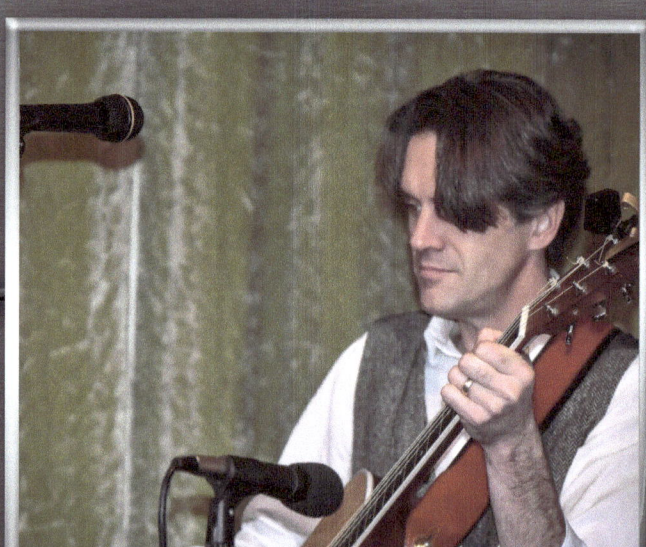
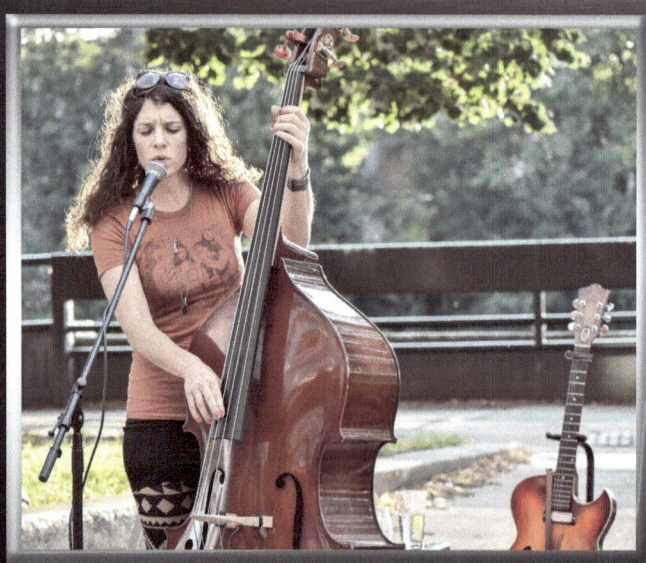
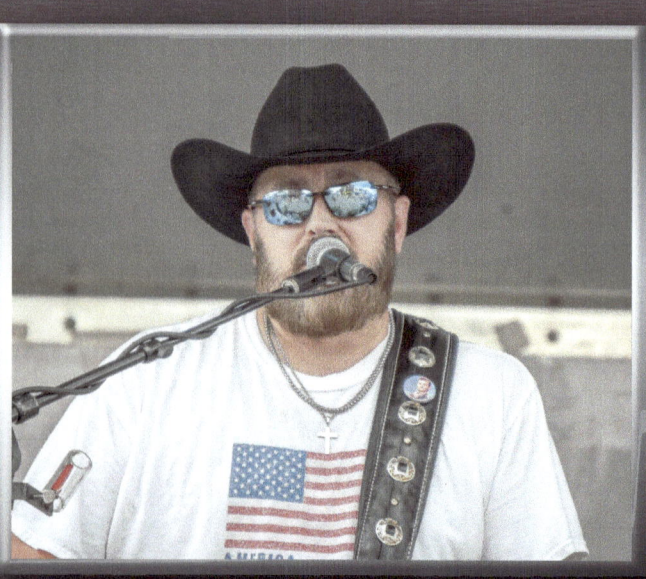

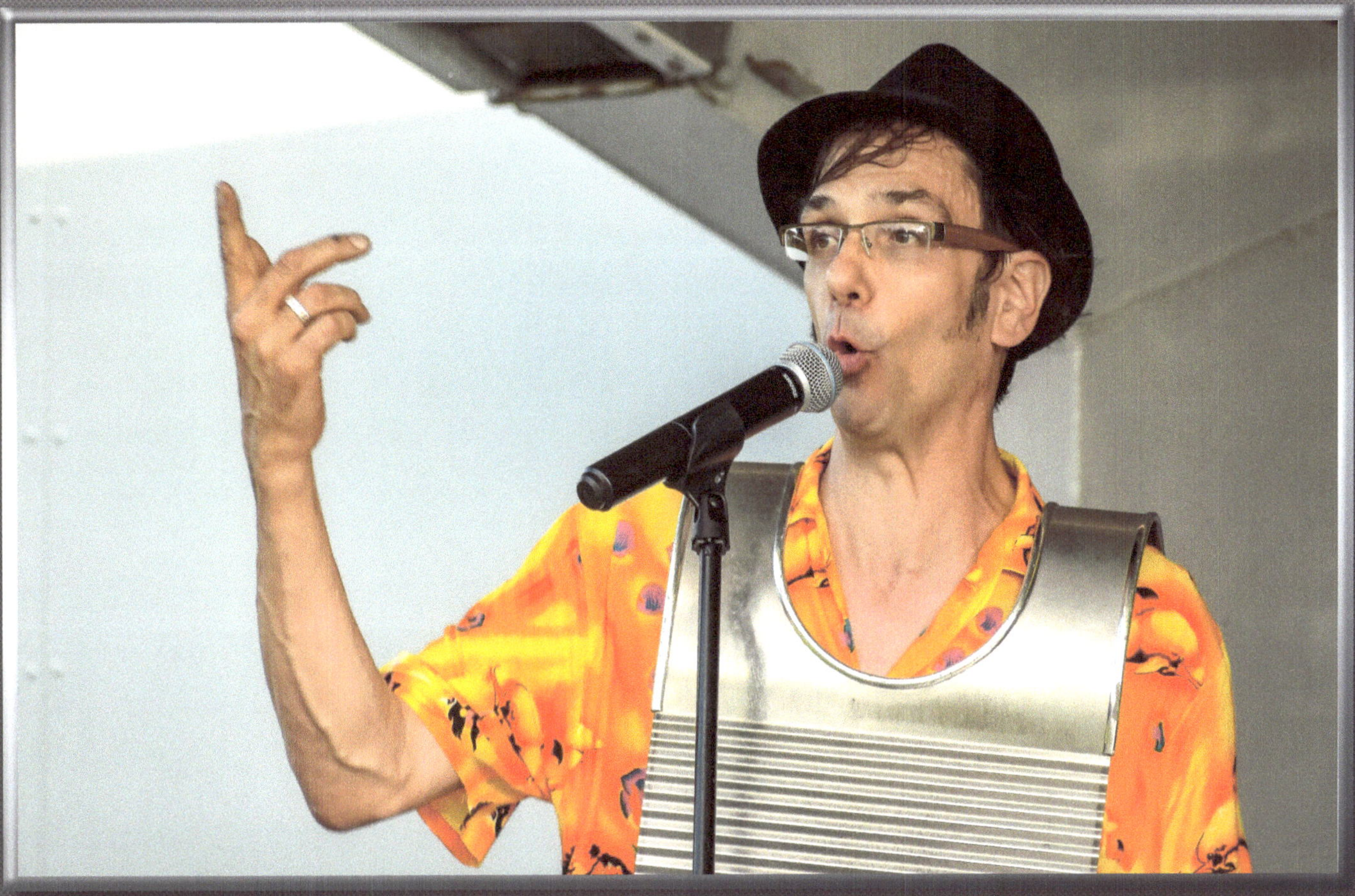

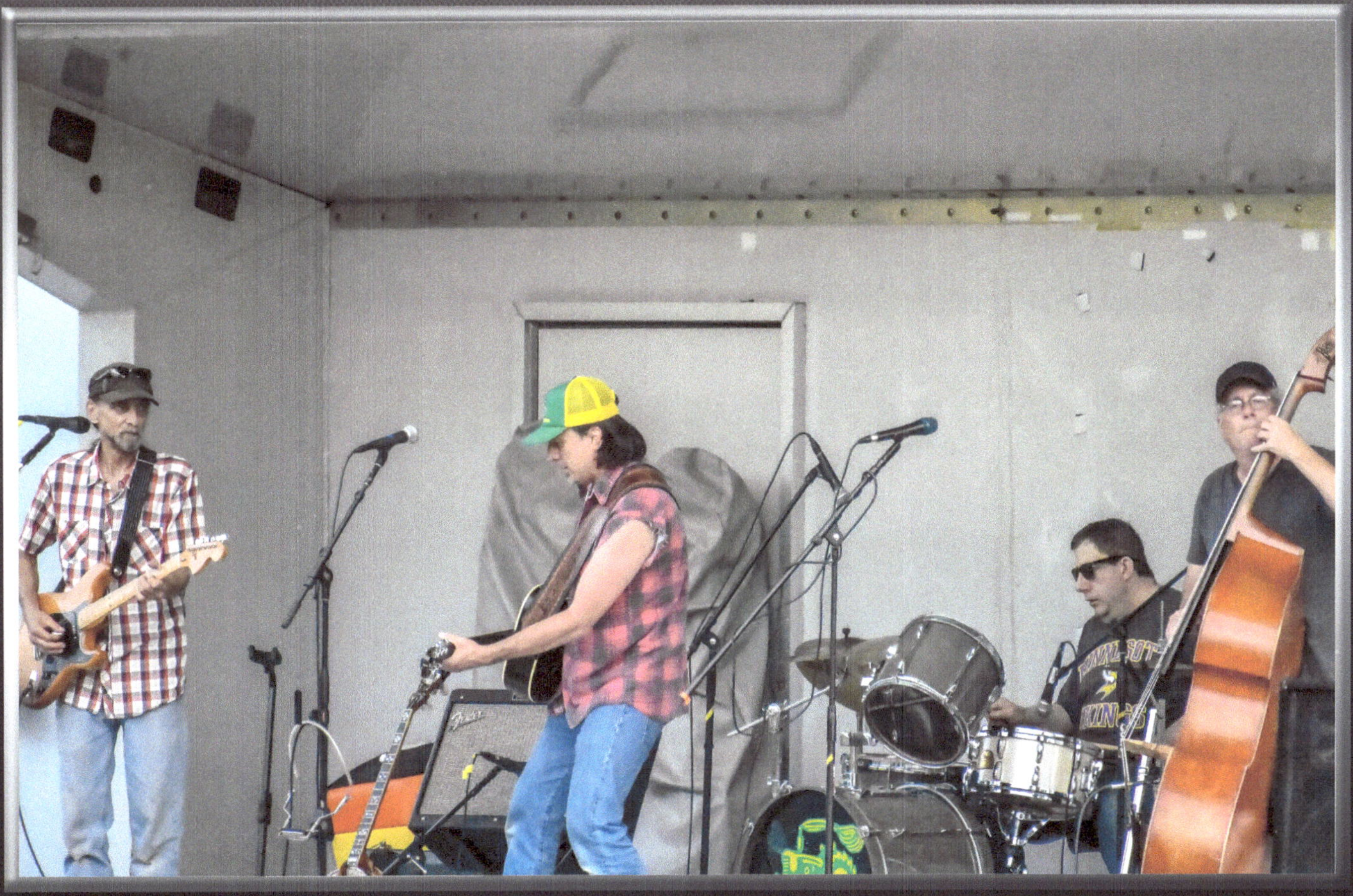

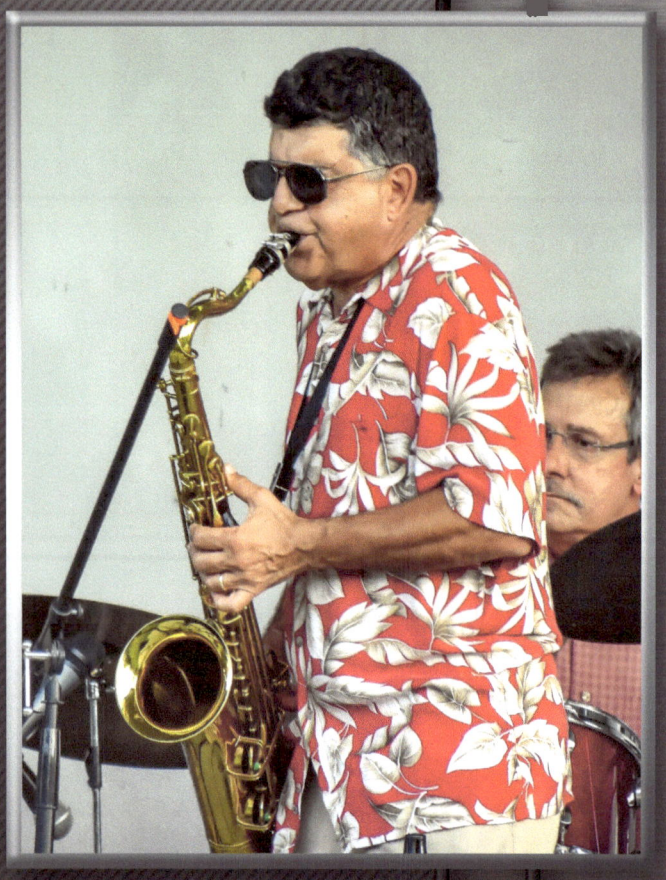
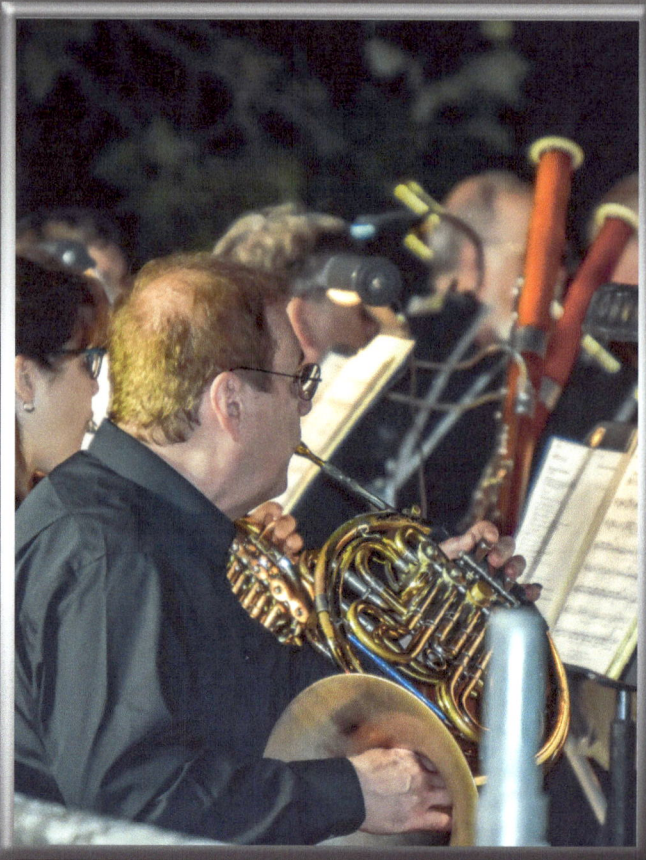

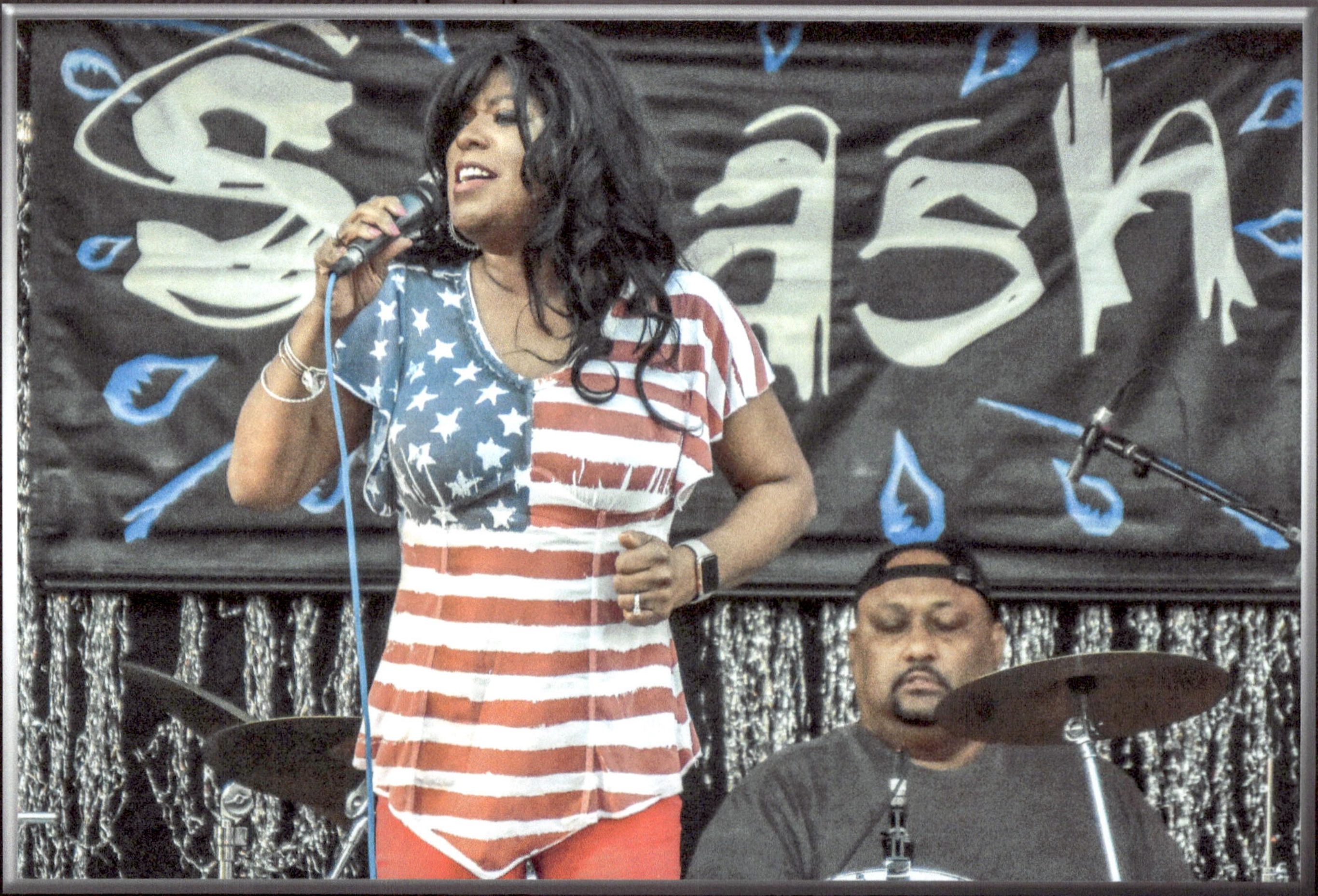

A huge thank you to all the local musicians in the Southern Tier who continue to provide us with their sweet sounds. You touch us in our souls and hearts.

www.ingramcontent.com/pod-product-compliance
Lightning Source LLC
Chambersburg PA
CBHW051211220526

45473CB00003B/984